MW01121354

CHILD ABUSE

HARM AND SOLUTIONS

CHILDREN'S ISSUES, LAWS AND PROGRAMS

CHILDREN'S ISSUES, LAWS AND PROGRAMS

CHILD ABUSE

HARM AND SOLUTIONS

ARTURO LOREDO ABDALÁ
HUGO JUÁREZ OLGUIN
AND
ABIGAIL CASAS MUÑOZ
EDITORS

nova
science publishers
New York

Library of Congress Cataloging-in-Publication Data

ISBN: 978-1-53614-271-6

Published by Nova Science Publishers, Inc. † *New York*

CONTENTS

PREFACE

Child abuse is a modality of violence against children and adolescents which remains to be comprehensively attended. The complexity of the problem implies not only the clinical manifestations (physical, sexual and psychological abuses and neglect), but also the social component (social determinants for health) as well as the judicial implication. This makes the suspicion, diagnosis, comprehensive care of each case, the physical and emotional rehabilitation of each patient, and the strategies for the prevention of this phenomenon very difficult. Undoubtedly, child abuse is fraught with enormous emotional and economic loads for the child, the family and society.

In the light of the abovementioned facts, the propositions in this book lie in the presentation and development of the most frequent and known modalities of child abuse. These modalities include physical, sexual and psychological abuses and neglect, as well as other forms like fetal abuse, ethnic maltreatment, abuse among peers, bullying, and parental alienation among others that are little known or barely considered; hence, these latter issues are not frequently seen by physicians, nurses, social workers, psychologists, lawyers, etc. In addition, some preventive programs that have been successful as viable strategies in many countries of the world are proposed.

The aim of this book is to give a wide vision on the knowledge concerning child abuse, based on the analysis of behaviors and attitudes and revising some new strategies ensuing from information furnished by research works. The authors are convinced that the consideration of these concepts would definitely permit the elaboration of optimum and specific management for this population.

Chapter 1 - Violence in all its manifestations is, unfortunately, the current situation that prevails in the world. Violence has been classified into three large groups, depending on the context in which it is inflicted: self-inflicted, interpersonal and collective violence. Violent acts can be physical, sexual, emotional or psychological or exercised by inattention. According to the International Classification of Diseases, it is a condition that integrates basically four modalities: physical abuse, sexual abuse, psychological abuse and neglect.

In the violence between humans, interpersonal and inter-community violence as well as violence among countries can be highlighted. Interpersonal violence is the most common among humans and can happen between members of the same family or between couples or friends. In all these forms of violence, physical violence (PA) stands out and this affects both children and adults. PA in children has been considered as an act or acts in which the caregiver has caused; intentionally or accidentally; pain, physical and/or emotional damage to a girl, a boy or a teenager. PA can be visible and invisible. However, its diagnosis is beclouded by confusion and lack of precise diagnostic instruments. To deal with this problem, the Comprehensive Care for Battered Child Clinic of the National Institute of Pediatrics (CAINM-INP), Mexico City has come up with a series of indicators that allow establishing or ruling out if the injuries suffered by a child were caused by an accident or PA. PA risk factors are classified into factors of the minor, factors of the parents and family and school or environmental factors.

Its consequences can be immediate or long-term. The probability of the victim having a negative cognitive performance and psychosocial functioning in his or her life in the short, medium and long term are, especially, when the victim has faced more than four adverse experiences in childhood (AEC). When PA in boys, girls and teenagers is well-founded, the management must be medico-legal. The prevention of PA is extremely important and must consist of both primary and secondary interventions so as to radicate or substantial reduce the occurrence of the phenomenon in the world. This chapter highlights the importance of recognizing child maltreatment, the modalities of childhood physical abuse and the way to prevent it.

Chapter 2 - Accidental traumatic brain injuries (TBI) are one of the main causes of death in children under one year old. Within TBI is the abusive head trauma (AHT) defined as an excessive shaking of the body and head of an infant due to anger developed by an adult as a result of excessive crying of the infant or the small child. Such shakings provoke a rotatory movement and an inertial force. The effect of these two actions is a friction between the dura mater and cerebral parenchyma leading to the rupture of the veins and thus, subdural and subarachnoid hemorrhage.

Depending on the degree of aggression, the child can present multiple clinical signs such as decreased appetite, irritability, lethargy and/or vomiting, or it can progress to severe and identifiable symptoms such as traumatic brain injury (TBI), seizures, loss of consciousness, respiratory and/or cardiorespiratory arrest, shock and even sudden or unexplained death of the infant. Moreover, research works have shown that half of the children who survived AHT develop sequels such as language disorder and delay in the acquisition of it, diverse motor deficit, spasticity, quadriparesia or hemiparesia, visual deficit or blindness, hearing loss, epilepsy, sleep disorder, attention deficit and behavioral disorder.

Ignorance of how to deal with a crying crisis is one of the main risk factors for shaking a baby. Anyone who is facing a crying baby is at risk of shaking him. Therefore, pediatricians, nurses, parents and other caregivers need to know this syndrome and know the strategies to deal with crying.

Since baby crying is the main trigger of shaking and that the ways in which parents or caregivers deal with it are the principal determinants for shaking to occur or not, the authors can then conclude that these two main points should be the focus for its prevention and where an intervention is required. In the light of this, adequate preventive programs based on universal primary prevention education to all parents of newborn babies are extremely necessary. This chapter reviews the mechanism of action of shaken child syndrome and how to prevent it.

Chapter 3 - The term fetal abuse (FA) refers to any action or omission caused in an intentional or negligent manner that may cause harm to the product of gestation. From time immemorial, the right to life has not always been recognized in newborns. In old cultures, infanticide was justified as a mechanism to get rid of newborns with malformation, neurological damage or simply for birth control. This denial continued in different countries and cultures until the establishment and recognition of Universal Declaration on Children´s Right which states that "a child, due to his physical and mental immaturity, requires special care including adequate legal protection before and after birth."

The vital question is, "Who should take care of the product of gestation before its birth? To provide the necessary conditions for a child to be born healthy, and fulfill one of his rights to lives evidently in the hands of the parents, the obstetricians and gynecologists, the general practitioners and the society itself. When this condition is denied either intentionally, by neglect or omission, fetal abuse is concreted. Paradoxically, the ideal attention to this problem is not simple, since the situations of ethical, social and legal natures come into play.

The intrauterine life of a product depends on whether the pregnant was desired, planed or accepted by the two parents. The absence of any of this can lead to a series of actions leading to FA. These series of action is usually directed to affect in adverse manner the Ecological system of the product which comprises of the microenvironment, the maternal environment and the macro environment. In the case of maternal environment, the action can be directed towards fertilization and implantation period, embryonic period or the fetal period. Usually, such actions may be in form of intentional or unintentional to propitiate Adverse Social Determinants (DSD) like consumption of licit and illicit" drugs, exposure to elevated concentrations of teratogenic substances and inappropriate nutrition among others.

The diagnosis of fetal can be established when there is a denial or pretension not to know of the pregnancy, history of various abortion attempts, plan to give the child for immediate adoption at birth, abandonment of the pregnant woman the father of the product or by her family, drug dependency or alcoholic woman and history of abuse, sociopathic parents or with psychiatric disorders, and finally, adolescent mothers who for family, personal or social reasons are under pressure to commit acts against themselves or against the product when they suspect or confirm the pregnancy.

To avoid the product of gestation being a victim of fetal abuse, it is fundamental that the pregnancy be planned, desired or accepted by the two parents within a social, civil and religious realities. Therefore, it is essential that the medical group, paramedical group, families and society in general should join hands in the prevention of unwanted pregnancy and guide pregnant women to successful and healthy end of their pregnancy.

When a pregnancy is not planned and agreed, there is a possibility that the future parents will resort to abortion, action that could be legal or illegal. The reasons to take this decision can be the rejection of the couple, the family or the society. The right of a child to be born healthy must be favored mainly by his parents, although it is also the responsibility of the obstetricians, pediatricians and the society in general. This right to health and welfare must be protected by the state. This chapter reviews the impact of the maternal lifestyle can have on the fetus that may result in fetal abuse.

Chapter 4 - Violence has been part of the lives of individuals. The term "bullying or peer abuse" is currently used to designate violence among children of about the same age at schools. It is characterized by the presence of an intentionally repeated and unjustified aggressive behavior of a child or group of children towards another with the objective of inflicting physical or emotional harm to the victim. In developed countries, the prevalence is very high. Usually, physical abuse is common among boys and young men while discrimination and psychological abuse are more frequent among girls and young women. In recent years, there has emerged a new form of bullying known as "cyberbullying." This form of bullying is defined as an aggressive act by a student or group of students using electronic devices

Customarily, the actors in play in the issue of bullying are constituted by the provokers, the aggressor, the victim, the observers or witnesses and the authorities. Usually, the authorities are the last to know about the situation and this normally happens when the victim´s parent raise their voice or file in a report.

Apart from the physical harm, victims of bullying may suffer different associated pathologies such as depression and suicidal attempts. For this reason, the development of a program of actions involving the participation of the school authorities, the students, parents and the society in general directed to the prevention of the phenomenon through communication with the responsible authorities, students supervision within the classrooms, the school environment and their immediate surroundings, and the psychological therapy of the victims if the need be.

In this chapter, the authors review all aspects of bullying, bringing into limelight the actors in play, the sites of occurrence, its modalities, and the basic and extreme clinical characteristics as well as the curative and preventive interventions necessary to curb this phenomenon.

Chapter 5 - Ritualism is considered a religious threat, which can generate physical, psychological and sexual abuse to the victims, most of them children. This type of violence evolved with the advance of time, beginning with religious fanaticism, witch hunts, change to religious sacrifices or exposure to children in unsafe situations or places of risk, as well as the risk of death by denying blood transfusions. The doctor and any professional who is in contact with the children must consider this type of violence; that would enable him to offer comprehensive management.

It is necessary that the medical community and the society in general be on alert because the children are at high risk of being physically, sexually or psychologically abused by adults, including their parents, who under a religious fanaticism violate the rights of children. Because of the complexities in the diagnosis and the resulting denunciation, there is no clear mechanism to fully attend these children and young people. However, it is the responsibility of doctors, jurists and sociologists to design an algorithm that allows the rescue of the victims and prevent them from suffering damage. This chapter analyzes the risks of religious fanaticism and how it can affect to children.

Chapter 6 - The National Center for Child Abuse and Neglect conceptualized sexual abuse (SA) in children as "a contact or interaction between a child and an adult, when the adult (aggressor) uses the child to sexually stimulate himself/herself or another person." It can also be perpetrated by a person under the age of 18, when he/she is significantly older than the child (victim) or when the aggressor is in a position of power or control over the child." The adult may use acts of violence, threat, surprise, deceit or seduction to ensure the participation of the victim in a sexual context taking advantage of the victim's inability to consent because of the age, difference in power or the nature of the relationship.

Sexual abuse is estimated to occur in 11% of women and in 2% of men. Children are more often abused by people they know than by strangers. The abuse in children impacts on their health in adult life. It can generate mental illnesses and even metabolic diseases given the constant exposure of stress. Hence, its prevention becomes essential. This chapter reviews the sexual abuse in children as part of child abuse and the impact on their health.

Chapter 7 - Parental alienation syndrome (PAS) is described as a mental illness in which a child is involved in the separation or violent divorce of the parents by psychologically manipulating him or her to be strongly associated with a parent (alienator) and to reject the relationship with the other parent (alienated) without legitimate justification. The child could be a victim of one or several types of child abuse such as sexual abuse, psychological abuse and neglect in the course of a separation and divorce of the parents. The magnitude of the child's problems can be associated with the type of separation, the age and gender of the child and the predominating inclination of the child's relationship (mother-child or father-child). Usually, there is an increase in emotional manifestations of the child such as depression, anxiety and aggression. Therefore, it is pertinent to consider the age of the child and the physical, intellectual, emotional and economic capacity of the parents to always ensure the best interests of the child. In this chapter the authors will discuss how the parents' divorce or separation affects the mental, emotional and physical health of the children in such a family.

Chapter 8 - Pregnancy in adolescents is a gestational process that occurs in the life stage of a girl who has not completely concluded her biopsychosocial growth and development. According to its administrative record, a gestation that occurs between 10 and 19 years of age should be considered as teen pregnancy. Its impact is reflected on the health, education, life project, social and cultural relations of the girl as well as on her and her family economy. Being an adolescent mother or father is usually fraught with and/or re-enforces, without social distinction, a series of associated conditions of vulnerability.

The processes of professionalization and adaptation, of education, health, communication and of other conditions that may serve as a vehicle for the application of preventive strategies to prevent the phenomenon are extremely necessary. The results obtained presume a partial success in the prevention of unwanted pregnancies in this stage of life thus, re-enforcing the achievements which can be obtained with additional strategies.

Due to the multifactorial nature of its genesis, teen pregnancy will have an individual expression. Generally, the magnitude of the impacts depends on the circumstances of the person, the couple, the family and the society as well as on the demographic circumstances of each country and its different regions. Hence, a general approach with an individual flexibility is required when dealing with teen pregnancy. This chapter reviews teen pregnancy, its predisposing factors and its prevention.

Chapter 9 - Child abuse (CA) in any of its modalities – physical abuse (PA), child sexual abuse (SA), psychological/emotional abuse (PsA/EA) and negligence (NE) – can have immediate and lifelong negative repercussions on the physical and mental health of the child or adolescent. CA is a factor that strongly contributes in the development of malnutrition (MN) which can be expressed like undernutrition (UNT), stunting, overweight and obesity. The presence of any of the aforementioned manifestations may be the physical expression of any of the forms of CA.

In this chapter the authors will review the relationship between childhood abuse and eating disorder, as well as the impact on adulthood.

Chapter 10 - Negligence is recognized as the most frequent form of Child Abuse (CA), but because of its clinical and social complexity, it is the CA most difficult to establish an accurate diagnosis, integral care and registration. It is defined as: the failure of a relative or a caregiver of a child to cover his needs for food, clothing, protection, medical care or to supervise his health, education, safety and to protect him from everyday dangers.

The basic expression of this form of CA is intentional action of the primary caregiver aimed at not covering in an adequate way the victim of fundamental biopsychosocial needs. The affectations of negligence can be social, emotional and economic. The effect on cognitive function can range from variable degree of neurodevelopmental delay to an affectation of variable degree in school or academic performance. The emotional involvement occurs approximately 80% of them, some mental health affectations such as anxiety and depression. It is clear that CA requires the implementation of a series of preventive strategies of moral, family, social and governmental nature, whose orientation will depend on the specific form in question. This chapter tells us about the psychological, emotional and physical damage caused in children by parents' lack of attention.

Chapter 11 - Child abuse is a universal problem that affects children of all nationalities and social status. One of the indicators of abuse in children is the oral health which could affect the mouth head and/or the neck. In children, these areas are the most affected sites in child abuse, especially physical and sexual abuse. Usually, the pediatric victims are afraid to denounce the mistreatment and most often resort to introverted or violent behavior. Therefore, it is extremely important that a complete physical examination of the patient and a psychological assessment be carried out; bearing in mind that access to medical care in these cases is not immediate. Assaults that affect oral health can occur in all forms such as physical abuse, sexual abuse and negligence.

It is essential to bear in mind that dental damage in childhood influences adult life. Therefore, it is very important to detect the warning signs, prevent continued abuse and treat the injuries. In this chapter, the authors will review how child abuse impact in oral health and pinpoint the etiological instruments in odontopediatric child abuse, its local and global incidence as well as the different forms of stomatognathic system lesions suggestive of CA and the preventive strategies to curb the phenomenon.

ACKNOWLEDGMENTS

As the saying goes "behind every achievement is the effort of not only one but many", we would like to express our profound gratitude to all that in one way or another collaborated in making this book a success. Our special thanks to Dr. Cyril Ndidi Nwoye Nnamezie, a native English speaker, for his untiring effort in translating and editing this work, and meticulously ensuring that the language herein used met the standard needed in a work of this magnitude. My thanks also go to Dra Mayra Santillán García and Dra Monica Punzo Soto for their marvelous medical assistance in the preparation of most of chapters included in this book. Your contributions have been a great help in bringing this project to a successful end.

In: Child Abuse: Harm and Solutions   ISBN: 978-1-53614-271-6
Editors: Arturo Loredo Abdalá et al. © 2018 Nova Science Publishers, Inc.

Chapter 1

CHILDHOOD PHYSICAL ABUSE: THE SERIOUS MODALITY OF CHILD ABUSE

Arturo Loredo Abdalá, Leslie Ramírez Angoa and Abigail Casas Muñoz*

Centro de Estudios Avanzados sobre Maltrato Infantil-Prevención del
InstitutoNacional de Pediatría (CEAMI-P-INP),
Ciudad de Mexico, Mexico

ABSTRACT

Violence in all its manifestations is, unfortunately, the current situation that prevails in the world. Violence has been classified into three large groups, depending on the context in which it is inflicted: self-inflicted, interpersonal and collective violence. Violent acts can be physical, sexual, emotional or psychological or exercised by inattention. According to the International Classification of Diseases, it is a condition that integrates basically four modalities: physical abuse, sexual abuse, psychological abuse and neglect.

* Corresponding Author Email: cainm_inp@hotmail.com.

In the violence between humans, interpersonal and inter-community violence as well as violence among countries can be highlighted. Interpersonal violence is the most common among humans and can happen between members of the same family or between couples or friends. In all these forms of violence, physical violence (PA) stands out and this affects both children and adults. PA in children has been considered as an act or acts in which the caregiver has caused; intentionally or accidentally; pain, physical and/or emotional damage to a girl, a boy or a teenager. PA can be visible and invisible. However, its diagnosis is beclouded by confusion and lack of precise diagnostic instruments. To deal with this problem, the Comprehensive Care for Battered Child Clinic of the National Institute of Pediatrics (CAINM-INP), Mexico City has come up with a series of indicators that allow establishing or ruling out if the injuries suffered by a child were caused by an accident or PA. PA risk factors are classified into factors of the minor, factors of the parents and family and school or environmental factors.

Its consequences can be immediate or long-term. The probability of the victim having a negative cognitive performance and psychosocial functioning in his or her life in the short, medium and long term are, especially, when the victim has faced more than four adverse experiences in childhood (AEC). When PA in boys, girls and teenagers is well-founded, the management must be medico-legal. The prevention of PA is extremely important and must consist of both primary and secondary interventions so as to radicate or substantial reduce the occurrence of the phenomenon in the world. This chapter highlights the importance of recognizing child maltreatment, the modalities of childhood physical abuse and the way to prevent it.

Keywords: physical abuse, sexual abuse, psychological abuse, neglect

INTRODUCTION

The current situation in the world has as predominant expression "violence" in all its manifestations and these can be natural, environmental, human and personal.

For example, nature plays a preponderant role on generating earthquakes, fires, floods, droughts, etc. in different parts of the world and these environmental conditions cause physical destruction but most importantly, death and desolation of human beings in the affected areas. This can generate violence between people and even against the children due to its devastating consequences such as lack of water, food, shelter and the absence of family members by death.

Day after day, different types of violence occur among the humans. Thus, we have family violence, school violence, inter-community violence and violence among countries. These situations cause varying degrees of morbi-mortality in girls, boys and teenagers as well as in adults and the elderly.

Within the violence between humans, interpersonal violence stands out. This type of violence has been in existence from time immemorial and can happen between members of the same family or between couples or friends. In recent time, the violence between humans is re-emerging in an escalating form and when it involves children, it is known as child abuse (CA). The latter is a pathology that can cause immediate physical and emotional damage to the victims and when a girl or a boy or a teenager manages to survive it, his or her physical and emotional health will remain affected, in varying degrees, throughout the life. Coupled with these consequences is the high percentage of the possibility of its transgenerational replication [1-4].

The World Health Organization (WHO) indicated that the abuse of girls, boys and teenagers must be registered as CA and in accordance with the International Classification of Diseases (ICD-10). This classification distinguished four modalities of CA: physical abuse, sexual abuse, psychological abuse and neglect thus, conglomerating all types of violence that generally affect people of this age group [5-6].

Violence is also classified into three large groups based on the context in which it is inflicted. On this basis, violence can be self-inflicted, interpersonal and collective violence. Regardless of the context, violent acts can be physical, sexual, emotional or psychological, or exercised by inattention (Figure 1).

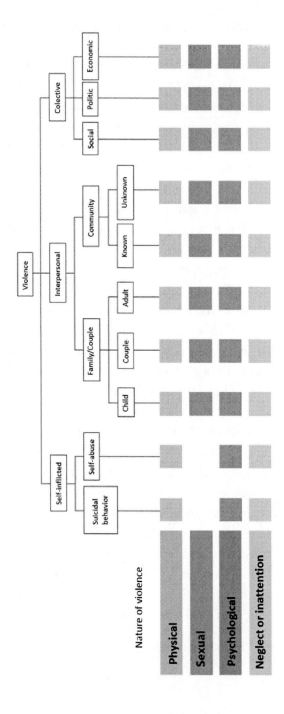

Figure 1. Typology of violence (WHO) Taken from Butchart A., 2009. Prevention of child abuse: What should be done and how gather evidence.

On the basis of the context of infliction, CA is should be seen and accepted as a medical-social-legal problem. This status is re-enforced and supported by the magnitude and nature of damage inherent CA acts especially when the physical and emotional damages that occur in the child, its emotional and economic consequences on the family and the social and economic impacts on the community are considered. These constitute the bases why in 1999, the World Health Organization catalogued CA as a world health public problem [7].

HISTORICAL REVIEW

Historically, there have been numerous medical, paramedical and legal reports on CA and on each of its modalities in almost all the countries of the world. Among these reports, we can highlight Ambrois Tardieu's case on the accusations of aggression against the children in the 19th century, the case of Mary Ellen in New York, the legal modifications to deal with the situations of violence against children in England; and later, in the 20th century, Caffeyen's descriptions of the phenomenon in the USA and in 1962, Kempe's publication on "The Battered-Child Syndrome" [8-12].

Within the clinical context of CA, the physical abuse (PA) stands out as the "tip of the iceberg" due to its seriousness and basically because, it is the most evident condition in the pediatric medical environment. It is graded as a CA type that inflicts the most physical and emotional damage in the pediatric victims that, if unchecked, may lead to death or bring about variable degrees of physical and emotional disabilities that can impact on their personal, professional and intellectual developments in the short, medium or long term [13-14].

Definition of PA

The predominant definitions of PA are from global institutions such as the World Health Organization (WHO), the Panamerican Health

Organization (PAHO), UNICEF, etc. The article 19 of the Convention on the Rights of the Child (CRC) defined violence as "any form of physical or mental prejudice or abuse, neglect or negligent treatment, bad treatment or exploitation, including sexual abuse" [17].

The WHO defined CA as the abuse and neglect of children under 18, and includes all types of physical, psychological, or sexual abuse; neglector negligent treatment and commercial exploitation or other types of exploitation that cause or may cause damage to the health, development or dignity of a child, or endangering his or her survival, in the context of a relationship of responsibility, trust or power. Exposure to violence is also included among forms of child abuse.

UNICEF defined it as "Children and teenagers up to the age of 18 who" suffer occasional or habitual acts of physical, sexual or emotional violence, either in the family or in social institutions [18]. On its part, the International Society for the Prevention of Child Abuse and Neglect (IPSCAN) (2009) construed CA as physical and emotional abuse, sexual abuse, neglect and negligent treatment of children, as well as their exploitation [18]. However, there are several difficulties to define physical abuse in a consistent manner. Taking into account the explicitness of its invasive nature, this problem has been considered as an act or acts in which the caregiver has caused, intentionally or accidentally, pain, physical and/or emotional damage to a girl, boy or teenager. Therefore, PA should be suspected when a girl, a boy or a teenager presents an external or internal injury as a result of intentional or accidental aggression, caused by another person who is generally an adult [19-22].

Frequency of PA

It is very difficult to specify the true and real frequency of PA at global level, especially in countries with developing economies. Most of the figures denoting the seriousness of the problem come from countries with leading economy. In England, for example, the annual frequency ranges from 3.7 to 16.3% [6]. In the USA, the registry of CA frequency is dated back to 1988. The National Child Abuse and Neglect Data System of this country reports an annual number of approximately 700,000 cases out of which 118,000 correspond to PA [15].

There are several limitations that hinder the obtention of reliable data on the frequency of PA. These limitations rotate on the fact that the severity of the clinical expression of the damage varies according to the intensity and frequency of the aggression, the insufficient legal denunciation, an incorrect record of the cases and for the fact that PA cases are frequently associated with other forms of CA, mainly negligence and psychological abuse.

The reality is that no country in the world escapes from this problem [6]. For its persistence in the second decade of the 21st century, its consequences on the health of the victim and their family; and the economic and social impact on the community it then becomes necessary that in the study of PA, its "medical-social-legal emergency" status must be understood and accepted and that it has not been contained or eradicated [16].

CLINICAL PICTURE

Several studies specifying the characteristics of the injuries a victim of PA can suffer which would help to establish the clinical diagnosis have been published [23-25]. However, children and teenagers with important physical damage are usually brought to the pediatric hospitals. The injuries are generally, but not always, the type that can put their lives or the function of the damaged structure in danger and so, warrants an integral medical attention. Nevertheless, it is pertinent to highlight at this point within the PA cases requiring medical attention that the cases of "shaken child syndrome," whose severity can cause the death of the victim, are exceptions [10, 26-30].

In order to better understand the physical damage that a victim of PA can have, the clinical manifestations of PA victims can be classified into 2 groups: "visible and invisible."

Visible Clinical Expressions

The visible lesions of PA can be located in anywhere of the body. In order of frequency they are found in the skull, face, buccal mucosa, upper extremities, lower extremities and in the genito-anal mucosa. Usually the damage can be localized in the skin and/or mucous membranes and this is expressed depending on the mechanism of the aggression. Generally, they are:

a) *Injuries caused by physical trauma with the fists, kicks, bites and with blunt objects, wires, belts or with sharp objects.*

   The clinical expression usually appears in the form of scratches, ecchymosis, mark of the object used, dental arch, an open wound on the skin or an injury in the oral mucosa and teeth or in the genito-anal area.

b) *Burns.* These may be the consequences of various mechanisms among which are: 1. Contact with boiling fluid. Normally, this mechanism produces injuries of variable degree and location in any part of the body. The injuries in the hands or the feet by immersion in very hot water are called "glove" or "sock" and are characterized by being symmetrical, well delimited and without "satellite" which is a manifestation of injuries caused by the splash of boiling liquid. 2. Direct contact with burning object. This can be produced by the flame of the stove, iron, cigarettes burns that are extinguished on the back of the victim and 3. Contact with hot objects. This may occur when hot food or drinks are deliberately introduced in the mouth of a child or when the aggressor intentionally touches the child with a very hot object [31-33].

Invisible Clinical Expressions

Bone Injury

In most cases, in addition to the visible expressions on the skin and mucous membranes, there may be a bone lesion (fracture) which is usually established by specific radiographic or gammographic study.

The injury or injuries can be found in the skull, ribs and vertebrae as well as in the bones of the upper and lower extremities. Its location, severity and age are variable. To determine if an invisible injury is as a result of PA, doctors should focus on the explanation given by the caretakers of the child. If the explanation of the mechanism is not convincing, then PA can be established.

In severely injuries, the fracture can be exposed thus, expressly establishing CA diagnosis of PA modality [34-35]. Table 1 shows the specificity of the injuries that will permit the establishment of PA diagnosis.

All injuries abruptly presented by children and teenagers must be consistent with the explanation of the adult who presents the child. Likewise, the age and sex of the victims, the tracing of the fracture, its location, the existence of more injuries and the time elapsed before the child is presented for medical attention should be taken into consideration in the establishment of PA diagnosis.

Table 1. Specificity of radiological findings in children

High Specificity	Moderate Specificity	Common/low specificity
• Metaphyseal injuries • Costal fractures (posteromedial) • Scapular fractures • Vertebral fractures (spinous processes) • • Sternal fractures	• Multiple fractures, especially bilateral ones • Old fractures • Epiphyseal fractures • Fractures or subluxations of vertebral bodies • Digital fractures • Complex skull fractures.	• Subperiosteal bone formation • Clavicular fractures • Diaphysis fracture of long bones • Lineal skull fractures

Table taken from Flaherty [35].

Table 2. Clinical indicators in children to differentiate injuries due to physical abuse or accidents

Indicator	Physical Abuse (%)	Accidents (%)	Assigned Value
Discordance First order Clinical radiology Clinical scintigraphy or both	85	15	p < 0.0001
Injuries and scars Second order ancient	62	25	p < 0.0001
Unwanted Product Second Order	59	7	p < 0.0001
Poor Hygiene Second Order	57	19	p < 0.0001
Short Stature Third Order	35	6	p < 0.0001
Poor Nutrition Third Order	27	5	p < 0.0001
Poor school performance Third Order	17	2	p < 0.001
Incomplete Vaccination Scheme Third Order	16	4.5	p < 0.001

First order = 75 to 100%; second order = 50 to 75%; t third order = 0 to 50%.

Table 3. Clinical indicators to differentiate physical abuse from accidents in the pediatric population (family history)

Indicator	Physical Abuse (%)	Accidents (%)	Assigned Value
Delayed Medical Attention First Order	85	2	p < 0.000001
Alcoholism or Drug Dependence of a parent or both Second order	55	26	p < 0.0001
Request for medical attention by an external family member or a stranger: Third Order	46	12.5	p < 0.0001
History of abuse In parents: Third order	45	1	p < 0.0001
History of abuse in other family member: Third order	35	3	p < 0.0001
Living together with stepparents: Third Order	35	1	p < 0.0001

First order = 75 to 100%; second order = 50 to 75%; Third order = 0 to 50%.

A dilemma to solve is when a girl, boy or teenager is presented in the emergency service, with a history that the injuries are as a result of an accident. However, with well-established clinical picture, the doctor may suspect or discard PA. There are several strategies to determine if the injuries that a child presents correspond to an accident or PA [36]. For example, at the Comprehensive Care for Battered Child Clinic of the National Institute of Pediatrics (CAINM-INP), Mexico City, a series of indicators that allow to establish or rule out if the injuries suffered by a child were caused by an accident or PA were set down.

The sensitivity and specificity of each of the variables and their association permitting the establishment of the type of variable, its hierarchy and its sum were employed to develop the following classification used in the daily clinic practice. The basic objective is to establish or rule out the diagnosis of PA: (Tables 2-3). These variables are based on:

1) The existence of two criteria of 1st Order; two of 2nd Order and two criteria of 3rd Order indicate a diagnostic certainty of 90-100%.
2) Two criteria of 1st Order, one of 2nd Order and one of 3rd Order indicate a diagnostic certainty of 80-89%
3) A criterion of 1st Order, one of 2nd Order and two of 3rd Order indicate a diagnostic certainty of 70-79%. Table 2 shows the characteristics of the same and their values [37-38].

Injury of Internal Organs

Trauma can cause injuries to the organs of the cranial cavity, eyes, thorax, abdomen or pelvic cavity. The clinical manifestations depend on the injured structure.

Probably the most frequent is neurological damage. Sudden and severe suffering of the central nervous system can usually be observed in children under 2 years of age, a situation that is exemplified by the cases of the shaken and impacted child syndrome. The damage is caused by the severe shaking of the skull and, occasionally, by impacting the head and the whole body on a hard surface. This causes cerebral edema, subdural hematoma, subarachnoid hemorrhage and in other areas of the brain. Characteristic lesions of this syndrome also occur in the eye which can be manifested by unilateral or bilateral retinal hemorrhage and occasionally, retinal detachment [26, 28-29, 39].

In all cases in which PA is suspected, a wide exploration of the oral cavity must be made to establish lesions in the teeth and mucosa [40-42].

The damage of abdominal entrails can generate a picture of acute belly, mainly by perforation of the appendix as a result of a kick in the abdomen, perforation of the second portion of the duodenum, injury that occurs when the child is kept lying down and upside down on adult's leg and receives blows at the back. In this case, the intestinal entrails is hit with the vertebral body causing perforation of that portion of the intestine. Similar damage can occur in the bladder when the upper part is injured.

There are cases of bursting of the liver or spleen that cause a picture of acute abdomen and/or hemorrhagic shock. As a consequence of abdominal trauma, cases of chylous ascites, pancreatic fracture in young children, the development of a non-accidental post-traumatic jejuno-jejunal fistula have been described and are difficult to diagnose etiologically [43-48]. Cases of suffocation, drowning or sudden poisoning should also be considered as an expression of PA [49-54].

In all cases of probable PA, clinical suspicion should be established with the following data:

a) Discrepancy of the clinical picture with the version given by the relative.
b) The type of injury, based on its location.
c) Delay to request medical attention.
d) The intellectual level of the minor and/or the person who takes care of him.

DIFFERENTIAL DIAGNOSIS

The research work during two decades has allowed the specification of some situations that should be ruled out before establishing the diagnosis of PA (Table 4).

**Table 4. Medical-social conditions that should be discarded before
establishing the diagnosis of PA**

Accidents
Disciplinary strategy
Educational strategy
Poverty
Ignorance
"Customs and habits"
Some pediatric diseases

**Table 5. Nosological entities to be considered in the differential
diagnosis of physical abuse trauma or accidental burn**

Some neurological or metabolic disease	*Diseases with bone repercussion*
- Glutaricacidemia	- Scurvy
- Congenital inference to pain	- Imperfect osteogenesis
- Lesh-Nyhan syndrome	- Renal rickets
- Spinal cord injury	
Disorders of coagulation	*Cultural*
- Hemophilia	- Applications of "suckers"
- Hypoprothrombinemia	- Treatment of the "fallen crown"
- Thrombocytopenic purpura	- Put lemon drops in the eyes
	- Made the child smell hot pepper
Various skin disorders	- Throbbing the tonsils
- Aplasia cutis	
- Contact dermatitis	*Others*
- Lyell syndrome	Syndrome of sudden infant death

In this context it is essential to make the differential diagnosis with the
conditions presented in Table 5 [55-56].

The medical problem that must be solved on a daily basis with patients
in whom PA is suspected is the establishment of a diagnosis of certainty. In
most cases, there may be a discrepancy between what is said by the adult
who brings the child with the clinical and imaging study findings. In this
way, the doctor must make an accurate diagnosis [57].

RISK FACTORS

It is very important that the doctor and the paramedic who care for these children know, at a given time, the risk factors that can denote PA. These variables are classified as factors of the minor, factors of the parents and family and school or environmental factors (Table 6).

Table 6. PA occurrence risk factors

- Be an unwanted product, planned or accepted by their parents or one of them.
- Be born with a congenital malformation of lesser or greater severity
- Have a chronic illness (cancer, asthma, seizures)
- Suffer from a global growth delay

Factors of the parents or the relatives
- History of CA by one or both parents.
- The girl, boy or teenager lives with stepfather and / or stepmother.
- Addiction to alcohol or to any illicit substance by the father or mother of the child.
- Witness or suffer family violence
- History of an emotional disorder or mental illness in one of the family members.
- The father or mother is in prison

Environmental factors
- Violence in the home
- Bullying at school
- Violence in the neighborhood
- Environmental rudeness
- Narco retail and drug trafficking
- Housing marginalization
- Extreme poverty

LONG-TERM CONSEQUENCES

For approximately two decades, the world literature has reiterated that the probability of the victim having a negative cognitive performance and psychosocial functioning in his or her life in the short, medium and long term are, especially, when the victim has faced more than four adverse experiences in childhood (AEC) [58-59]. Table 7 shows a summary of 10 AEC situations [58].

Victims of PA who have four or more of the indicated elements are more prone to develop, in adult life, depression, addictions or some attempt or suicidal culmination compared with the general population [58, 60-62].

When we consider that PA is an adverse experience suffered in the first years of life that generally occur at home where violence predominates, there are chances that this form of CA will also favor the development of anxiety disorders, aggressive behaviors and depression at various times in the life of the victim [63-66].

Table 7. Adverse experiences in childhood

– Physical Abuse in childhood
– Sexual Abuse in childhood
– Psychological Abuse in childhood
– Emotional Negligence
– Physical Negligence
– Family member with mental illness at home
– Family member in prison
– Exposed to violence at home
– Substance abuse at home
– Parental separation/divorce

LEGAL NOTIFICATION

When there is a well-founded suspicion that a girl, a boy or a teenager is a victim of PA, a legal complaint must be made. Once the diagnosis of certainty is established, the complaint is medico-legal and the responsibility to establish the legal status of the minor, his family and even the possible aggressor falls on the responsible legal authority. However, this action may be different depending on each country.

Several authors maintain the notion that the transgenerational replication of CA exists in a proportion of 55-85%. This figure depends on the studies analyzed. Moreover, the existence of numerous variables that intervene in this phenomenon such as the type of abuse, its chronicity, who was the aggressor, the environment, protective actions, etc., have been specified. Therefore, it is extremely necessary to dauntlessly continue investigating the consequences of CA in the victims and those of them that can manifest in adult life. Probably, this is the reason why the prevention of this pathology has not been successful [4, 67-68].

PREVENTION

Despite the important progress so far made at worldwide level in research on child's early-life development as well as in the development of public policies and services, the results are still not so favorable to develop an effective primary prevention campaign against child abuse, due mainly to their inadequate and inequitable employment. An effective preventive action can only be developed when PA risk factors are detected, whether at the family or community level [69-71]. However, in spite of all these hindrances, there are successful interventions based on the medical and paramedical surveillance of children and teenagers who have been victims of PA that have worked to curb the repetition of the problem. In any case, such interventions only corresponds to a "secondary prevention" of the phenomenon [72-73] and do not address the "primary prevention" which is the hallmark for the eradication or substantial reduction of the phenomenon in the world.

REFERENCES

[1] *Informe Sobre la Situación Mundial de la Prevención de la Violencia 2014*. Organización Mundial de la Salud 2014. [*Report on the world situation of the prevention of violence 2014*. World Health Organization. 2014].

[2] *Salud para los adolescentes del mundo Una segunda oportunidad en la segunda década*. Organización Mundial de la Salud. 2014 [*Health for the world's teenagers A second chance in the second deca*de. World Health Organization. 2014].

[3] Dixon L, Browne K, Hamilton-Giachritsi C. Risk factors of parents abused as children: a meditational analysis of the intergenerational continuity of child maltreatment (Part I). *J Child Psychol Psychiatr.* 2005; 46:47–57.

[4] Bartlett JD, KotakeCh, Fauth R, Easterbrooks A. Intergenerational transmission of child abuse and neglect: Do maltreatment type, perpetrator, and substantiation status matter? *Child Abuse Neglect* 2017; 63:84-94.

[5] *Clasificación Internacional de Enfermedades 10° (CIE-10). Revision.* Organización Panamericana de la Salud/Organización Mundial. [*International Classification of Diseases (ICD-10) Review.* Pan American Health Organization/World Organization].

[6] Gilbert R, Spatz Widom C, Browni K. Burden and consequences of child maltreatment in high income countries. *Lancet* 209; 373:68-80

[7] McMenemy MC. WHO recognizes child abuse as a major problem. *Lancet* 1999;353:1340.

[8] Tardieu A. Etude medico-legal esur les services et mauve is traitement exercessur les infants. *Ann Hyg Publ Med.* 1860; 13:361-398.

[9] Caffey J. Multiple fractures in the long bones of infants suffering from chronic subdural hematoma. *Am J Roentgen* 1946; 56:163-173.

[10] Kempe CH, Silverman FN, Steel BE. The battered child syndrome. *JAMA* 1962; 181:17-24.

[11] Loredo Abdalá A. Maltrato físico. En: Loredo Abdalá A. *Maltrato en niños y adolescentes.* [Physical abuse. In: Loredo Abdalá A. *Abuse in children and adolescents*] Editores de Textos Mexicanos 2004 pp 28-74.

[12] Berkowitz CD. Physical Abuse of Children. *N Engl J Med.* 2017; 376:2659-2666.

[13] Dubowitz H, Bennett S. Physical abuse and neglect of children. *Lancet* 2007; 369:1891-1899.

[14] Black M, Walker S P, Fernald LC H, Andersen CT, DiGirolamo A. Early childhood development coming of age: science through the life course. *Lancet* 2017; 389:77–90.

[15] Administration for Children and Families, Administration on Children, Youth and Families, Children's Bureau. *Child maltreatment 2015 - data tables.* Washington, DC: Department of Health and Human Services, 2017.

[16] Acker S, Roach J, Partrick D, Karrer F, Bensard D, Sirotnak A. Beyond morbidity and mortality: The social and legal outcomes of non-accidental trauma. *J Pediatr Surg,* 2015; 50:604-607.

[17] Centro de Prensa, OMS: *Maltrato infantil;* 2016 [actualizada en septiembre 2016; acceso el 25 julio 2017]. http://www.who.int/ mediacentre/factsheets/fs150/es/ [Press Center, WHO: *Child abuse;* 2016 [updated September 2016; Access on July 25, 2017] http://www.who.int/mediacentre/factsheets/fs150/es/].

[18] Butchart A, Phinney H, Mian M, Fürniss T. Prevención del maltrato infantil: qué hacer, y cómo obtener evidencias. [Prevention of child maltreatment: what to do, and how to obtain evidence] *Catalogo Biblioteca de la OMS,* 2009.

[19] Hansen DJ, Sedlar G, Warner-Rogers JE. Childphysical abuse. In R. T. Ammerman & M. Hersen (Eds.), *Assessment of family violence: A clinical and legal sourcebook.* New York Wiley. 1999: 127-156.

[20] Widom CS. Child abuse, neglect and adult behavior: Research design and findings on criminality, violence and child abuse. *Am J Orthopsychiatr,* 1989;58:260-270.

[21] Widom CS. Understanding the consequences of childhood victimization. In: RM Reece (Ed.) *Treatment of child abuse*. Baltimore, 2000; 339-361.

[22] Cicchetti D, Lynch M. Toward an ecological/ transactional model of community violence and child maltreatment: Consequences for children's development. *Psychiatry* 1993;56:96-118.

[23] Mc Gee AH, Wolfe SA, Yuen SK, Carnachan J. Measurement of maltreatment. *Child Abuse Neglect* 1995;19:233-49.

[24] Trocme N Mac Millan H, Fallon B. Nature and severity of physical harm caused by child abuse and neglect results from de Canadian Incidence Study. *Can Med Assoc J* 2003; 169:911-915.

[25] Trokel M, Waddimba A, Griffith J, Sege R. Variations in the diagnosis of child abuse and severity injured infants. *Pediatrics* 2006; 117:722-728.

[26] Guthkelch AN. Infantile subdural haematoma and its relationship to whiplash injuries. *BMJ* 1971; 2:430-1.

[27] Caffey J. On the theory and practice of shaking infants: its potential residual effects of permanent brain damage and mental retardation. *Am J Dis Child* 1972;124:161–9.

[28] Duhaime AC, Alario AJ, Lewander WJ, Schut L, Sutton LN, Seidl TS. Head injury in very young children: mechanisms, injury types, and ophthalmologic findings in 100 hospitalized patients younger than 2 years of age. *Pediatrics* 1992; 90:179-85.

[29] King WJ, MacKay M, Sirnick A, Canadian Shaken Baby Study Group. Shaken baby syndrome in Canada: clinical characteristics and outcomes of hospital cases. *Can Med Assoc J* 2003;168:155-9.

[30] Simonnet H, Laurent-Vannier A, Yuan W, Hully M, Valimahomed S, Bourennane M, Chevignard M. Parents' behavior in response to infant crying: Abusive head trauma education. *Child Abuse Neglect* 2014; 38:1914-22.

[31] Renz BM, Sherman R. Abusive scald burns in infants and children: a prospective study. *Am Surg* 1993; 59:329-334.

[32] Malik JA. Emergency department evaluation of child abuse. *Emerg Med Clin North Am.* 1999; 17:575-593.

[33] Titi N, Niekerk A, Ahmed R. Child understandings of the causation of childhood burn injuries: Child activity, parental domestic demands, and impoverished settings. *Child Care Health Dev* 2017; 1:1-7.

[34] Section on Radiology, American Academy of Pediatrics. Diagnostic imaging of child abuse. *Pediatrics* 2009; 123:1430-5.

[35] Flaherty EG, Perez-Rossello JM, Levine MA, Hennrikus WL, and the American Academy Of Pediatrics Committee On Child Abuse And Neglect, Section On Radiology, Section On Endocrinology, And Section On Orthopaedics, And The Society For Pediatric Radiology. Evaluating children with fractures for child physical abuse. *Pediatrics* 2014; 133:e477- e489.

[36] Woodman J, Pitt M, Wentz R. Performance and screening test for child physical abuse in Accident and Emergency Department. *Health Technol Assest* 2008; 12:1-118.

[37] Loredo Abdalá A, Trejo Hernández J, Castilla Serna L. Children injured: abuse or accident? Diagnosis through indicators. *Bol Med Hosp Infant Mex* 2003; 60:368-379.

[38] Loredo Abdalá A, Perea Martínez A, Trejo Hernández J, Bustos Valenzuela V. Maltrato físico y accidentes como causas de lesiones en el niño y utilidad de los indicadores clínicos para el diagnóstico diferencial. En: Loredo Abdalá A. *Maltrato en el niño. Temas de Pediatría.* [Physical abuse and accidents as causes of injury to children and the usefulness of clinical indicators for differential diagnosis. In: Loredo Abdalá A. *Abuse in the child. Pediatrics Topics.*] Asociación Mexicana de Pediatría. Mc Graw- Hill Interamericana. Mexico. 2001; 191-203.

[39] Levin AV, Christian CW, Committee on Child Abuse and Neglect, Section on Ophthalmology. The eye examination in the evaluation of child abuse. *Pediatrics* 2010;126:376-80.

[40] Needleman HL. Orofacial trauma in child abuse: types, prevalence, management, and dental proffesions involment. *Ped Dent* 1986; 8: 71-79.

[41] Fonseca MA, Feigal RJ, Bensel BW. Dental aspects of 1248 cases of child maltreatment in file at a major country hospital. *Ped Dent J* 1992;14:152-157.

[42] American Academy of Pediatrics. Committee on child abuse and Neglect and American Pediatric Dentistry. Oral and Dental aspects of child abuse and neglect. *Pediatrics* 1999; 104:248-350.

[43] Baeza Herrera C, Ortiz Zúñiga A, Osorio Agüero CD. Enfermedad quirúrgica por abuso. En: Loredo Abdalá A. *Maltrato en niños y adolescentes*. [Surgical disease due to abuse. In: Loredo Abdalá A. *Abuse in children and adolescents*] Mexico. 2004, Editores de Textos Mexicanos. Pp 120-149.

[44] Kondolot M, Yagmur F, Yikilmaz A, Turan C. A life-threatening presentation of child physical abuse jejuna perforation. *Pediatr Emer Care* 2011;27:1075-1077.

[45] Baeza-Herrera C, Cortés-García R, Martínez-Leo B, Arcos-Aponte A, García-Cabello LM. Ascitis quilosa causada por maltrato físico. Estudio de un caso y revisión de la literatura. [Chylose ascites caused by physical abuse. Study of a case and review of the literature] *Acta Pediátrica de Mexico*: 2011; 32:130-135.

[46] Sowrey L, Lawson KA, Garcia-Filion P, Notrica D. Duodenal injuries in the very young: Child abuse? *J Trauma Acute Care Surg* 2012;74:136-142.

[47] Solaiman Z, Kulaylat FN, Santos MC. Delayed presentation of jejuno-jejunal fistula with structure after physical child abuse. *Pediatr Emerg Care* 2015; 1-3.

[48] Touloukian RJ. Abdominal visceral injuries in battered children syndrome. *Pediatrics* 1968; 42:642-646.

[49] Meadow R. Suffocation. *BMJ* 1989; 298:1572-1573.

[50] Krugman SD, Lantz PE, Sinal S, De Jong AR, Coffman K. Forced suffocation of infants with baby wipes: A previously undescribed form of child abuse. *Child Abuse Neglect* 2007; 31:615-621.

[51] Boos SC. Constrictive asphyxia: a recognizable form of fatal. *Child Abuse Neglect* 2000; 24:1503-1507.

[52] McClure RJ, Davis PM, Meadow SR, Sibert JR. Epidemiology of Munchausen syndrome by proxy, non-accidental poisoning, and non-accidental suffocation. *Arch Dis Child* 1996;75:57-61.

[53] Bellemare S. Child abuse by suffocation: A cause of apparent life-threatening events. *Paediatr Child Health* 2006; 11:493-495.

[54] Oral R, Koc F, Smith J, Sato Y. Abusive suffocation presenting as new-onset seizure. *Pediatr Emerg Care* 2011; 27:1072-1074.

[55] Loredo Abdalá A, Casas Muñoz A, Monroy Llaguno DA. *Maltrato infantil. Conocimientos básicos de una patología médico-social-legal vigente.* [*Child abuse. Basic knowledge of a current medical-social-legal pathology*] Precop SCP 2017; 13:46-51.

[56] Loredo Abdalá A, Casas Muñoz A, Figueroa Becerril ZE, Vargas Flores J. Maltrato infantil: su estudio y manejo en el Instituto Nacional de Pediatría. [*Child abuse: A study and management at the National Institute of Pediatrics*] Mexico. Colombia Forense 2016; 3:41-49.

[57] Loredo Abdalá A, Bustos Valenzuela V, Trejo Hernández J, Sánchez Velázquez A. Maltrato al menor: una urgencia médica y social que requiere atención multidisciplinaria. [Child abuse: a medical and social emergency that requires multidisciplinary care] *Bol Med Hosp Infant Mex* 1999; 56:131.

[58] Felitti VJ, Anda R F, Nordenberg D. Relationship of childhood abuse and house hold dysfunction to many of the leading causes of death in adults: The Adverse Childhood Experiences (ACE) Study. *Am J Prev Med* 1998; 14:245-258.

[59] McKelvey LM, Whiteside-Mansell L, Conners-Burrow NA, Swindle T, Fitzgerald S. Assessing adverse experiences from infancy through early childhood in home visiting programs. *Child Abuse Neglect* 1998; 51:295-302.

[60] Felitti VJ, Bremner JD. The enduring effects of abuse and related adverse experiences in childhood. *Eur Arch Psychiatr Clin Neurosci* 2006; 256:174-186.

[61] Hornor G. Childhood trauma exposure and toxic stress: whatthePNP needstoknow. *J Pediatr Heal Care* 2015; 29:191-8.

[62] Kerker B, Storfer-Isser A, Szilagyi M, Stein R, Garner A, O'Connor K, Hoagwood K, Horwitz S. Do pediatricians ask about adverse childhood experiences in pediatric primary care? *Acad Pediatr.* 2016;16:154-60.

[63] Johnson J, Cohen P, Brown J. Childhood maltreatment increases risk for personality disorders during early adulthood. *Arch General Psychiatr* 1999; 56:600-606.

[64] Golier JA, Yehuda R, Bierer LM, Mitropoulou V. New AS, Schmeidler J. A relationship of borderline personality disorder to posttraumatic stress disorder and traumatic events. *Am J Psychiatr* 2003; 160:2018-2024.

[65] Scarpa A, Haden SC, Abercromby JM. Pathways linking child physical abuse, depression, and aggressiveness across genders. *J Aggression Maltreat Trauma* 2010; 19:757-776.

[66] Gaxiola J, Frias M. Las consecuencias del maltrato infantil: Un estudio con madres mexicanas. [The consequences of child abuse: A study with Mexican mothers] *Revista Mexicana de Psicología* 2015; 22:363-374.

[67] Voncina MM, Milovancevic MP, Maravic Tosevski DL. Timeline of intergenerational child maltreatment: the mind–brain–body interplay. *Curr Psychiatr Rep* 2017; 19:2-12.

[68] SpatzWidomC,Czaja SJ, DuMont KA. Intergenerational transmission of child abuse and neglect: Real or detection bias? *Science* 2015;347:1480-1485.

[69] Reading R, Bissel S, Holdhagen J. Promotion of children s rights and prevention child maltreatment. *Lancet* 2009; 373:332-343.

[70] Gilbert R, Fluke J, O Donnell M, González Izquierdo A. Child maltreatment: variation in trends and policies in six developed countries. *Lancet* 2012; 379:758-775.

[71] Shawar YR, Shiffman J. *Generation of global political priority for early childhood development: the challenges of framing and governance.* Published online October 4, 2016 http://dx.doi.org/ 10.1016/S0140-6736(16)31574-4.

[72] Loredo-Abdalá A, Cisneros MM, Rodríguez HR, Castilla SL. Multidisciplinary care for the battered child: An evaluation of three years in Mexican children. *Bol Med Hosp Infant Mex* 1999; 56:129-134.

[73] Black MM, Walker SP, Fernald LCH. Advancing early childhood development: from science to scale 1. Early childhood development coming of age: science through the life course. *Lancet* 2016; 31:1-14.

In: Child Abuse: Harm and Solutions   ISBN: 978-1-53614-271-6
Editors: Arturo Loredo Abdalá et al. © 2018 Nova Science Publishers, Inc.

Chapter 2

ABUSIVE HEAD TRAUMA AND THE STRATEGIES FOR ITS PREVENTION

Abigail Casas Muñoz, Juan Alan Román Olmos and Noé González García*

Centro de Estudios Avanzados sobre Maltrato Infantil-Prevención
del Instituto Nacional de Pediatría (CEAMI-P-INP),
Ciudad de Mexico, Mexico

ABSTRACT

Accidental traumatic brain injuries (TBI) are one of the main causes of death in children under one year old. Within TBI is the abusive head trauma (AHT) defined as an excessive shaking of the body and head of an infant due to anger developed by an adult as a result of excessive crying of the infant or the small child. Such shakings provoke a rotatory movement and an inertial force. The effect of these two actions is a friction between the dura mater and cerebral parenchyma leading to the rupture of the veins and thus, subdural and subarachnoid hemorrhage.

Depending on the degree of aggression, the child can present multiple clinical signs such as decreased appetite, irritability, lethargy

---

* Corresponding Author Email: abycas_md@hotmail.com.

and/or vomiting, or it can progress to severe and identifiable symptoms such as traumatic brain injury (TBI), seizures, loss of consciousness, respiratory and/or cardiorespiratory arrest, shock and even sudden or unexplained death of the infant. Moreover, research works have shown that half of the children who survived AHT develop sequels such as language disorder and delay in the acquisition of it, diverse motor deficit, spasticity, quadriparesia or hemiparesia, visual deficit or blindness, hearing loss, epilepsy, sleep disorder, attention deficit and behavioral disorder.

Ignorance of how to deal with a crying crisis is one of the main risk factors for shaking a baby. Anyone who is facing a crying baby is at risk of shaking him. Therefore, pediatricians, nurses, parents and other caregivers need to know this syndrome and know the strategies to deal with crying.

Since baby crying is the main trigger of shaking and that the ways in which parents or caregivers deal with it are the principal determinants for shaking to occur or not, we can then conclude that these two main points should be the focus for its prevention and where an intervention is required. In the light of this, adequate preventive programs based on universal primary prevention education to all parents of newborn babies are extremely necessary. This chapter reviews the mechanism of action of shaken child syndrome and how to prevent it.

Keywords: excessive crying babe, head trauma, infantile irritability, shaken baby syndrome, subarachnoid hemorrhage.

INTRODUCTION

In children under one year old, accidental traumatic brain injuries (TBI) represent the main cause of death in this age group [1]. Some calculations performed have established that between 64 and 95% of these injuries are related with child abuse (CA) [2, 3].

In 1972, Caffey J. used for the first time the term "whiplash-shaken infant syndrome" to describe the association of intracranial lesions, retinal hemorrhage and certain fractures of long bones and skull attributable to CA in infants, the majority being younger than 1 year of age [4]. Subsequently, this syndrome has been recognized as: shaken baby syndrome, inflicted cerebral trauma, non-accidental head trauma, abusive head injury, non-accidental head injury and currently as Pediatric Abusive Head Trauma (AHT) [5].

WHY DOES ABUSIVE HEAD TRAUMA (AHT) OCCUR AND HOW IS IT MANIFESTED?

AHT results from excessive shaking of the body and head of an infant for the anger which an adult developed as a consequence of excessive crying of the infant or the small child (in most of cases, this crying is perceived by the adult as inconsolable). Such shakings provoke a rotatory movement (described as centrifugal force), while the sudden turn due to the shaking produces an inertial force. The resultant effect of these two actions, the rotatory movement and inertial force is a friction between the dura mater, covering the brain, and cerebral parenchyma. This friction gives rise to the rupture of the veins and thus causes subdural and subarachnoid hemorrhage [6]. In rare occasions, this syndrome is caused by involuntary actions such as throwing the baby up to make him laugh, by vehicle accident or by resuscitation maneuvers.

Depending on the degree of aggression, the child can present moderate and unspecific clinical signs such as decreased appetite, irritability, lethargy and/or vomiting, or it can progress to severe and identifiable symptoms such as traumatic brain injury (TBI), seizures, loss of consciousness, respiratory and/or cardiorespiratory arrest, shock and even sudden or unexplained death of the infant [7, 8].

CONSEQUENCES OF AHT

As already mentioned, AHT is the leading cause of death in children under one year old with a mortality rate between 10 and 38%. This damage is greater than that caused by *Haemophilus influenza* type b meningitis (approximately 5%) [9-11]. Therefore, infants who experience AHT are five times more likely to die and eight times more likely to have prolonged hospital stay for the injuries that occur [12].

The severity of the damage that children who survived AHT develop is also important since probably half of them present different sequels. Such sequels include language disorder and delay in the acquisition of it (49%); diverse motor deficit (45%); spasticity, quadriparesia or hemiparesia; visual deficit or blindness (45%) and hearing loss; epilepsy (38%); sleep disorder (17%); attention deficit (79%) and behavioral disorder (53%) [2, 13, 14]. In a retrospective study, it was reported that after suffering AHT, most of these children (83%) attended some kind of rehabilitation and 30% required special education services [15].

FREQUENCY OF ABUSIVE HEAD TRAUMA

In western countries, brain injury by AHT has an estimated rate between 17 and 30 cases per every 100,000 children under 12 months of age [16, 17]. Incidence studies in the United States and in other countries have reported rates that range from 24 to 29.7 cases in every 100,000 person-years in the first year of life. There are reports from North Caroline, USA, whose frequency is 2.6% for children <two years of age [17]; from Netherland, 3.4% in six-month old infants and from Japan, 3.4% for four-month-old babies [10]. In developing countries like Mexico, there are only reports of cases attended in second and third level pediatric hospitals [18].

WHO ARE THE MOST SUSCEPTIBLE TO SUFFER AHT?

Due to the anatomical characteristics of the children (large head, short neck, and weak and little developed muscles), the infants are the most vulnerable age group with a clear predominance of the male sex group. The average age of the victims is from 5 to 9 months and most of the victims are under 36 months of age, although it can occur even in children under 5 years of age.

WHICH ARE THE RISK FACTORS?

Crying is one of the manifestations of the children that most leads the parents to make a visit to the doctors or emergency rooms in the first years of life. A significant proportion of parents consider that excessive crying is the consequence of "colic". Despite decades of research, most cases of excessive crying are not diagnosed as such, because they can be confused in the emergency room or referral clinics for organic diseases [19]. Although, persistent episodes of unexplained crying can occur at any hour of the day, their intensity and duration are predominantly during the night hours. Factors like gastrointestinal (gastroesophageal reflux), allergy to cow's milk protein or lactose intolerance have been suggested as the possible causes [20].

This type of infantile irritability occurs in approximately 15% to 25% of all newborns and is equally distributed among ethnic groups and both sexes. The problems of sleep and crying of the baby, the frequency of nocturnal vigil and uncontrollable episodes of crying are common situations in the first months of life and are considered as the main trigger of shaking.

Postpartum depression is also a predisposing and important factor in the cases of AHT, child abuse and neglect. Mothers who report that their children have more than 20 minutes of "inconsolable crying" a day are twice likely to suffer symptoms of postpartum depression than those who describe it as "excessive crying". Excessive crying is defined as uneasiness and crying of more than three hours daily plus the duration of inconsolable crying [21].

The presence of a crying child has a direct effect on the patterns and response of the parents or the adult caregivers, as well as in the functioning of the family. Inappropriate management of unexplained and persistent crying in an infant can lead to maternal depression, disorganized response from the parents and helplessness towards the infant and unsafe attachment of the parents [22].

Parents' anguish is often exacerbated by the lack of information on the etiology of persistent crying in the infant. Therefore, instructing parents on how to know the patterns of normal crying and help them to develop coping strategies form part of the strategies for the prevention of AHT.

It is insisted that anyone who is facing a crying baby is at risk of shaking him. Therefore, pediatricians, nurses, parents and other caregivers need to know this syndrome and know that they can develop strategies to deal with crying.

It is very important to consider that in the first world countries, approximately between 25% and 50% of the parents or future parents do not know that the act of shaking a baby can cause brain damage in the infant and even death [23]. In a study conducted in Mexico (data not yet published), the percentage of ignorance of this information was between 70 and 89%. Thus, the ignorance of how to deal with a crying crisis becomes one of the main risk factors for shaking a baby.

In this pathology, the gender of the caregiver can also be a risk factor. Parents or stepparents are responsible of 37% of the cases, the couples of the mothers 21%, mothers 37% and the rest is attributed to other caregivers such as babysitters [24].

HOW MUCH DOES THE CARE OF AHT PATIENTS COST?

The report of the initial hospitalization costs for inpatients range from $18,000 to $70,000 per child. The average medical cost can exceed $300,000 per child [24]. The lifelong cost of a child victim of AHT treated in the United States of America is estimated in $13.5 billion dollars. Finally, when a child survives AHT, his families and/or caregivers should bear in mind the potentially very high cost and the need for lifelong care. These needs include devices for their mobility, controlled medications, physical therapy and special schools just to mention a few [25].

Table 1. Initiatives focused on reducing baby crying

Initiative, country or countries where it has been used and authors	Characteristics of the intervention, to whom it is directed and material used	Evidence of its effectiveness
Rest Routine for Infant Irritability United States Keefe et al. 2006 [32]	Directed to the parents. Nurses make four home visits to guide parents on baby-care routine. This they do through an individualized routine. The parents are encouraged to promote concordance in the father-child dyad following four principles: Regulation, Entrainment, Structure and Touch. They are provided with daily schedules and educational material for the family consisting of the video "Fussy Babies and Frantic Families" and a workbook	Reduction in the frequency of crying (in 1.7 hours per day) and improved the parent´s perception about resolution of the problems related to the crying of their children.
Swadding the Infant The Netherlands Van Sleuwen et al. 2006 [33] Blom et al. 2009 [34]	Directed to parents. Parents are guided on the care routine through clinical visits and via telephone. For the implementation of a care routine characterized by a) sleeping the baby wrapped b) feeding the baby c) playing with the baby and having positive interaction, and d) lying the tired baby even awake on his crib or playpen. A guide on the correct way to wrap the baby before the sleep periods is provided. This consists of tightly wrapping the shoulders and the hands and leaving the hip and legs a little loose.	Crying frequency was reduced specifically in babies of 1 to 7 weeks old, while in babies of 8 to 13 weeks old, crying frequency was reduced when they are not wrapped.
Acupuncture Sweden Landgren et al. 2010 [20]	Aimed at babies with colic. Six sessions of acupuncture for 3 weeks were given to babies in a clinic.	There was a reduction in the number of crying hours per day.
Baby Business Australia Cook et al. 2014 [35]	Directed to parents. *The Happiest Baby* video is mailed to teach the parents a method to calm their babies. It is based on actions that simulate the conditions of the utero. Strategies like 1) wrapping the baby, 2) positioning him by the side or decubitus, 3) shushing (making a constant sound close to the baby´s ears), 4) gently rocking the baby and 5) offering the baby something to suck are progressively followed until the baby calms down.	There was a decrease in depressive symptoms in the caregivers. There was also a decrease in the number of times in which the baby woke up during the night and less concern of parents about their baby´s sleep.
The Happiest Baby United States McRury&Zolotor, 2010)[36]		It showed no evidence of change in the crying of the babies or in the stress of the parents who received the intervention when compared with a control group.

Taken from Rodríguez et al. [5].

Faced with this reality, it is insisted that the prevention programs are very important to save lives and also reduce costs. "Out-of-pocket benefits of existing prevention program would exceed its costs if it prevents 2% of cases" [25].

HOW CAN IT BE PREVENTED?

Knowing that baby crying is the main trigger of shaking and that the way in which parents or caregivers deal with it are the principal determinants for shaking to occur or not, we can then conclude that these two main points should be the focus for its prevention and where an intervention is required [26].

Several AHT prevention initiatives have been developed [24, 27, 28]. Such initiatives can be classified according to their objectives and based on these objectives, they can be grouped into three categories [5]:

1. *Initiatives focused on decreasing baby crying.* Only two of these initiatives showed a significant reduction in baby crying (Table 1). These initiatives have the disadvantage of having a high cost and that their implementation is more complex. In addition, they require longer interventions and specialized personnel with specific training.

2. *Strategies that favor emotional regulation of the caregivers and help them to deal with crying.* These initiatives showed modest results with little significance in AHT prevention (Table 2).

3. *Programs whose main objective is to increase the awareness and knowledge about AHT.* These programs showed the evidence that an increase in the knowledge about child crying, the consequences of shaking a child and the changes that the caregivers experience on how to cope with child crying are programs that have shown a decrease in the number of AHT cases in two places where they were implemented (Table 3). The education of the parents on baby crying and the risks of shaking a child are strategies that seem to

be more promising for AHT prevention. Among them, the "The Period of Purple Crying" program stands out for its evidence to prevent AHT.

Table 2. Strategies that favor emotional regulation of the caregivers

Initiative and country or countries where it has been used	Characteristics of the intervention, to whom it is directed and material used	Evidence of its effectiveness
Wholistic and Mindfulness based Stress Reduction United States William-Orlando, 2012 [37]	Directed to parents and caregivers. Readings that teach the strategies to reduce the daily stress levels are provided through major changes in the diet (indication of stress preventing foods), in the lifestyle (practicing physical activities, consumption of stress reducing supplements and search for social interactions) and relaxation training and meditation in Mindfulness-based Stress Reduction. The training was for 1.5 hours for six weeks.	Participants perceived improvement in their ability to relax, deal with stress, pain and anxiety.
Early Parenting Program Japan Okamoto et al. 2013 [22]	Directed to parents. It consists of verbal and written material intervention. A 10-page booklet which shows with illustrations the strategies to calm the baby is given to the parents. It includes a 3-hour lesson on: 1) the changes in the pattern of child crying, 2) approaches or resources to deal with crying of the baby and 3) support resources for parenting (regional resources available to the parents as support).	Helped the participants minimize their lack of self-confidence as mothers.
NHS Direct United Kingdom Smith, 2010 [38]	Directed to parents and caregivers. Through health support telephone line, nurses used the organizational protocols of decision making, according to the complaints of the parents or caregivers regarding the crying of the baby. The nurses who answered the telephone compiled these complaints in a system and this system offered guidance to the parents using algorithms on the best way to proceed.	It did not show evidence of effectiveness.

Taken from Rodríguez et al. [5].

Table 3. Programs whose main objective is to increase awareness on and knowledge of Pediatric Abusive Head Trauma

Initiative and country or countries where it has been used	Characteristics of the intervention, to whom it is directed and the material used	Evidence of its effectiveness
Prevent Shaken Baby Syndrome! United States Dias et al. 2005 [24], Altman et al. 2011 [39]	Directed to parents of newborns. It is focused on AHT in maternity wards. It consists on showing the video "*Portrait of a Promise*", handing out booklets on AHT and the risks of shaking a baby (with maternity nurse) is discussed and signing a certificate of commitment not to shake your baby.	The number of AHT cases reduced by 47% in the places where the program was implemented. When the program was replicated in New York, reduction in the number of AHT cases was 70%.
The Period of Purple Crying United States, Japan, Canada, Australia Barr, et al. 2009 [40], Barr, et al. 2009 [41], Runyan et al. 2009 [42], Hennink-Kaminski and Dougall, 2009 [43], Stewart, et al. 2011 [44], Shanahan, et al. 2011 [45], Fujiwara et al. 2012 [46], Reese et al. 2014 [11], Stephens et al. 2014 [47], Fujiwara, 2015 [10], Barr, et al. 2015 [19]	Directed to parents and caregivers (Families and friends). Education is provided to the parents on the crying patterns of babies and how to cope it. The materials of the workshop include a video of 12 minutes and an educative booklet that describe AHT and the consequences of the same on the health of the baby. The booklet also addresses normal crying, suggests the strategies to make the baby feel comfortable, re-enforce the idea that these strategies do not always work, describe the reasons why inconsolable crying is frustrating and suggests the three steps to deal with baby crying as 1) console, carry, lull and talk to try to calm the baby, 2) if the crying intensifies or becomes frustrating, keep the baby in a safe place and get away and 3) never shake or hurt the baby. The material was transformed and also adapted for a mass media campaign to disseminate and increase awareness on the patterns of child crying and AHT among friends and families of new parents, considering that they can be potential caregivers of these babies. Moreover, it offers emotional support to the parents. It also focuses on dissemination of information by caregivers.	Increased the knowledge of the participants on AHT and their abilities to cope the crying. There was greater knowledge about the crying of the baby, the risks of shaking and greater exchange of information about babies. Abilities to deal with the crying: more frequent responses about getting away from the baby when frustrated and/or face a baby with inconsolable crying.
Shaking Your Baby is Just Not the Deal Australia, Greece,	Directed to parents and caregivers. Education about crying and AHT is provided. It describes the characteristics of a	The participants showed an adequate increased knowledge

Initiative and country or countries where it has been used	Characteristics of the intervention, to whom it is directed and the material used	Evidence of its effectiveness
Brazil, Turkey, and Hungry Tolliday et al. 2010 [48], Foley et al. 2013 [49]	physiological crying, the risks of shaking an infant and encourages the caregivers to look for help in times of irritability. It includes the video "*Shaking Your Baby is Just Not the Deal*" (it is animated and short). It uses the film script elaborated by the International Society for the Prevention of Abuse and Negligence (ISPAN). In addition, brochures are provided and posters are put in strategic places of the maternity wards.	on AHT and in the crying.
All Babies Cry (ABC) United States Morrill et al. 2015 [50]	Directed to parents. It is a prevention program of child abuse based on mass media. It has four objectives: 1) Foster attachment; 2) improve parent´s response to baby crying and 3) normalize and mitigate the stress of the parents. It provides the strategies to reduce the stress of the parents and to calm the baby. The intervention consisted of: a) An 11-minutes video projected in the hospital to explain the topics that would be covered at home; b) The parents took home a video with four short modules based on the acquisition of skills and 28-page booklet to re-enforce the messages in mass media. Three evaluations are made. The first intervention in the hospital and the other two at 5 and 17 weeks via telephone.	There was an increase in the knowledge about parenting.
Love Me... Never Shake Me United States Deyo et al. 2008 [31]	Focused on hospitals, schools and prisons. It provides education to the parents on AHT, the typical patterns of infant crying, relaxation techniques to deal with crying (holding, rocking, singing, caressing, stimulating with soft music and/or feeding) and coping strategies towards crying (doing exercise, call a friend or a family member, take a rest, meditate or breathe deeply and/or listen to music).	The participants showed increased knowledge about crying.
Colombia Prevention Program Colombia Monsalve and Alvarado, 2010 [51]	Directed to caregivers. A 45-minute educational intervention is provided. It addresses: the definition of child abuse, the concept of AHT, the mechanism of its production, causes, consequences and its prevention with insistence on appropriate games and the techniques to calm uncontrollable crying in children under two years of age.	The participants increased their knowledge about child crying and the consequences of AHT.

Table 3. (Continued)

Initiative and country or countries where it has been used	Characteristics of the intervention, to whom it is directed and the material used	Evidence of its effectiveness
Take five Safety Plan for Crying United States Bechtel et al. 2011 [52]	Directed to parents and caregivers. The intervention consisted of giving education about AHT, the beliefs about child crying and about avoiding harmful coping responses for the baby. The intervention was given by a resident in the maternity wards and a magnet for the refrigerator was provided with the same points of intervention.	The participants increased their behavior of getting away from the baby when they are frustrated.
The Hand Project: More Hugs, No Shakings Puerto Rico Rodriguez et al. 2011 [53]	Directed to parents of newborns. It was carried out in the maternity wards. Education to the parents about AHT was provided through an educational video and the strategies to deal with crying were discussed.	There was an increase in knowledge about AHT and the consequences of shaking the baby.
Saint Maurice Maternity Hospital France Simonnet et al. 2014 [54]	Directed to parents. It consisted of education for the parents in the maternity wards. A session and a brochure with the key points of the intervention are provided. It focused on the characteristics of child crying and the ability of the caregivers to deal with it, as well as knowledge about AHT. The impact of the intervention or the second and third days was evaluated.	Participants showed increased knowledge about AHT and the consequences of shakinga baby.

Taken from Rodríguez et al. [5].

A good part of these programs is taught as universal primary prevention education during the postpartum period to all parents of newborn babies [26, 29]. Others focused on AHT education for the parents and high risk families during their visit to health service providers [30]. Finally, others are directed to men who are future or new fathers and who are specifically in the army, prison or juvenile detention centers [31]. Tables 1, 2 and 3 summarize the characteristics of the most widely disseminated programs as well as those in which empirical evidence (favorable or not) on their effectiveness have been reported.

CONCLUSION

With all the evidence herein mentioned, we can conclude that AHT is preventable and therefore should be prevented. The prevention strategies that have shown the best results are mainly focused on: a) increasing the awareness on the injury produced when a baby is shaken, b) informing the caregivers on the normal course of crying in children and c) offering coping strategies towards baby crying. In addition, it is necessary to provide timely, clear and precise message at a certain time to the caregiver. The caregiver should know that "when a baby does not stop crying despite all effort to lull or calm him/her, she/he should leave the place and first relax". She can request the presence of another person while she is out of the place. Moreover, the caregiver should be explained that there is a possibility that the babies sometimes do not stop crying.

The transcendence of the aforementioned interventions can contribute to reducing not only risky behavior for AHT, but also can serve as basis to focus on other inappropriate behaviors that occur in the context of parenting that may have both transversal and long-life substantial impact in the health of the population.

In view of its implications, interventions or campaigns to prevent AHT should be indicated for all people that directly and indirectly participate in the care of a baby or a small child. These programs must be accessible and brief in their administration. If based on evidence, it can serve as a powerful message, administered in the right moment, and meaningful to those who receive it and thus increase the chances of success. An efficient prevention campaign could save the lives of many children and improve the lives of many others. The cost of the programs can be recovered from the economic savings that the society derives from them.

REFERENCES

[1]   American Academy of Pediatrics &CoCAaN. Shaken baby syndrome: inflicted crebral trauma. *Pediatrics* 1993; 62:872-875.

[2]   American Academy of Pediatrics &CoCAaN. Shaken baby syndrome: rotational cranial injuries-technical report. *Pediatrics.* 2001; 108:206-208.

[3]   Randel A, Levitt C, Smith W. Abuse head trauma. In R R, Ludwing S. *Child abuse: medical diagnosis and management.* Philadelphia: Lippincott Williams & Wilkins; 2001.

[4]   Caffey J. On the theory and practice of shaking infants. *Am J Dis Chil* 1972; 124:161-169.

[5]   Rodrigues Laterza Lopes N, Cavalcanti de Albuquerque Williams L. Pediatric Abusive Head Trauma Prevention Initiatives: A Literature Review. *Trauma Violence Abus* 2016; 6:1-12.

[6]   Noriko K. Prevalence of infant shaking among the population as a baseline for preventive interventions. *J Epidemiol* 2016; 26:2-3.

[7]   Blumental I. Shaken baby syndrome. *Postgrad Med J* 2002; 78:732-735.

[8]   Fujiwara T, Okuyama M, Miyasaka M. Characteristics that distinguish abuse from nonabusive head trauma among children who underwent head computed tomography in Japan. *Pediatrics* 2008; 122:841-847.

[9]   Hennes H, Kini N, Palusci V. The epidemiology, clinical characteristics and public health implications of shaken baby symdrome. *J Aggress Maltreat T* 2001; 5:19-40.

[10] Fujiwara T. Effectiveness of public health practices against shaken baby symdrome/abusive head trauma in Japan. *Pub Health* 2015;5:475-482.

[11] Reese L, Heiden E, Kim K, Yang J. Evaluation of Period of PURPLE Crying, an abuse head trauma prevention program. *J Obstet Gynecol Neonatal Nursing* 2014; 43:752-761.

[12] Niederkrotenthaler T, Xu L, PS, Sugerman D. Descriptive factors of abusive head trauma in young chldren-United States, 2000-2009. *Child Abuse Neglect* 2013; 37:446-455.

[13] Keenan H, Hooper S, Wetherington C, Nocera M, Runyan D. Neurodevelopmental consequences of early traumatic brain injury in 3-year-old children. *Pediatrics* 2007; 119:616-623.

[14] King W, M. M, Sirnick A. Shaken baby syndrome in Canada: clinical characteristics and outcomes of hospital cases. *Can Med Assoc J* 2003; 168:155-159.

[15] Lind K., Toure H, Brugel D, Meyer P:LVA, Chevignard M. Extended follow-up of neurological, cognitive, behavioral and academic outcomes after severe abusive head trauma. *Child Abuse Neglect* 2016; 51:358-367.

[16] Keenan H, Runyan D, Marshall S, Nocera M, Merten D, Sinal S. A population-based study of inflicted traumatic brain injury in young children. *J Am Med Assoc* 2003; 290:621-626.

[17] Zolotor A, Runyan D, Shanahan M, Durrance C, Nocera M, Sullivan K, et al. Effectiveness of a statewide abusive head trauma prevention program in North Carolina. *JAMA Pediatrics* 2015; 169:1126-1131.

[18] Loredo-Abadalá A, Casas-Muñoz A, Trejo-Hernández J, Melquiades-Parra I, Martín-Martín V. Síndrome del niño sacudido: cuadro clínico y evolución de 17 casos en el Instituto Nacional de Pediatría. [Shaken baby syndrom: clinical picture and evolution of 17 clinical cases in National institute of pediatrics. Pediatric´s record of Mexico] *Pediatric Act of Mexico* 2015; 36:72-80.

[19] Barr R, Rajabali F, Aragon M, Colbourne M, Brant R. Education about crying in normal infants is associated with a reduction in pediatric emergency room visits for crying complaints. *J Dev Behav Pediatr* 2015; 36:252-257.

[20] Landgren K, Kvornign N, Hallström I. Acupunture reduces crying in infants with infantile colic: a randomised, controled, blind clinical study. *Acupunct Med* 2010; 28:174-179.

[21] Hiscock H, Cook F, Bayer J, Le H, MF, Cann W, Symon B. Preventing early infant sleep and crying problems and postnatal depression; a randomized trial. *Pediatrics* 2014; 133:e346-354.

[22] Okamoto M, Ishigami H, Tokimoto K, Matsuoka M, Tango R. Early parenting program as intervention strategy for emotional distress in first-time mothers: a propensity score analysis. *Matern Child Health J* 2013; 17:1059-1070.

[23] Goulet C, Frappier J, Fortin S, Déziel L, Lampron A, Boulanger M. Development and evaluation of a shaken baby sydrome prevention program. *J Obstet Gynecol Neonatal Nursing* 2009; 38:7-21.

[24] Dias M, Smith K, DeGuehery K, MP, Liv V, Shaffer M. Preventing abusive head trauma among infants and young children: a hospital-based, parent education program. *Pediatrics* 2005; 115:e470-407.

[25] Miller TR, Steinbeigle R, Lawrence BA, Peterson C, Florence C, Barr M, et al. *Lifetime cost of abusive head trauma at ages* 0-4, USA. Prev Sci J 2017.

[26] Barr RG. Crying as a trigger for abusive head trauma: A key to prevention. *Pediatr Radiol* 2014; 44:S559-S564.

[27] Gutierrrez F, Clements PAJ. Shaken baby syndrome: Assessment, intervention & prevention. *J Psychosoc Nur Men* 2004; 42:22-29.

[28] National Center on Shaken Baby Syndrome. *National Center on Shaken Baby Syndrome.* [Online]; 2018. Available from: https://www.dontshake.org/.

[29] Kent H. Edmonton tackles shaken baby syndrome. *Can Med Assoc J* 2002; 168:207.

[30] Taşar M, ŞF, Polat S, İlhan M, Çamurdan A, Dallar Y, et al. Long-term outcomes of the shaken baby syndrome prevention program; Turkey's experience. *Turk Pediatri Arsivi* 2014; 49:203-209.

[31] Deyo G, Skybo T, Carroll A. Secondary analysis of the "Love Me. Never Shake Me" SBS education program. *Child Abuse Neglect* 2008; 32:10017-225.

[32] Keefe MR, Lobo ML, Froese-Fretz A, Kotzer AM, Barbosa GA, Dudley WN. Effectiveness of an intervention for colic. *Clin Pediatr* 2006; 45:123-133.

[33] van Sleuwen BE, L'Hoir MP, Engelberts AC, Busschers WB, Westers P, Blom MAMSTW, et al. Comparison of behavior modifications with adn without swaddling as interventions for excessive crying. *J Pediatr* 2006; 149:512-517.

[34] Blom MA, Van Sleuwen BE, De Vries H, Engelberts AC, L'Hoir MP. Health care interventions for excessive crying in infants: Regularity with and without swaddling. *J Child Health Care* 2009; 13:161-176.

[35] Cook F, Bayer J, Le HND, Mensah F, Cann W, Hiscock H. Baby Bussiness; A randomised controlled trial of a universal parenting program that aims to prevent early infant sleep and cry problems and associated parental depression. *BMC Pediatrics* 2012; 12:1-9.

[36] McRury JM, Zolotor AJ. A randomized, controlled trial of a behavioral intervention to reduce crying among infants. *J Am Board Fam Med* 2010; 23:315-322.

[37] Williams-Orlando C. Wholistic medicine for infants: Wholisytic- and Mindfulness-based Stress Reduction (WMBSR), for parents. *Integr Med* 2012; 11:32-37.

[38] Smith S. Helping parents cope with crying babies: Desicion-making and interaction an NHS Direct. *J Adv Nurs* 2010; 66:381-391.

[39] Altman RL, Canter J, Patrick PA, N. D, Butt NKM, Brand DA. Parent education by maternity nurses and prevention of abusive head trauma. *Pediatrics* 2011;128:e1164-e1172.

[40] Barr RG, Barr BISM, Fujiwara T, Conway J, Catherine NMBR. Do educational materials change knowledge and bejavioral about crying and shaken baby syndrome? A randomized controlled trial. *Can Med Assoc J* 2009; 180:727-733.

[41] Barr RG, Rivara FP, Barr M, Cummings P, Taylor J, Lengua LJ, et al. Effectiveness of educational materials designed to change knwoledge and behaviors regarding crying and shaken-baby syndrome in mothers of newborns: A randomized, controlled trial. *Pediatrics* 2009; 123:972-980.

[42] Runyan DK, Hennink-Kaminski HJ, Zolotor AJ, Barr RG, Murphy RA, Barr M, et al. Designing and testing a shaken baby syndrome

prevention program - The period of PURPLE crying; Keeping babies safe in North Carolina. *Social Marketing Quarterly* 2009; 15:2-24.

[43] Hennink-Kaminski HJ, Dougall EK. Tailoring hospital education materials for the period of purple crying: Keeping babies safe in North Carolina media campaing. *Social Marketing Quarterly* 2009; 15:49-64.

[44] Stewart TC, Polgar D, Gilliland J, Tanner DA, Girotti MJ, Parry N, et al. Shaken baby syndrome and a triple-dosage strategy for its prevention. *J Trauma* 2011; 71:1801-1807.

[45] Shanahan ME, Nocera M, Zolotor AJ, Sellers CJ, Runyan DK. Education on abusive head trauma in North Carolina hospitals. *Child Abuse Neglect* 2011; 20:290-297.

[46] Fujiwara T, Yamada F, Okuyama M, Kamimaki I, Shikoro N, Barr RG. Effectiveness of educational materials designed to change knowledge and behavior about crying and shaken baby syndrome: A replication of a randomized controlled trial in Japan. *Child Abuse Neglect* 2012; 36:613-620.

[47] Stephens A, Kaltner M, Liley W. Infant abusive head trauma prevention: Acceptability of the period of PURPLE Crying ® program in far North Queensland, Australia. *Rural Remote Health* 2014; 14:2603.

[48] Tolliday F, Marine S, Foley S, Benson S, Stephens A, Rose D. From inspiration to action: The shaken baby prevention project in western Sydney. *Communities Children and Families Australia* 2010; 5:31-47.

[49] Foley S, Kovács Z, Rose J, Lamb R, Tolliday F, Simons-Coghill M, et al. International collaboration on prevention of shaken baby syndrome - an ongoing project/intervention. *Pediatr Intern Child Health* 2013; 33:233-238.

[50] Morril AC, McElaney L, Peixotto B, VanVleet M. Evaluation of All Babies Cry, a second generation unviersal abusive head trauma prevention program. *J Commun Psycol* 2015; 43:296-314.

[51] Monsalve-Quintero DS, Alvarado-Romero HJ. Effect of patient education and support for caregivers of children under two year on

the prevention of shaken baby syndrome. *Investigación en Enfermería: Imagen y Desarrollo*. [*Nursing research: image and development*] 2010; 12:43-58.

[52]   Bechtel K, Le K, Martin KD, Shah N, Leventhal JM, Colson E. Impact of an educational intervention on caregiver's beliefs about infant crying and knowledge of shaken baby syndrome. *Acad Pediatr* 2011; 11:481-486.

[53]   Rodriguez BM, Marrero AP, Ortiz ED, Rios J, Rivera GM. The hand project: More hugs, no shakings. *Newsletter of the Medical Association of Puerto Rico* 2011; 103:9-13.

[54]   Simonnet H, Laurent-Vannier A, Yuan W, Hully M, Valimahomed S, Bourennane M, et al. Parent's behavior in response to infant crying: Abusive head trauma education. *Child Abuse Neglect* 2014; 38:1914-1922.

In: Child Abuse: Harm and Solutions   ISBN: 978-1-53614-271-6
Editors: Arturo Loredo Abdalá et al. © 2018 Nova Science Publishers, Inc.

Chapter 3

FETAL ABUSE: AN IGNONIMIOUS PHENOMENON

Arturo Loredo Abdalá[1,], Angélica Aguilar[1],*
Hugo Juárez Olguín[2] and Fernanda Reyes González[2]
[1]Centro de Estudios Avanzados Sobre Maltrato Infantil-Prevención
del Instituto Nacional de Pediatría (CEAMI-P-INP),
Ciudad de Mexico, Mexico
[2]Laboratorio de Farmacología, Instituto Nacional de Pediatría,
Facultad de Medicina, Universidad Nacional Autónoma de Mexico,
Ciudad de Mexico, Mexico

ABSTRACT

The term fetal abuse (FA) refers to any action or omission caused in an intentional or negligent manner that may cause harm to the product of gestation. From time immemorial, the right to life has not always been recognized in newborns. In old cultures, infanticide was justified as a mechanism to get rid of newborns with malformation, neurological damage or simply for birth control. This denial continued in different

* Corresponding Author Email: cainm_inp@hotmail.com.

countries and cultures until the establishment and recognition of Universal Declaration on Children´s Right which states that "a child, due to his physical and mental immaturity, requires special care including adequate legal protection before and after birth."

The vital question is, "Who should take care of the product of gestation before its birth? To provide the necessary conditions for a child to be born healthy, and fulfill one of his rights to lives evidently in the hands of the parents, the obstetricians and gynecologists, the general practitioners and the society itself. When this condition is denied either intentionally, by neglect or omission, fetal abuse is concreted. Paradoxically, the ideal attention to this problem is not simple, since the situations of ethical, social and legal natures come into play.

The intrauterine life of a product depends on whether the pregnant was desired, planed or accepted by the two parents. The absence of any of this can lead to a series of actions leading to FA. These series of action is usually directed to affect in adverse manner the Ecological system of the product which comprises of the microenvironment, the maternal environment and the macro environment. In the case of maternal environment, the action can be directed towards fertilization and implantation period, embryonic period or the fetal period. Usually, such actions may be in form of intentional or unintentional to propitiate Adverse Social Determinants (DSD) like consumption of licit and illicit" drugs, exposure to elevated concentrations of teratogenic substances and inappropriate nutrition among others.

The diagnosis of fetal can be established when there is a denial or pretension not to know of the pregnancy, history of various abortion attempts, plan to give the child for immediate adoption at birth, abandonment of the pregnant woman the father of the product or by her family, drug dependency or alcoholic woman and history of abuse, sociopathic parents or with psychiatric disorders, and finally, adolescent mothers who for family, personal or social reasons are under pressure to commit acts against themselves or against the product when they suspect or confirm the pregnancy.

To avoid the product of gestation being a victim of fetal abuse, it is fundamental that the pregnancy be planned, desired or accepted by the two parents within a social, civil and religious realities. Therefore, it is essential that the medical group, paramedical group, families and society in general should join hands in the prevention of unwanted pregnancy and guide pregnant women to successful and healthy end of their pregnancy.

When a pregnancy is not planned and agreed, there is a possibility that the future parents will resort to abortion, action that could be legal or illegal. The reasons to take this decision can be the rejection of the couple, the family or the society. The right of a child to be born healthy must be favored mainly by his parents, although it is also the responsibility of the obstetricians, pediatricians and the society in general.

This right to health and welfare must be protected by the state. This chapter reviews the impact of the maternal lifestyle can have on the fetus that may result in fetal abuse.

Keywords: fetal care, gestational care, intrauterine life, negligently, pregnancy

INTRODUCTION

When Kempe coined the term "Battered child syndrome" (BCS), the study of one of the topics that generated the most controversy in pediatrics was born [1]. Since then, numerous studies have been carried out to define a little-considered modality denominated "fetal abuse" (FA) [2].

At the global level, the dissemination of an interest in the topic is growing each time. In view of this, numerous civil societies, governmental institutions, promotional campaigns with preventive educational announcements in radios and televisions, as well as scientific meetings have been created, and although, most of them carry out only informative and protective actions, there are others that try to play a preventive role.

In the world, this problem develops and manifests in different form because it depends on the place where it is studied. In fact, the socioeconomic and cultural conditions as well as the lifestyles of each country are determinant factors. This makes it difficult to establish the frequency of the same.

Similar problem occurs when it comes to specify the global frequency of Child Abuse (CA); however, it is more feasible to indicate approximate frequency of some modalities of CA. For example, in the developed nations, it is likely that sexual abuse (SA) is reported more frequently than in developing countries. Finkelhor et al. [3], conducted a study in the United States and reported that of 17,645 cases of CA, sexual abuse occurred in 7%. Similar figures were reported in Sweden [4].

On the other hand, in some underdeveloped countries like Mexico [5] and Nigeria [6], it is likely that physical abuse, emotional or dietary deprivations are the predominant forms of CA.

In the last decades of the twentieth century, significant advances were made in favor of this problem and its understanding. In 1989, the United Nation Organization (UNO) established the Declaration of Children's Rights which was universally accepted [7].

Moreover, International Classification of Diseases (ICD-10) [8], has pointed out that the topic of specific violence against boys and girls must be registered as Child Abuse and has specified the following four basic modalities: Physical abuse, sexual abuse, psychological abuse and negligence extended up to the fetal life. Thus the term "fetal abuse and neglect (FA)" was created to understand any action or omission caused in an intentional or negligent manner that may cause harm to the product of gestation [9]. This new concept of CA allows us to better understand the first article of the Universal Declaration on children's Rights which states that "a child, due to his physical and mental immaturity, requires special care including adequate legal protection before and after birth" [7].

From time immemorial, the right to life has not always been recognized in newborns. In old cultures, infanticide was justified as a mechanism to get rid of newborns with malformation, neurological damage or simply for birth control [10].

Faced with this reality, an immediate question arises: Who should take care of the product of gestation before its birth? Currently, it is evident that the parents (father and mother), the obstetricians and gynecologists, the general practitioners and the society itself are who must provide the necessary conditions for a child to be born healthy, and fulfill one of his rights to live. Paradoxically, the ideal attention to this problem is not simple, since the situations of ethical, social and legal natures come into play [11].

DEFINITION

It is understood by fetal abuse (FA) any act that internationally or negligently affects the gestation product in any of its stages. Such action can be directly caused by the mother, some member of the family, a doctor or someone who interferes with the pregnancy. It is pertinent to remember that such action could have a cultural, social, political or legal basis [9].

During the prenatal stage, the product is influenced by a series of closely related maternal and environmental factors that constitute the Ecological System (SE). To study this system, it is necessary to divide it into 3 groups: the micro environment, the maternal environment and the macro environment, since each of these has specific characteristics that affect the fetus in one way or another [12].

1) Micro environment

   It is constituted by the uterus and its contents (umbilical cord, placenta, amniotic membranes and amniotic fluid). Any alteration in any of these structures will directly affect the fetus.

2) Maternal environment

   This refers to the rest of anatomic and physiological structures of the maternal organism. Any alteration in them can compromise the proper growth and development of the product.

3) Macro environment

   This is constituted by the environmental, cultural, social, economic, political and legal characteristics that surround any pregnant woman.

Before starting the complete analysis of the intrauterine life of a product, it is necessary to specify if the pregnant was desired, planed or accepted by the two parents. On these depends the normal uterine and extrauterine development and growth of the future new life [13-21].

In the course of the intrauterine life, there are three periods that are necessary to remember, since any intrinsic or extrinsic factor that acts on any of them will alter the product [22]:

a) Fertilization and implantation period

It begins at the moment of fertilization and ends on the 14th day of gestation. It is characterized by high mitotic activity and cellular multi potentiality. A teratogenic action can affect, in varying degree and severity, the product of gestation, and sometimes may impede the progress of the pregnancy (which ends in abortion) [22].

b) Embryonic period

This begins in the 2nd week of gestation and ends in the 10th week. In this period, the processes of morphological differentiation or organogenesis take place. It is a particularly vulnerable period, since it is influenced by different harmful agents that interfere in the proper development of the embryonic structures, thus giving rise to various malformations whose characteristics will be related to the duration and the moments when such agents acted on the product as well as the nature of them [22].

c) Fetal period

This period begins on the 10th week of gestation and ends at the moment when the baby is born. This stage is characterized by the growth and development of the product,and therefore, the fetus cannot suffer malformations; nevertheless, the presence of some nocive agents (infectious, physical, chemical, etc.) can cause growth alterations, which may result in fetopathies and intrauterine growth retardation or even intrauterine or extrauterine fetal death [22].

PROBLEM ANALYSIS

There are four basic approaches for the development and study of FA.

a) The medical aspect of the pregnancy and the product of gestation.
b) Physical and mental health of the father and the mother.

c) Social determinants for the family health.
d) Legal considerations of the pregnancy

Each of these approaches can have different possibilities.

Medical Approach

This consists of different facets namely: the role of the doctor, exposition to drugs, genetic diseases and technological advances.

Doctor's Role and Drug Prescriptions

The obstetrician gynecologist and all practitioners who control the evolution of a pregnancy are ethically bound to provide the best possible care to the mother-son binomial, since the continued growth and development of the fetus can be affected if there is any deficiency. It has been report that psychomotor injury can occur in up to 62% of the newborns if the gestational care is not properly attended [23]. Prenatal diagnosis offers family members and medical staffs several opportunities to determine the existence of congenital, genetic or acquired anomalies.

Exposure to Prescribed Drugs or by Self-Medication

The list of drugs that a pregnant woman cannot receive is very long and includes some ecological agents that are potentially capable of causing various effects on the developing product.

The doctor must know and analyze the different effects that a drug can have on the product of gestation to correctly analyze its prescription during pregnancy [24-27].

In Table 1, a list of products capable of having teratogenic effect is presented.

Genetic Diseases

The risk for genetic disease to reoccur in the same family is the result of not providing proper and sufficient information on some genetic problems as the Down's syndrome (mother over 36 years old), pancreatic cystic fibrosis, congenital deafness, Tray Sachs disease, progressive muscular dystrophy, etc. This situation gives rise to the concept of "mistaken" life or birth [18].

Faced with these diseases, the parents must be adequately informed in a timely manner, so that they can take decision regarding the continuity of the pregnancy.

This type of diseases can be classified into four groups [29].

1) Numerical and structural anomalies of the Chromosome (Down's syndrome or trisomy 21). In the group of structural alteration of the chromosomes is "Cri du Chat" syndrome.
2) Genopathies or monogenic diseases.

This group of genetic diseases is subdivided into two:

a) Dominant autosomal diseases
   Included in this subgroup are polycystic kidney disease, achondroplasia, neurofibromatosis and familial hyper-cholesterolemia. Moreover, dominant X-linked chromosomal diseases such as glucose-6-phosphate dehydrogenase deficiency, rackits and vitamin D resistance are among this subgroup.
b) Recessive Autosomal diseases
   This subgroup is comprised by cystic fibrosis of the pancreas and most inborn errors of metabolism; recessive X-linked hemophilia A and B, Duchenne progressive muscular dystrophy and Bruton agammaglobulinemia [12].

3) Polygenic or multifactorial diseases

This group consists of congenital acetabular dysplasia, congenital heart diseases, hypospadias, congenital pyloric stenosis and hydrocephalus [22]. Table 1 shows the drugs and substances with potential teratogenic effect.

Table 1. Relationship of the medications and substances that affect the product in utero and their effects

Drugs	Effects
Fetal death or serious malformation	
Aminopterin	
Cyclophosphamide	
Adrenal steroids	
Other cytotoxic drugs (methotrexate)	
Quinine	
Trimetadione	
Metabolic changes with well-known anatomical effects	
Androgens	Masculinization of the female fetus
Chlorpropamide	
Lead (Environmental pollution?)	Embryotoxic and teratogenic in the human being
	Skeletal malformations
	Bone abnormalities
	Microcephaly
Diazepam	Diaphragmatic hernia
Diphenlhydatoin (DPH)	Hypoplasia of fingers
	Harelip
	Cleft palate
Diazoxide	Alteration in hair growth
	Delayed bone age
	Masculinization of the female fetus
Estrogens	Adenocarcinoma of the cervix and vagina
	Cleft palate
Glucocorticoids	Harelip
	Masculinization of the female fetus
Progestogens	Hypospadias
	Congenital anomalies
	Vascular, renal and skeletal defects
Quinine	Thrombocytopenia
	Dysmelia, phocomelia, amelia, hemimelia, adactilia
Thalidomide	and hypoglycemia
	Cleft palate
Vitamin A	Eye injury
	Syndactyly
Metabolic changes with probable teratogenic effect	Heart disease and biliary atresia
Antacids	Possible skeletal or chromosomal
Amphetamines	malformation

Table 1. (Continued)

Drugs	Effects
Cumarinics	Probable teratogenicity
Fenmetrazine	Possible teratogenicity (affects CNS)
Lisergida (LSD)	Probable teratogenicity
Meclizine	Skeletal and cardiac abnormalities
Influence on fetal growth	
Busulfan	Low size and low weight
Tetracyclines	
Smoking	
Interference in the adaptation of the newborn	
Tricyclic antidepressants	Platelet dysfunction
Barbiturates	Defects of coagulation
Hexamethonium bromide	Ileus, death
Ammonium chloride	Acidosis
Lithium carbonate	Lithium poisoning
Chlorodiacephoxide	Suppression syndrome
Chloramphenicol	Gray child syndrome
	Encephalopathy
Caffeine	Hyperbilirubinemia
Fenformin	Increase in lactic acid production
Thyroid substances (thiouracils, iodides, T3)	Hypothyroidism, suppression of the hypothalamic-pituitary-thyroid axis
	Neonatal goiter, mechanical compression of the trachea and fetal death
Imipramine	Urinary retention
Isoniazide	Hemolysis
Kanamycin	Hyperbilirubinemia
Mepivacaine	Depression and seizures
	Neonatal depression
Meperidine	Decreased saturation of neonatal O_2 Hypertiroidism
Methimazole	Supression Syndrome
Methadone, narcotics and barbiturates	Hyperbilirrubinemia
Nitrofurantoin	Hyperbilirrubinemia
Oxacillin	Dependence fenomenon
Pyridoxine	Low Apgar at birth
Propranolol	Hemolysis
Primaquine	Increased nasal discharge
Reserpine	Thoracic retraction
	Cyanosis
	Lethargy, bradycardia and death

Drugs	Effects
Salicylates	Hemorrhagic disorders
	Platelet Dysfunction,
	Decreased factor XII
	Competes with albumin in its binding to bilirubin
	(may alter platelet adhesiveness, vascular fragility
	and prolonged prothrombin time)
Magnesium sulphate	CNS depression
Sulfonamides	Hepatic and splenic necrosis, hyperbilirubinemia
	Congenital Cataracts
Thiazides	Depletion of Na, K and water
	Thrombocytopenia
Vitamin D	Hypercalciuria and hypercalcemia
Vitamin K	Hyperbilirubinemia if administered at a high doses
	to the mother before delivery
Injuries that manifest late	
Aminoglycosides	Injury of VIII par
Chloroquine (large doses)	Cochlear lesion
Tetracycline	Alteration of dental enamel

4) Technological advances.

In the last two decades, perinatal medicine has witnessed important advances and development. This has been achieved thanks to the advances in the use of equipment as the high resolution ultrasound and the development of technics for taking fetal samples [30]. These advances have not only allowed an early diagnosis of intrauterine anomalies, but also have led to an increase in their possible corrections [31]. Such advances have also made it possible to incorporate the consideration of a fetus as a patient, since some ailments in this stage of life can be diagnosed as well as the feasibility to receive different treatment alternatives [32]. Table 2 shows a list of medical problems that can be treated during the intrauterine life [30, 33-36]. Table 3 depicts some medical-surgical problems that have been treated intrauterine [34, 37-46].

Presently, intrauterine surgical interventions in animals have been performed. For example, the intrauterine correction of neural tube defects, suspected due to alpha-fetoprotein increase, that was diagnosed by ultrasound [47-53].

Table 2. Fetal states that could require medical treatment before birth

Problem	Treatment
Fetal erythroblastosis	Intraperitoneal, intravenous blood transfusion
Pulmonary immaturity	Transplacental glycocorticoids and glycocorticoids administered to the mother
Neural tube defects	Periconceptional administration of folic acid (4mg / day) Betamimetics (experimental)
Acute intrapartum fetal distress	
Metabolic problems:	Transplacental vitamin B
Methylmalonic acidemia	Transplacental biotin
Carboxylase deficiency	Digital
Cardiac arrhythmias	Propranolol
Supraventricular tachycardia	Transplacental procainamide
Endocrine deficit:	
Hypothyroidism	Transaninotic thyroid hormone
Adrenal hyperplasia	Transplacental corticosteroids
Nutritional deficiency	Hyperproteic or hypercaloric diet (experimental)
Delay in growth	Betamimetics (experimental)

Table 3. Anatomical defects that can be corrected with early surgical interventions

Problem	Consequences	Diagnostic method	Treatment
Urethral obstruction	Hydronephrosis Pulmonary hypoplasia	Ultrasound at 12- 15 weeks	Surgical
Diaphragmatic hernia	Pulmonary hypoplasia	Ultrasound	Surgical at 22 - 28 weeks of gestation
Stenosis of Silvio aqueduct	Hydrocephalus	Ultrasound at 15-18 weeks	Surgical
Oligohydramnios	Fetal suffering	Ultrasound	Intrapartum amniotransfusion
Compression of the umbilical cord			
Meconium amniotic fluid		Ultrasound	Surgical resection
Sacrococcygeal teratoma	Premature delivery		
Fetal-fetus transfusion syndrome	Fetal death Discordant growth due to hypoxia, dropsy in one or both fetuses	Ultrasound at the end of the third trimester of pregnancy	Serial amniodrainage or laser electrocoagulation of vascular communications

Better indicators for intrauterine diagnosis of congenital renal diseases are being sought for. For example, the combination of amniotic liquid volume measurement and ultrasonographic study yields a result with a certainty close to 90% [54].

In this situation, the doctor and the future parents must know and understand perfectly the dangers of this kind of surgical interventions such as hemorrhage, intestinal perforation, the development of chorioamnionitis, sepsis, premature abortion and fetal or maternal death [55-56].

PERSONAL AND FAMILY ENVIRONMENTS OF THE MOTHER

The health of the father and mother as well as the maternal environment is decisive in the development and growth of the fetus.

Other conditions that affect the growth and development of the fetus in synergistic way are: the nutritional deficiency of the mother (anemia, deficiency of vitamins A and B, folic acid, zinc), tobacco smoking, marijuana, addiction to substances and sexually transmitted infections [57].

During the pregnancy, the mother should be surrounded by the family and social environment that are propitious. Frequently, this condition is not always feasible due to the accumulation of Adverse Social Determinants (DSD) as [58-60]:

a. Nutritional insecurity
b. Housing insecurity
c. Educational deficit
d. Family violence
e. The existence of a family member with addictions
f. A parent in prison

Within the licit addictions are prejudicial to the fetus, the following can be highlighted:

Alcoholism

The consumption of alcohol during pregnancy may cause prenatal and postnatal alterations. The first group is constituted by alcoholic embryo fetopathy or fetal alcoholic syndrome (FAS) which is an alteration with the following characteristics [61-62]:

1) Delayed prenatal and postnatal growth.
2) Global delay of development or learning disabilities in 90% of the cases [63-66].
3) Craniofacial dysmorphia characterized by microcephaly, microphthalmia, short palpebral fissure, strabismus, palpebral ptosis, epicanthus, saddle-shaped nose, short and wide bridge, hypoplasia of the upper lip, fallen labial commissures, ogival palate, posterior rotation of the propeller and micrognathia [67].
4) Various malformations. These can be located in different areas of the economy such as the skin, joints, bone-muscular tissue, kidney, heart and genital (Table 4) [43-47].

The exact mechanism of alcohol toxicity is not known. However, attempts have been made to link it with the level of unmetabolized ethanol. Probably the amount of alcohol, apparently higher, can increase the risk of injury in the product. Nevertheless, no "safe" level has been clearly established during pregnancy. Therefore, the so called "social alcoholism" should be avoided by a pregnant woman [68].

In Mexico, there is certain predilection for women to consume beer, a drink indicated as a specific trigger of some adverse effects on the product of gestation and it is reported that about 6% of the women tend to intense alcoholism in the last month of gestation [69-70].

Table 4. Manifestations of fetal alcohol syndrome

Area	Frequency (25-50%)	Ocasional (1-25%)
Eyes	Ptosis, strabismus, epicanthus	Myopia, microphthalmia, blepharophimosis Scarce shaping of the auricular pavilion
Ears	Rear rotation	
Mouth	Lateral prominence of palatine bridges	Cleft lip or palate, small teeth with enamel hypoplasia
Heart	Atrioseptal defect	Defect of the ventricular wall, anomalies of large vessels, tetralogy of Fallot
Urogenital	Hypoplasia of labia minora	Hypospadias, small and malrotated kidneys, hydronephrosis
Skin	Hemangiomas	Hirsutism
Skeleton	Aberrant palm ridges, pectum excavatum	Limited joint movement in fingers and elbows: nail hypoplasia, polydactyly, radial synostosis, scoliosis
Muscular		Diaphragmatic and umbilical hernia, diastasis of recti
SNC	Attention deficit disorder and hyperactivity	Psychomotor retardation, personality disorder

The fetal alcohol syndrome (FAS) has been well noted in the literature since 1973. The basic characteristics of this are presented in Table 4 and Figure 1 [71-74].

Smoking

It is currently estimated that cigarette smoking took place in approximately one-third of pregnant woman; in spite of campaigns and programs on its harmful effects [75].

The alterations that have been demonstrated in the product of a woman who smokes are: low prenatal and postnatal weight, shorter stature at birth for the gestational age, decreased cephalic perimeter, increase in the hematocrit and umbilical cord blood carbon monoxide. These data would help to diagnose the feto-fetal smoking syndrome [76-79]. Possibly, the decrease in the uterine perfusion, caused by tobacco, triggers an alteration in the fetal nutrition [79]. Nicotine causes peripheral and uterine vasoconstriction with decreased utero-placental perfusion [75].

Another harmful substance is carbon monoxide, which, when bound to hemoglobin forms carboxyl-hemoglobin and this leads to decreased transplacental oxygen transport, a mechanism that causes fetal morbidity [80]. If the effect is acute, this can result in spontaneous abortion, prematurity, placental detachment or alterations in the implantation and fetal death [81].

The long-term effects include the feto-fetal smoking syndrome characterized by low weight before and after birth, short stature and microcephaly. It has also been reported that that sudden infant death syndrome is twice more frequent in children of women who smoked during pregnancy [75]. The consumption of more than five cigarettes per day is enough to cause alterations in the good development of the fetus [82, 83].

Ilicit Drug Consumption

This phenomenon has widely spread worldwide. The defects and alterations reported in children of women who have been exposed to various substances are numerous [84, 85]. The consumption of illicit drugs can cause congenital malformations of variable degree and severity, chromosomal breaks or abstinence syndrome, among others.

Cocaine

This drug crosses the placenta and accumulates in the amniotic liquid [86]. In the mother, it produces alpha adrenergic effects, which result in decreased blood supply, hypertension and tachycardia, with direct repercussion in the product by causing vasoconstriction of placental vessels, hypoxemia and decreased nutrient passage. The consequences are delayed intrauterine growth and microcephaly [87].

The consumption of cocaine increases the incidence of spontaneous abortions, placental detachment, prematurity and fetal death [88-90]. Malformations of the urogenital and gastrointestinal tracts, musculoskeletal and the central nervous system may also develop [91].

Crack

Like the cocaine, crack is a drug that causes episodes of apnea and bradycardia in newborns, phenomena that have been associated with sudden infant death syndrome.

Marihuana

Children of mothers addicted to marijuana have intrauterine growth retardation for carbon monoxide hypoxia, whose concentrations exceeds those of the consumption of cigarettes of tobacco [92]. Visual defects, behavioral disorders and psychomotor development have also been reported in children of these mothers [93].

Opioids

Opioids comprise a group of alkaloids naturally derived from opium and their chemically related components, morphine, heroine, codeine and meperidine hydrochloride. Their consumption during pregnancy causes intrauterine growth retardation and various congenital malformations [94].

The long-term effects in children are hyperactivity, aggressiveness and lack of social adaptation [95]. Likewise, a higher risk of sudden death in infants and children of mothers addicted to opioids as well as the possibility of acquiring infections such as hepatitis B, syphilis and HIV has been report [96].

These babies can also develop the withdrawal syndrome, phenomenon that can cause death if not timely and correctly treated [97].

LSD

With the consumption of LSD, chromosomal breaks and various alterations in the central nervous system have been reported. It is necessary to emphasize that the suppression or withdrawal syndrome occurs in the first hours of life and can cause death of the newborn if it is not treated properly.

Nutritional Status of the Mother

Maternal malnutrition during pregnancy can influence the fetal brain cellular development in an irreversible form. For this reason, it is important that doctors and expectant mothers be watchful of this and make sure that their diet contains adequate caloric-protein intake, because, although the growth of fetal structures is determined by genetic code, these structures can be negatively modified by improper nutrition.

Since the late '90s of the twentieth century, the need for future parents to consume folic acid and B complex was established. In young women, this favors the proper development of the placenta and its correct implantation which permits an adequate feeding of the product of gestation. In the woman, it prevents the development of congenital malformations, mainly of the neural tube.

Aggregated Risks

This category includes the sudden death syndrome of the infant and neonatal abstinence syndrome.

1) Infant sudden death syndrome
   This syndrome had been a very frequent phenomenon until the strategy of how to lay the babies was modified. It was pointed out that the best way to avoid this pathology is to lay the babies in dorsal decubitus. Nevertheless, it is the exposure of the mother to drugs like morphine is principally the precipitating factor [98-100].

2) Neonatal abstinence syndrome
   This problem is triggered when a baby from a mother addicted to illicit drugs is born and abruptly the supply of the drug is suspended. Heroin was the drug initially studied and in the recent decades, the involvement of multiple non-opioid pharmacological agents such as phenobarbital, benzodiazepines, marijuana, cocaine and alcohol has been clearly demonstrated [101].

The time of onset of the symptoms depends on the drug involved, the doses consumed, the time elapsed between the last dose and birth, the type and amount of anesthesia or analgesic administered during the delivery, and the presence of pathologies in the newborn. Generally, the clinical signs begin in the first 72 hours, but can also appear immediately after the delivery or any time during the next two weeks [102].

FETAL ABUSE. HIGH RISK FUTURE MOTHERS

Currently, doctors can identify the people that can cause this type of CA. Schmit has proposed a series of data oriented for their identification [103]:

1) A woman who denies being pregnant or pretends not to know that she was pregnant.
2) A woman with various abortion attempts
3) A woman who plans to give the child for immediate adoption at birth
4) A pregnant woman who is abandoned by the father of the product or by her family.
5) Drug dependent or alcoholic woman who refuses medical or psychiatric treatment
6) Parents with a history of abuse
7) Sociopathic parents or with psychiatric disorders
8) Adolescent mothers who for family, personal or social reasons are under pressure to commit acts against themselves or against the product when they suspect or confirm the pregnancy.

It is essential to insist on the medical group, paramedical group, families and society in general on the need to guide pregnant women to avoid the use of "licit and illicit" drugs as well as exposing themselves to elevated concentrations of lead, mercury, pesticides, ionizing radiations and X-rays, considering the mutagenic and teratogenic effects of all these elements [104-105].

BASIC CONCEPTS

To avoid the product of gestation being a victim of fetal abuse, it is fundamental that the pregnancy be planned, desired or accepted by the two parents within a social, civil and religious realities [106].

When this planning does not occur, there is a possibility that the future parents will resort to abortion, action that could be legal or illegal. The reasons to take this decision can be the rejection of the couple, the family or the society [107].

Poverty

As a consequence of this diversity, malnutrition of the mother and thus, of the product can occur and the consequences of this can be so severe leading to damage to the growth and development of the fetus.

Teenage Pregnancy

Teenage pregnancy can affect the health, education, life project, social and cultural relationships, and the economy among other aspects of the young woman. Frequently, as this is not a condition expected by the couple, there is physical and emotional rejection of the product [108-110].

Understanding the positive and negative aspects that are involved in the phenomenon of teenage pregnancy would permit to diagnose, control and prevent FA. In Figure 1, the basic aspects of the problem are presented [111-114].

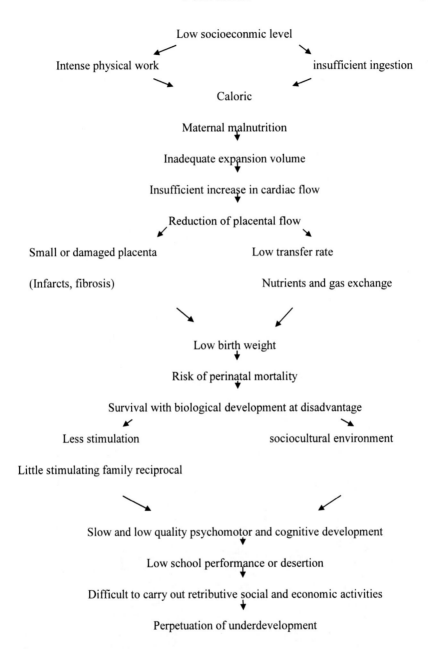

Figure 1. Natural evolution of low birth weight in developing countries. (Modified Rosso scheme) This sequence of events suggests that material misery is a social disease that is biologically inherited through the placenta.

Legal Situation

The right of a child to be born healthy must be favored mainly by his parents, although it is also the responsibility of the obstetricians, pediatricians and the society in general. This right to health and welfare must be protected by the state.

In some countries of the world there may be problems when you need to accept or reject abortion, regardless of the reason.

The problem arises because for some human groups, the acceptance and legal protection of abortion represents an obvious abuse and is probably the most widespread form of injustice or fetal abuse.

This condition has become a complex and heterogeneous issue, since the ethical evaluation of fetal life varies dramatically in each society, in such a way that a fetus can be susceptible to legal protection depending on the political, moral or ethical values of each society.

Finally, a scheme of this theme is presented in next figure.

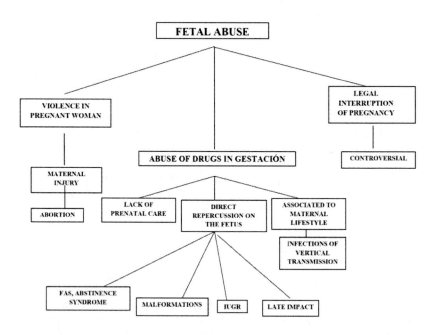

Figure 2. Scheme of fetal abuse.

REFERENCES

[1] Kempe HC, Silverman FN, Steele BF, Droegemueller W, Silver HK. The battered child syndrome. *JAMA* 1962 7; 181:17-24.

[2] Sierra GQJ, Loredo Abdalá A, Carbajal RL. Abuso y negligencia en el desarrollo fetal: Nueva controversia acerca del síndrome del niño maltratado. [Abuse and neglect in fetal development. New controversy about battered child syndrome] *Rev Méx Pediatr.* 1989; 56:311-320.

[3] Finkelhor D, Hortalin G. The national incidence study of child abuse and neglect. *Child Abuse Negl.* 1984; 8:23-33.

[4] Gelles R, Edfeldt A. Violence toward children in the United States and Sweden. *Child Abuse Negl.* 1986; 10:501-511.

[5] Loredo Abdalá A, Reynés NJ, Carbajal RL. El niño maltratado, una realidad actual en Mexico. [The abused child, a current reality in Mexico] *Act Pediatr Méx* 1984; 5 :28-37.

[6] Okeahialam T. Child abuse in Nigeria. *Child Abuse Negl.* 1984; 8:69-73.

[7] United Nations Organization (UNO). *Preamble: Declaration of the Rights of the Child.* New York: UN, 1959:4354.

[8] Clasificación *Internacional de Enfermedades 10° (CIE-10). REVISION.* Organización Panamericana de la Salud/Organización Mundial [*International Classification of Diseases 10th (ICD-10). Review.* Pan American Health Organization / World Organization].

[9] Landwirth J. Fetal abuse and neglect: an emerging controversy. *Pediatrics* 1987; 79:508-514.

[10] Langer I. Infanticide: a historical survey. *History of childhood quarterly 1974*; 1:353-362.

[11] Moreno J. Ethical and legal issues in the care of the impaired newborn. *Clin Perinatol* 1987; 14:345-360.

[12] Zuckerman BS, Walter DK, et al. Adolescent pregnancy: bio behavioral determinants of autocome. *J Pediatr* 1985; 105: 587.

[13] Langer A. El embarazo no deseado: impacto sobre la salud y la sociedad en América Latina y el Caribe. [Unwanted pregnancy:

impact on health and society in Latin America and the Caribbean] *Rev Panam Salud Publica/Pan Am J Public Health* 2002; 11:192-204. 14.

[14] Díaz-Sánchez V. El embarazo no deseado y el aborto como problema de salud pública. [Unwanted pregnancy and abortion as a public health problem] *Gac Méd Méx* 2003; 139: S1:23-28].

[15] Núñez-Urquiza RM, Hernández-Prado B. García-Barrios Celia, González D, Walker D. Unwanted adolescent pregnancy and post-partum utilization of contraceptives methods. *Salud Pub Mex* 2003;45:S94-S102.

[16] Oye-Adeniran BA, Adewole IF, Umoh AV. Community-based survey of unwanted pregnancy in southwestern Nigeria. *Afr J Reprod Health* 2004; 8:103-115.

[17] Segal SJ, LaGuardia KD. Termination of pregnancy. A global view. *Balliere Clin Ob Gy.* 1990;4:235-247.

[18] Rosenberg M, Waugh MS. Long S. Unintended pregnancies and use, misuse and discontinuation of oral contraceptives. *J Reprod Med* 1995;40:355-360.

[19] Villaseñor M, Alfaro N. Factores socioculturales que intervienen en la determinación del deseo o no deseo del embarazo en la adolescente. En: Lartigue T, Avila H, ed. *Sexualidad y reproducción humana en Mexico.* [Sociocultural factors that intervene in the determination of the desire or not desire of pregnancy in the adolescent. In: Lartigue T, Avila H, ed. *Sexuality and human reproduction in Mexico.*] Mexico, D. F., UIA-Plaza Valdés, 1996; Capítulo IV:143-162.

[20] Orozco López MA, Mendoza Reséndiz MT, Ramos Galván RI, López López A, Ruelas González G. Embarazo no deseado a término en mujeres atendidas en dos hospitales del Distrito Federal. [Unwanted pregnancy at term in women seen in two hospitals in the Federal District] *Revista de Especialidades Médico-Quirúrgicas* 2011;16:240-247.

[21] Briere J, Runtz M, Eadie E, Bigras N, Godbout N. Disengaged parenting: Structural equation modeling with child abuse, insecure

attachment, and adult symptomatology. *Child Abuse Neglect* 2017; 67:260–270.

[22] Moore KL. *Embriología clínica* [*Clinical embryology*] 2a. ed. Mexico: Interamericana, 1979:13-96.

[23] Loredo Abdalá A. Efecto de drogas e infecciones en el producto *in utero*. En: Rodríguez RS (ed.). Nueva guía para el diagnóstico y tratamiento del paciente pediátrico. [Effect of drugs and infections on the product in utero. In: Rodríguez RS (ed.). *New guide for the diagnosis and treatment of the pediatric patient*] 5th. ed. Mexico: Méndez Cervantes, 1983: 21.

[24] Sutton R, Buzdar AU, Hortobagyl GN. Pregnancy and off spring after adjuvant chemotherapy in breast cancer patients. *Cancer* 1990;65:847-850.

[25] Pomerance J, Yaffe S. Maternal medication and its effect on the fetus. *Current Prob Pediatrics* 1973;4:38-42.

[26] Loredo Abdalá A. Efecto de medicamentos sobre el feto en desarrollo. En: Salas M (ed.). *Guía para el diagnóstico y terapéutica en Pediatría*. [Effect of medications on the developing fetus. In: Salas M (ed.). *Guide for diagnosis and therapy in Pediatrics*] Prensa Médica Mexicana, 1977:10-14.

[27] Bowman WC, Rand MJ. Farmacología: bases bioquímicas y patológicas. [*Pharmacology: biochemical and pathological bases*] 2nd. ed. Mexico: Interamericana, 1985:2039-2043.

[28] Fleisher LD. Wrongful births. When is there liability for prenatal injury? *AM J Dis Child* 1987;141:1260-1265.

[29] Mckusick VA. Mendelian inheritance in man and its online version, OMIM. *Am Hum Genet.* 2007; 80:588-604.

[30] Leis MM, Gallardo GJ, Guzmán HM, Acevedo GS, Velásquez TB, García BC. Tratamiento fetal. En Ahued A, Fernández C (eds.) Obstetricia y ginecología aplicadas. [Fetal treatment. In Ahued A, Fernández C (eds.) *Applied obstetrics and gynecology.*] 1st ed. Mexico: JGH Editores, 2000:67-79.

[31] Harrison MR, Villa RL. Transamniotic fetal feeding. Development of an animal model: continous amnioticin fusion in rabbits. *J Pediatr Surg* 1982; 178:376-380.

[32] James D. Medicina fetal. [Fetal medicine] *BMJ* 1998;6:271-275.

[33] Adzick NS, Harrison MR, Flake AW, Howell LJ, Golbus MS, Filly RA. Recent advances in prenatal diagnosis and treatment. *Pediatr Clin North Am* 1985;32:1106-1107.

[34] Harrison MR, Golbus MS, Filly RA, Callen PW, Katz M, de Lorimier AA, Rosen M, Jonsen AR. Fetal surgery for congenital hydronephrosis. *N Engl J Med* 1982; 306:591-593.

[35] Lumbley J, Watson L, Bower C. Periconcepcional supplementation with folate, and/or multivitamins for preventing neural tube defects. *Cochrane Db Syst Rev.* 2000; (2): CD001056.

[36] Gulmezoglu AM, Hofmeyr GJ. *Betamimetics for suspected impaired fetal growth* (Cochrane Review; Inssue 2; Update software). Oxford: The Cochrane Library, 1999.

[37] Diamond DA, Saunders R, Jeffs RD. Fetal hydronephrosis: considerations regarding urologic intervention. *J Urol* 1984; 131:1155-1159.

[38] Natera G, Terroba GG. Prevalencia de consumo y variables demográficas asociadas en la ciudad de Monterrey, N. L. [Prevalence of consumption and associated demographic variables in the city of Monterrey, N. L.] *Salud Mental* 1982; 5: 82-86.

[39] Adzick NS, Harrison MR. Diaphragmatic hernia in the fetus: prenatal diagnosis and outcome of 94 cases. *J Pediatr Surg* (in press).

[40] Nakayama DK, Harrison MR. Berger MS, Chinn DH, Halks- Miller M, Edwards MS Correction of congenital hydrocephalus in utero. I. The model: intracisternal kaolin produces hydrocephalus in fetal lambs and rhesus monkeys. *J Pediatr Surg* 1983;18:331-338.

[41] Nakayama DK, Harrison MR. Seron- Ferre. Fetal surgery in the primate. II. Uterine electromiographic response to operative procedures and pharmacologic agents. *J Pediatr Surg* 1984;19:333-339.

[42] Flake AW, Harrison MR. Fetal surgery. *Annu Rev Med* 1995;46:67-78.

[43] Hyett J, Ville Y, Sebire N, Sepúlveda W, Nicolaides K. Management of severe twin transfusion syndrome. *Fet Mat Med Rev* 1996;8:67-77.

[44] De Lia JE, Kuhlman RS, Harstat TW, Cruikshank DP. Fetoscopic laser ablation of placental vessels in severe twin-twin transfusion syndrome. *Am J Obstet Gynecol* 1995;172:1202-11.

[45] Hofmeyer GJ. Amnioinfusion: a question of benefits and risks. *Br J Obstet Gynaecol* 1992;92:449-51.

[46] Hofmeyer GJ. Amnioinfusion for meconium-stained liquor in labour. En: Neilson JP, Crowther CA, Hodnett DE, Hofmayer GJ, Keirse MJNC, Renfrew MJ (eds.) *Pregnancy and childbirth module. Cochrane Database of Systematic Reviews* (update software, update 6 june 1996). Oxford: The Cochrane Library, 1996.

[47] Hodger GD. Antenatal diagnosis and treatment of fetal skeletal malformations with special emphasis in utero surgery for neural tube defects and limb bud regeneration. *JAMA* 1981; 246:1079-1083.

[48] Milinsky A. Prenatal detection of neural tube defects: VI. Experience with 20 000 pregnancies. *JAMA* 1980;244:2731-2735.

[49] Bellinger MF, Comstock GH, Grosso D, Zaino R. Fetal posterior urethral valves and renal dysplasia at 15 weeks gestational age. *J Urol* 1983;129:1238-1239.

[50] Mathew OP. Pharyngeal airway obstruction in preterm infants during mixed and obstructive apnea. *J Pediatr* 1982;100:964-967.

[51] Editorial. When ultrasound shows fetal abnormality. *Lancet* 1985;2:1618-1619.

[52] Ruiz-García M, Garza S, Sánchez O, Loredo Abdalá A. Conclusiones del Consenso de Expertos sobre el tratamiento farmacológico del trastorno por déficit de atención con o sin hiperactividad. [Conclusions of the Expert Consensus on the pharmacological treatment of attention deficit disorder with or without hyperactivity] *Bol. Med Hosp Infant Mex.* 2003; 60: 349-355.

[53] Boyer M, Guest G, Lestage F. Prenatal diagnosis of urinary tract malformations. *Adv Nephrol* 1985;14:21-38.

[54] Grupe WE. Dilema del diagnóstico intrauterino de enfermedad renal congénita. [Dilemma of intrauterine diagnosis of congenital kidney disease] *Clin Pediatr North Am* 1987;3:675-683.

[55] Kramer SA. Current status of fetal intervention for congenital hydronephrosis. *J Urol* 1983;130:641-646.

[56] International Fetal Surgery Registry (IFSR). Report of the IFSR. Catheter shunts for fetal hydronephrosis and hydrocephalus. *N Engl J Med* 1986;315:336-340.

[57] Hanson JW, Jones KL, Smith DW. Fetal alcohol syndrome experience with 41 patients. *JAMA* 1976;235:1458.

[58] Urbina Fuentes M, Sánchez Kobashi R. Antecedentes y Contexto. En: Urbina Fuentes M. Los Determinantes Sociales de la Salud y la Equidad en Salud. [*Background and Context.* In: Urbina Fuentes M. *The Social Determinants of Health and Equity in Health*] Documento de Postura. Academia Nacional de Medicina. Mexico. 2017, 7-14.

[59] Parkes MW, Horwitz P. Water, ecology and health: ecosystems as settings for promoting health and sustainability. *Health Promot Int.* 2009; 24:94-102.

[60] Blouin C, Chopra M, van der Hoeven R. Trade and social determinants of health. *Lancet* 2009;373:502-7.

[61] Day NL, Richardson GA, Fetal alcohol syndrome. *Seminar in perinatology* 1991;15:271-279.

[62] Sokol RJ, Clarren SK. Guidelines for use terminology describing the impact of prenatal alcohol on the offspring. *Alcohol Clin Exp Res* 1989;13:597-598.

[63] Abel EL, Sokol RJ. Fetal alcohol syndrome now leading cause of mental retardation. *Lancet* 1986;2:1222.

[64] Aronson M, Olegard R. Children of alcoholic mothers. *Pediatrician* 1987;14:57-61.

[65] Sulik KK, Johnston MC. Sequence of developmental alterations following acute etanol exposure in mice: craniofacial features of the fetal alcohol syndrome. *Am J Anat* 1983;166:257-269.

[66] Nanson JL. Autism in fetal alcohol syndrome: a report of six cases. *Alcohol Clin Exp Res* 1992;16:558-565.

[67] Clarren SK, Smith DW. The fetal alcohol syndrome. *N Engl J Med* 1978;298:1063-1067.

[68] Hanson JW, Jones KL, Smith DW. The effects of moderate alcohol consumption during pregnancy on fetal growth and morphogenesis. *J Pediatr* 1978;92:457-59.

[69] Borges G. Consumo moderado de bebidas alcohólicas por mujeres embarazadas. Una controversia epidemiológica. [Moderate consumption of alcoholic beverages by pregnant women. An epidemiological controversy] *Salud Pública Mex* 1988;30:14-24.

[70] Calderón G, Campillo SC. Respuestas de la comunidad ante los problemas relacionados con el alcohol. Mexico: OMS [*Community responses to problems related to alcohol.* Mexico: WHO] Instituto Mexicano de Psiquiatría, 1981.

[71] Jones KL, Smith DW. Pattern of malformations in off spring of chronic alcoholic mothers. *Lancet* 1973;1:1267-1271.

[72] Chasnoff L, Landress HJ, Harvey J, Mark E. Barret. The prevalence of illicit drug or alcohol use during pregnancy and discrepancies in mandatory reporting in Pinellas Country, Florida. *N Engl J Med* 1990; 322:1202-1206.

[73] Rosett HC. A clinical perspective of the fetal syndrome. *Alcoholism* 1980; 4:119-112.

[74] Milis J, Graubard BI. Is moderate drinking during pregnancy associated with an increased risk for malformations?. *Pediatrics* 1987;80:309-314.

[75] Rodríguez HR. Repercusiones del tabaquismo durante el embarazo. [Repercussions of smoking during pregnancy] *Acta Ped Mex* 1999; 20:67.

[76] Neiberg S, Mark JS, McLaren NM. The fetal tobacco syndrome. *JAMA* 1985;253:2998-2999.

[77] Haddon W, Nesbitt R. Smoking and pregnancy: Carbon monoxide in blood during gestation and at term. *Obst and Gynec* 1961;18·262.

[78] Doberezak TM, Thornton JC, Bernstein J. Impact of maternal drug dependency on birth weight and head circumference of offspring. *Am J Dis Child* 1987;141:1163-1167.

[79] Naeye RL. The duration of maternal cigarette smoking in fetal and maternal disordes. *Early Hum Dev* 1979; 33:229-237.

[80] Howard RB, Hosokawa T, Maguire H. Hypoxia-induced feto placental vasoconstriction in perfused human placental cotyledons. *Am J Obstet Gynecol* 1987; 157: 1261-1266.

[81] Van der Veen F, Fox H. The effects of cigarette smoking on the human placenta: a light and electron microscopic study: *Placenta* 1982; 3:243-256.

[82] Delgado A. *Vida clandestina*. [*Life clandestine*] España Imprenta BOAN, 1996:93-95.

[83] Taylor SE. The life long legacy of childhood abuse. *Am J Med* 1999;7:399.

[84] Van der Bor M, Walther FJ, Sims ME. Increased cerebral blood flow velocity in infants of mothers who abuse cocaine. *Pediatrics* 1990; 85:733-736.

[85] Bingol N, Fuchs M, Diaz V. Teratogenicity of cocaine in human. *J Pediatr* 1987;110:93-96.

[86] Casado FJ, Baño RA. Padres adictos a drogas: heroína, cocaína y marihuana. En: Loredo Abdalá A. Maltrato en el niño. [*Parents addicted to drugs: heroin, cocaine and marijuana*. In: Loredo Abdalá A. *Abuse in the child*] Mexico: McGraw-Hill Interamericana, 2001:31-42.

[87] Kain ZN, Rimar S, Barash PG. Cocaine abuse in the parturient and effects on the fetus and neonate. *Anesth Analg* 1993;77:835-845.

[88] Farrar HC, Kearns L, Cocaine: clinical pharmacology and toxicology. *J Pediatr* 1989;115:665-675.

[89] Acker D, Sachs BP, Tracey K, Wise WE. Abruptio placentae associated with cocaine use: *Am J Obstet Gyneacol* 1983; 146:220-221.

[90] Chouteau M, Namerow PB, Leppert P. The effect of cocaine abuse on birth weigth and gestacional age. *Obstet Gyneacol* 1988;72:351-354.

[91] Legido A. Trastornos neurológicos del hijo de madre toxicómana (alcohol, cocaína, heroína y marihuana). En: Casado FJ, Días HJ, Martínez C. *Niños Maltratados*. [Neurological disorders of the child of a drug addicted mother (alcohol, cocaine, heroin and marijuana). In: Casado FJ, Diaz HJ, Martínez C. *Mistreated children*] Madrid: Díaz de Santos, 1997:225-228.

[92] Cornelius MD, Taylor PM, Geva D, Day NL. Prenatal tabaco and marijuana use among adolescents: effects on offspring gestacional age, growth, and morphology. *Pediatrics* 1995; 95:738.

[93] Hutchings DE, Morgan B, Brake SC. Delta-9, tetra hydro cannabinol during pregnancy in the rat: differential effects on maternal nutrition, embryo toxicity and growth in the offspring. *Neurotoxicol Teratol* 1987;9:39-43.

[94] Little BB, Snell LM, Klein VR. Maternal and fetal effects of heroin addiction during pregnancy. *J Reprod Med* 1990; 35:159-162.

[95] Kaltenback K, Finnegan L. Neonatal abstinence syndrome, pharmacotherapy and developmental outcome. *Neurobehavioral Toxicology and Teratology* 1986; 8:353-355.

[96] Lam SK, To WK, Duthie SJ. Narcotic addiction in pregnancy with adverse maternal and perinatal outcome. *Aust NZ J Obstet Gynaecol* 1992; 32:216-221.

[97] Finnegan LP. Maternal and neonatal effects of alcohol and drugs. In: Lowinson JH, Ruiz P, Milliman RB, Langrod JG. *A comprehensive text book of sustance abuse*. 2nd ed. Baltimore: Williams and Wilkins, 1992:628-656.

[98] Kahn A, Blum D. Fenotiazinas y síndrome de Muerte súbita del lactante. [Phenothiazines and sudden infant death síndrome] *Pediatrics*. 1982; 14:65-68.

[99] Thomas DB. Narcotic addiction and the sudden infant death syndrome. *Med J Aust* 1998;149:562.

[100] Rajegowda BK, Kandall SR, Falciglia H. Sudden infant death in infants of narcotic addicted mothers. *Pediatr Res* 1976; 10·199

[101] Chassnoff I. Perinatal addiction: consequences of intrauterine exposure to opiate and monopiate drugs. In: Chassnoff I. *Drug use in pregnancy: mother and child.* Lancaster: MTP Press, 1987:52-63.

[102] Finnegan LP. *Drug addiction and pregnancy and parenting.* Boston: Kluwer Academin Publisher, 1988:59-71.

[103] Smith DW. Fetal alcohol syndrome. In: Smith DW. *Recognizable patterns of human malformations.* Philadelphia: WB Saunders, 1982:411-414.

[104] Carbajal RL, Sierra JJ. Intoxicación por mercurio. [Mercury poisoning] *Acta Pediatr Mex* 1990;11:52-59.

[105] NIOSH. Recommendations for occupational safety and health standars. *MMWR* 1985; 34:5S315S.

[106] Loredo Abdalá A, Casas Muñoz A, Navarro Ampúdia P, Villanueva Clíft H, García Carranza A. Maltrato infantil: riesgo y prevención [*Child abuse: risk and prevention*] Academia Mexicana de Pediatría, A. C. Mexico. Medigraphic.com.

[107] Dolz I, Cerezo MA, Milner JS. Mother-child interac- tional patterns in high and low risk mothers. *Child Abuse Neglect.* 1997; 20:1031-1048.

[108] Pacheco-Sánchez CI. Embarazo en menores de quince años: Los motivos y la redefinición del curso de vida. [Pregnancy in children under fifteen years: The reasons and the redefinition of the course of life] *Salud Pública Mex.* 2016;58:56-61.

[109] Gómez P, Molina R, Zamberlin N. *Factores relacionados con el embarazo y la maternidad en menores de 15 años en América Latina y el Caribe.* [*Factors related to pregnancy and maternity in children under 15 years old in Latin America and Caribbean,* Centro de Promoção e Defesa dos Direitos Sexuais e Reprodutivos] 1a Ed. Mexico: Centro de Promoción y Defensa de los Derechos Sexuales y Reproductivos PROMSEX; 2011.

[110] Rosende GV. Embarazo adolescente y pobreza rural. *E-Rural. Educación, cultura y desarrollo local.* [Teenage pregnancy and rural

poverty. *E-Rural. Education, culture and local development*] 2016;1:1-11.

[111] Alcázar L. *Consecuencias socio-económicas de la maternidad adolescente: ¿Constituye un obstáculo para la formación de capital humano y el acceso a mejores empleos?* Instituto Nacional de Estadística e Informática (INEI), Centro de Investigación y Desarrollo (CIDE): Lima, Perú [*Socioeconomic Consequences of Adolescent Maternity: Is it an obstacle to the formation of human capital and access to better jobs?* National Institute of Statistics and Informatics (INEI), Center for Research and Development (CIDE)] 2006:7-85. 2006: 7-85].

[112] Ramos-Gutiérrez RY, Barriga-Marín JA, Pérez- Molina J. Embarazo en adolescentes como factor de riesgo para maltrato fetal. [Pregnancy in adolescents as a risk factor for fetal maltreatment] *Ginecol Obstet Mex.* 2009;77:311-316.

[113] Moyeda IXG, Sánchez BM, Cervantes DMO, Vega HAR. Relación entre maltrato fetal, violencia y sintomatología depresiva durante el embarazo de mujeres adolescentes y adultas: un estudio piloto. [Relationship between fetal maltreatment, violence and depressive symptomatology during pregnancy in adolescent and adult women: a pilot study] *Psicología y Salud.* 2013;23:83-95.

[114] Loredo-Abdalá A, Vargas-Campuzano E. Casa-Muñoz A, González-Corona J, Gutiérrez-Leyva CJ. Embarazo adolescente: sus causas y repercusiones en la diada. [Adolescent pregnant: its causes and repercussions in the dyad] *Rev Med Inst Mex Seguro Soc.* 2017;55:161-69.

In: Child Abuse: Harm and Solutions   ISBN: 978-1-53614-271-6
Editors: Arturo Loredo Abdalá et al. © 2018 Nova Science Publishers, Inc.

Chapter 4

BULLYING OR PEER ABUSE

Hugo Juárez Olguín[1],, Arturo Loredo Abdalá[2]
and Miroslava Lindoro Silva[1]*
[1]Laboratorio de Farmacología, Instituto Nacional de Pediatría,
Facultad de Medicina, Universidad Nacional Autónoma de Mexico,
Ciudad de Mexico, Mexico
[2]Centro de Estudios Avanzados sobre Maltrato Infantil-Prevención del
Instituto Nacional de Pediatría (CEAMI-P-INP),
Ciudad de Mexico, Mexico

ABSTRACT

Violence has been part of the lives of individuals. The term "bullying
or peer abuse" is currently used to designate violence among children of
about the same age at schools. It is characterized by the presence of an
intentionally repeated and unjustified aggressive behavior of a child or
group of children towards another with the objective of inflicting physical
or emotional harm to the victim. In developed countries, the prevalence is
very high. Usually, physical abuse is common among boys and young
men while discrimination and psychological abuse are more frequent

---

*Corresponding Author Email: juarezol@yahoo.com.

among girls and young women. In recent years, there has emerged a new form of bullying known as "cyberbullying." This form of bullying is defined as an aggressive act by a student or group of students using electronic devices.

Customarily, the actors in play in the issue of bullying are constituted by the provokers, the aggressor, the victim, the observers or witnesses and the authorities. Usually, the authorities are the last to know about the situation and this normally happens when the victim´s parent raise their voice or file in a report.

Apart from the physical harm, victims of bullying may suffer different associated pathologies such as depression and suicidal attempts. For this reason, the development of a program of actions involving the participation of the school authorities, the students, parents and the society in general directed to the prevention of the phenomenon through communication with the responsible authorities, students supervision within the classrooms, the school environment and their immediate surroundings, and the psychological therapy of the victims if the need be.

In this chapter, we review all aspects of bullying, bringing into limelight the actors in play, the sites of occurrence, its modalities, and the basic and extreme clinical characteristics as well as the curative and preventive interventions necessary to curb this phenomenon.

Keywords: aggressive children, discrimination, peer abuse, physical abuse, violence

INTRODUCTION

Violence has been part of the lives of individuals, their communities and population settlements since the record of human existence. Within the society, it is used as a way to impose and exercise power on others and to bring order. By definition, violence is a deliberate use of physical force or power as a threat either on oneself, another person, a group of people or a community. The consequences on the victim can be injuries of varying severity, alteration on his/her physical and emotional development, psychological damage and even death [1-6].

Violence in the school among children of about the same age is known as "bullying" or peer abuse. This problem is characterized by the presence of an intentionally repeated and unjustified aggressive behavior of a child to physically or emotionally harm a classmate or schoolmate with less power or strength either in the classroom or in other areas of the school. Because of its worldwide frequency, peer abuse is regarded as a public health problem [7-9].

The origin of the study of this type of child abuse is dated back to 1973 when Dan Olweus started to study it in Norway. Olweus was concerned to know why some adolescents had committed suicide. He discovered that such adolescents were people who had suffered bullying during their childhood. In the decade of the 1980, the problem was studied in some European countries, North America and Japan, as well as in Australia. The clinical, social and economic results of those studies were very similar to what were initially described [10-11].

On analyzing the frequency of the problem in 40 countries in North America and Europe, it was found that this varies from 8.6% to 45.2% in boys and from 4.8% to 35.8% in girls [12-15].

RECENT STUDIES

A report of the Swedish National Agency for Education established that 9% of 4th and 6th grade students, ages 10 to 12, and 3% of 7th to 9th grades with ages ranging from 13 to 15 years have been assaulted by other students [16]. In some places in China, the frequency ranges from 2% to 66% and in Hong Kong, it is from 24% to 50% [17].

Recently in the Czech Republic, there has been a clear decline in reported cases from 1994 to 2014. It is pointed out that probably this change was secondary to the modification in the political regime of this country, the establishment of a school program, the preventive action of the police and to a clearer understanding of the problem by the society [18].

In recent years, a new form of bullying problem known as "cyberbullying" has emerged and is defined as an aggressive act by a student or group of students using electronic devices. The evolution of this modality of bullying and its consequences on the victims have increased and it is changing in line with the advances in electronic devices [19-24].

In Mexico, "bullying" became known through some research works carried out in primary schools in the cities of Guadalajara, Colima and Mexico [25-27]. Considering that in Mexico, 24% of the children and adolescent population is in school age, the distribution of bullying is 92% in public schools and the remainder in private schools.

In a pilot study of 485 students (51% males and 49% females, aged 11 to 16) conducted by the Comprehensive Care and Abused Children Clinic of National Institute of Pediatrics (CCACC-NIP) in a secondary school located in Coyoacan Local Government Area, Mexico city, it was found that:

- There was "bullying" in 30% of the students.
- The behavioral distribution of the studied population was aggressive in 11%, provokers in 11%, victims in 8.4% and the rest were observers.
- Aggression types were verbal in 53%, physical in 20%, social in 18% and others 9%.
- The places where the phenomenon occurred were mainly in the classroom in 62% and in the school yard in 18%.
- The reported frequency of aggression was one to two acts per week in 30%.
- The physical aggression predominated in boys and psychological in girls (data not published).

This behavior of the victims is very similar to the report of research works performed in other countries [28-29].

Violence experienced in the schools or in their classrooms is a situation that has always happened and traditionally it is regarded as something normal. The perpetuation of this type of negative conducts is simply because it is often a common treatment between students and teachers [30].

ACTORS IN BULLYING

In this type of abuse (bullying or peer abuse), there are always three actors:

The Victim

The victim is a minor of any sex with some physical, racial, emotional or religious characteristics that make him or her appear weaker than and different from the aggressor. These peculiarities can be skin color, short stature, very thin or fat, use of eye lens, shyness or timid, insecure and unsociable.

In a series of 35,013,000 students studied in the USA, there was no significant difference in the gender (boys 12,862,000 and girls 12,151,000) of the victims however; the aggression was slightly more frequent in girls [12, 31-33].

The behavior of the victim changes remarkably as a consequence of the type of aggression, its frequency and severity. Usually, the victim suddenly becomes sad and shy, loses some personal or school objects without justification and unlike before, asks money from the parents.

These changes should points of alert to the parents, the teachers, the school authorities and the classmates or peers; however, most adults very often say, "it also happened to me" or "it is a good experience for him or her to learn to defend himself/herself from others" or "if we intervene, in the school, they will attack him/her more" or even say, "nothing will happen to him/her" [34].

Finally, we must consider in these cases the racial difference that exists in some countries of the world. In the US, the problem has been shown to be more common in African-American adolescents than in Asian and Latin adolescents [35].

The Aggressor

The aggressor is the minor who carries out the aggression or induces it and obviously he or she is physically and emotionally superior to the victim. The aggression could be physical, emotional, intellectual or economic. Usually, the aggressor is characterized by lacking the sense of guilt and by having impulsive and aggressive temper with uncontrolled anger. Frequently they are people who come from homes that are characterized by their high aggressiveness, violence and lack of love among the family members as well as an absence of operating rules of conducts or norms in the family and hence, they cannot control their temper. In most of the cases, they are bad students and have no interest in studies. Despite these characteristics, a high percentage of them have a history of living or suffering from family violence or being physically, emotionally or sexually abused in their homes.

Usually, the aggressor is surrounded by other school mates that support him and in occasions, these supporters carry out the aggression on his or her behalf for fear of or to please the aggressor and in this way avoid being a victim of the phenomenon. Literature report shows that the aggressor enjoys the grief of the aggravated partner (60%) and that he or she is able to inflict pain regardless of the suffering of the victim, while 65% of them do it in order to "demonstrate their power and strength" over other school mates.

Boys and young men generally perpetrate physical abuse while girls and women deal with discrimination and psychological abuse.

An English study showed large differences between women victims of bullying in England with Pakistan and Caribbean women being the most assaulted when compared with women from other ethnic groups [36].

It should be emphasized that the most aspect of this situation is that, in all likelihood, the aggressor does not know the short, medium and long term consequences of his or her attacks on the child or the partners and these could at times be lethal and may, in part, explain the high level of juvenile suicide [37-38].

On the hand, the influence exerted by various situations or actions of the actors in some societies of the world must be born in mind. For instance, it is very evident that high consumption of alcohol and marijuana as well as the location of the school plays a vital role in this. If the school is located in a poor neighborhood and with a high level of delinquency, this will undoubtedly exert an influence in this situation [39-42].

The Witnesses

They are usually schoolmates of almost the same age and sex who witness the aggression without doing something about it due to fear or inability to stop it. Nevertheless, sometimes some of the witnesses may brave it and go to the teacher to inform him what is happening or talk about it at home and ask their parents for active and effective intervention with the school authorities. Frequently, the intervention of these adults is very minimal. It is also likely that the observer students are unaware of the consequences and the severity of the problem in the short, medium and long term.

It has been established that the passive reaction of the observer students may be associated with a low moral level and inability to defend themselves. Other factors may be the existing empathy with the other actors, inability to see and consider the negative consequences of "bullying" and lack of moral disagreement with the subject [43-45].

It may be interesting to point out a characteristic event that happened for many years in Mexico which lies on the tolerance of school authorities, teachers and students for actions known as "hazing". This action or harassment was usually towards newly admitted students in secondary and high schools or in colleges or universities. In this event, newly admitted adolescent students were the victims of physical, emotional or moral aggressions which though did not put their physical integrity at risk but affected their emotions and rights. Traditionally, this action was considered as a celebration of welcome to the newly admitted students to a school. Presently, such activities have almost disappeared from national schools.

SITE OF OCCURRENCE OF THE PHENOMENON

The problem of "bullying" is usually staged inside the schools, especially in the classrooms, hallways, staircases and in lesser degree in the yards, bathrooms, cafeteria, on the streets near the schools or in the school buses. The type of school, its academic quality and the neighborhood in which it is located should be considered when the school is being evaluated.

In an analysis of 49,698,000 public and private schools in the United States, it was shown that "bullying" occurred more frequently in private schools and even more in non-Catholic private schools [12, 46-47].

In the face of this knowledge, it must be emphasized that the primary function of the school authorities and the teachers is to detect and to directly or indirectly intervene, as soon as they are aware of "bullying" situation.

MODALITIES OF BULLYING

Bullying types can be diverse and regularly depend on the age of the victims and the school grade of the actors. On these bases, we can distinguish the following types of bullying:

- Physical abuse. It is more often observed in primary schools and less frequent in middle and upper schools (junior and senior high schools and the university). The type of aggression normally observed in this abuse is characterized by injuries caused by blows, pinching, pushing, and damage to various personal objects of the victim, theft of personal school materials and demand of money. The victims can be threatened with white weapons or firearms. In this modality, in addition to the aggressor, there are "guards or beaters" who carry out the act of intimidation.

- Psychological, moral and sexual abuse. Usually, this type occurs inside secondary schools or higher education. The main characteristics of this modality of abuse are: spreading malicious rumors about the victim, insults, prohibit the victim from integrating in the school dynamics or extreme isolation. An associated modality to the above is the incorrect use of social webs known as "cyberbullying." This medium propitiates the staging of aggressive attacks through mockery, threats and discredit.
- Sexual abuse is characterized by harassment, induction to sex, touching or sexting which is the sending of sexual materials by electronic means.
- Homophobic bullying or gay bashing. It refers to any kind of psychological, physical and moral damage for having or pretending to have a different sexual orientation.

The basic characteristics of bullying are presented in Table 1 and the clinical characteristics in Table 2 [48-51].

There are other manifestations that the minor refers to and that parents and teachers should know and consider. In this way, they can establish the suspicion of abuse among peers or confirm their existence (Table 3) [52].

Table 1. Basic facts of bullying

a) There is a clear imbalance in physical, emotional, intellectual or economic between victims and perpetrators.
b) The phenomenon is frequent and repeated.
c) There is little or no peer intervention to detain the action.
d) There is little intervention of the parents or little likelihood that they are attended by the school authorities and teachers.
e) Usually, the teachers are unaware or the last to know that the phenomenon occurs.
f) School authorities generally do not accept or bluntly negate the existence of the problem. This situation is more common in private schools.

Table 2. Clinical characteristics of bullying

a) The child attacked offers little or no resistance to the aggression due to fear or unequal power with the perpetrator.

b) There is intentionality of the aggressor. The purpose of the actions is to physically and emotionally harm the victim and to inspire fear, distress and physical or emotional suffering. Apparently in this way, the aggressor enjoys or derives pleasure.

c) The aggressor ignores the physical and emotional development of the victim as well as the severity of the long-term consequences.

d) The classmates have a passive attitude towards the existence of the problem.

e) The teacher and the school authorities usually do not want to get involved in the problem for the mere fact that they are ignorant of how to resolve the situation, afraid of losing the enrollment of the problematic student and not willing or wanting to face the parents of the aggressor student.

Table 3. Behavior of the victim of bullying

a) The child reports that he is being assaulted by one or more of his classmates.

b) The child has problem making friends and greater difficulty in relating to peers.

c) A sudden drop in school performance is observed.

d) The victim tells the parents that he/she does not want to attend school and manifests that he/she is suffering various discomfort, usually subjective, such as abdominal pain, headache, nausea, diarrhea, feeling tired, etc.

e) Suddenly, he/she requests to be changed from school on flimsy reasons that he/she does not understand the teachers, because the courses are more difficult and because he/she has no friends.

f) Sometimes, even if he/she changes school, the child or the adolescent says that he/she no longer want to go to the new school or continue schooling and that probably he/she wants to work, play sports or rest.

EXTREME ACTIONS

It is very probable that the aggressor students or classmates, the teachers, the school authorities and parents do not know the extreme behaviors of the victims of "bullying." In Table 4, we present the most important of these extreme behaviors [53-56].

Table 4. Extreme clinical aspects of the victim of bullying

a) On quitting school, the child may begin the consumption of licit and illicit drugs.
b) The child may begin to go with groups of youths that do not study or work and begins with criminal activities.
c) The child may fall into a state of major depression.
d) A state of psychosis can become evident.
e) The child thinks in suicide attempts and may succeed in carrying it out.
f) The child can decide to injure the schoolmates with white arm or firearm in his/her possession without the permission of the parents.

As previously pointed out, the behavior of the child or adolescent should alert the parents, the teachers, the school authorities, the pediatric physicians and the family members to intervene immediately, dynamically and effectively.

INTERVENTION OF THE PARENTS

Initially, parents must assume a real responsibility and begin a talk with the child to know what is happening to him/her. The following action must be carried out:

1) If parents become aware that their child has problems with one or more of his/her classmates, they should listen and believe the child, go to the school to speak with the teacher, the higher authorities of the school and with the parents of the child shown as the aggressor.

2) The parents should take the child to be checked by a pediatrician or family doctor to rule out a disease that explains the clinical manifestations already noted. The doctor must issue a certificate of physical and emotional health. If necessary, the physician should refer the child to a mental health professional (psychiatrist or psychologist).

3) The teacher and the school authorities should be involved in investigating the problem and listen to the parents on both sides. Often, the parents of the aggressor child are violent, with history of different addictions and generally do not accept their child's actual behavior.

4) When the victim presents data suggestive of important alteration in his/her self-esteem, depression, anxiety or distress, he/she and the family should be attended by a mental health professional.

5) The mental health professional should analyze and try to resolve the situations of family violence, different addictions in any of the progenitors, the existence of any modality of child abuse and attend the problem of school dropout as well as possible contact with illicit drugs and organized crime.

6) At school, a general program should be developed to explain to all students what bullying is and its consequences.

7) School authorities should make an effective decision in the event that the parents of the aggressor child refuse to accept the measures indicated at school. Certainly in private schools, this action is very difficult to carry out because there is a possibility that the parents remove the child from the school on knowing about the problem and therefore the school loses the enrollment and hence the corresponding income.

What Should Be Done Once the Diagnosis Is Established?

Without doubt, all the actors in this problem need to have complete information on the subject and the school must have a group of professionals trained to resolve the physical, emotional and legal situations.

In all cases, adults should carry out the following actions:

a) The victim must be attended by the family and teachers with affection, interest and knowledge of the cause so as recover his/her self-esteem, social security and attachment to school. The existence of depression, anxiety and distress requires (in some cases) the intervention of a psychiatrist or psychologist, qualified in the subject, to attend and resolve the situation of the child or adolescent. The parents and the pediatricians should be attentive to the progress achieved on the emotional and physical condition of the child.

b) As a personal action, the victim should try to improve his/her physical aspect by engaging in sports and in correct form, eat suitable diet.

c) Another fundamental situation arises from the need for the aggressor child or adolescent to receive the necessary family and professional support to treat some psychological pathology aimed at avoiding that he/she continues having or showing arrogant attitude and with that, avoid that the child direct his/ her interest towards the consumption of licit and illicit drugs, engaging with gangs, delinquents etc.

In the face of bullying, the parents of the victim and the perpetrator, the teachers and the school authorities must understand and accept that these children have a problem and that it must be effectively attended in order to gain their trust. Channeling him/her towards practicing a sport, artistic activities (playing guitar, piano and drum or enrolling him/her in a choir, musical band or theater group) or participating in social support activities to the community can be extremely useful actions.

School officials should understand that the parents of both the victim and the aggressor can develop frustration when they do not receive specific and adequate attention on the problem that their children are experiencing. Therefore, we must emphasize on the development of a two-way intervention to confront the problems inherent in bullying [57].

The existence of an emotional disorder such as autism or attention deficit hyper-reactivity disorder (ADHD) must be medically treated depending on the severity of the problem [58].

PREVENTIVE PROGRAM

We must be aware that measures to combat bullying through punishment, sanctioning and lawsuit do not seem to be the ideal strategy.

Several programs have been developed and published for the prevention of this problem. Nevertheless, few indicate positive results because the socio-cultural and economic differences of the people are a major barrier [59-60].

Faced with this global reality, development and implementation of practical and low-cost programs for the prevention of bullying is imperative. It is important that such program should consider boys and girls, adolescents, parents, teachers and school authorities.

At the CEAMI center of the National Institute of Pediatrics, a comprehensive care project has been designed to prevent bullying. It proposes the development of a strategy with transversal axis that, though involves all the actors who take part in the same, suggests considering in a primordial way the students, even when the basic actions fall on the school authorities. This proposal differs from the traditional vertical action that begins with the school administrative authorities and ends with the students – people who are not given the importance they deserve.

Obviously, to be successful with this program or similar programs; an active, dynamic and consensual participation of all the actors living and coexisting in an educational establishment is required. It is also desirable that the implementation of any program considers and involves primary and higher educational institutes, both officials and privates.

BASIC ACTIONS

Although the initiative begins almost always with the school staff, the novelty proposed is the primordial intervention of the students as well as the thinking and actions of the parents. In this way, it is insisted that the parents and children develop an active and purposeful intervention.

Initial Activity

Obviously, the initial action must fall, as already mentioned, on the administrative authorities of the school. These authorities and the teachers must propose and conduct an initial interview with the parents and members of the student society (if it exists) to present the general idea of the project.

The people involved are:

a) Students
b) Parents
c) Educators and teachers
d) Officials of the school.

The materials required are:

a) Handbook of Procedures for the Prevention of Bullying. Every school must have this handbook which must contain basic aspects of the subject.

b) Handbook of Values. Also every school and colleges must have this kind of handbook that reiterates and emphasizes the values of the school.

c) Academic Program. The schools must have academic program which contains the basic theme of Civics.

SPECIFIC ACTIONS

1) All the school staff – the principal, the teachers, the administrative staffs and the quartermaster - must know and analyze the "The Handbook of Procedures for the Prevention of Bullying" before the beginning of each school year.

2) The handbook of Procedures for the Prevention of Bullying will be given to parents or guardians upon enrollment of the students and before the beginning of the school year.

3) At the beginning of the school year, the administrative authorities will hold a meeting with the tutors, parents and some senior students to explain the strategy that has been designed to detect and prevent bullying, as well as the importance of engaging all the people involved to participate actively.

4) Parents must sign an internal register testifying that they have received, read and totally understood the "The handbook of Procedures for the Prevention of Bullying."

5) The handbook would establish the participation and commitment that the following people acquire:
   - School authorities
   - Tutors
   - Parents
   - Students

PROCEDURE

Students

A. Actions of the Administrative Authority

1) All members must have and know the Handbook of Procedure for prevention of Bullying.

2) A basic program of civics and values will be implemented in all groups in the school. The teachers may make a brief interview on the impact achieved in the students and in the families. Value information must be included as a subject in the school curricula. Its basic focus is to reach the projection of the best of every human being incorporated in the society.

3) Complaints or expressions of violence among peers, whether verbal, written and electronic or by direct observation is detected and analyzed. In addition, strategies will be implemented to resolve them and in this way, prevent the problem from increasing.

4) Direct and permanent contact is maintained with the teachers, parents and students following an established schedule. The academic board must include a section that evaluates the strategies outlined for the healthy coexistence of students, analyzes the strengths and weaknesses of the program and adjusts the action plans according to the results obtained during the period under review.

5) It is proposed that the administrative authority of the school names two teachers who will anonymously develop the supervision of the students. This function could be rotating and will last the period the school authority considers pertinent.

6) The naming of two students from each group of higher grades of basic education (4th, 5th and 6th) and senior high (7th, 8th and 9th) and their coexistence should be supervised to ensure that they carry out an anonymous monitoring. These students must be changed in a pre-established period.

7) Two parents will be requested to make analysis of the comments of their children, peers, other students and parents.

B. Actions of School Teachers

1) The teachers should emphasize with their students the meaning and the consequences of bullying and keep a close watch on the behavior of the students, especially in the class room, and of course, the spaces the students occupy in the recess and breaks should not be neglected. In this period, situations of violence should be monitored because the students think that they are less watched. Other areas to monitor in addition to the yard and playground are mainly the stairs, restrooms and school buses.

2) The teachers should listen to students' opinions on peer behavior. This constitutes a tool for data collection for making proposals that would help to establish and maintain healthy students' coexistence. The anonymity of such opinions should be strictly maintained.

3) Also, the teachers should constantly reinforce the concepts established in the Handbook of Procedures for the Prevention of Bullying.

4) With the periodicity established in the program, the teachers should emphasize and reiterate compliance with the Program of values and Civics of the school.

5) The teachers will maintain an environment of healthy coexistence through each and every one of the activities, emphasizing the positives of the group and helping to create in every one a healthy self-esteem.

6) The teachers will formulate and encourage strategies that will permit the students to express their feelings through painting, music, dance and sports. The aim is to detect the emotional situations which the students of each group are passing through.

C. Actions of the Teachers Assigned to Surveillance

The surveillance teachers will detect, register and notify (at a pre-established periodicity) to the administrative authority of the events and results of their intervention.

D. Actions of the Students

1) The selected students will receive a talk supported with pictures to explain the importance of knowing the risks of bullying among school children and the need to develop a harmonious coexistence within a framework of respect and responsibility.
2) They should maintain constant contact with the surveillance teachers and the school administrative authorities.
3) They will actively be part of permanent campaigns that address and encourage ethical values essential for coexistence among peers.

E. Parents

1) The selected parents will receive a talk supported with pictures to explain the importance of knowing the risks of bullying and the need to develop a harmonious coexistence within a framework of respect and responsibility in the school.
2) They should maintain constant contact with the surveillance teachers and the school administrative authorities.
3) They will actively participate in permanent campaigns that address and encourage ethical values essential for coexistence among peers.

Considering the consequences of bullying which can be observed in the victim and the perpetrators, a maximum and integral effort must be made to promote the development of socio-personal skills, the teaching of values and individual attention to the actors in the conflict.

It should be borne in mind that any innovative change generates rejection and criticism, but it is better to face them than doing nothing. Remember that if we fail in this action, the future of the school children will be very somber and they do not deserve it [61-63].

FINAL CONSIDERATIONS AND STRATEGIES

Parents should be attentive to the presence of this phenomenon, whether their child is the victim or the perpetrator. Also, it should be mentioned that the family is fundamental in the job of instilling principles and values that will make it possible to avoid and, sometimes, to confront bullying.

Remember that the family influences the socio-affective development of the children, since the models, values, norms, roles and abilities are learned during this period of life and are related to handling and resolving conflicts principally with the social and adaptive abilities, with the pro-social behaviors and with the emotional regulation [64].

On the other hand, there is evidence that adults who perpetrate bullying in their childhood develop family violence.

According to the proposals described, it will be possible to identify, stop and prevent school, environmental and family violence. For that, it is necessary to:

1) Involve the parents, teachers, physicians and families.
2) Promote the development of protocols of detection and attention. To propose cycles of conferences on violence, licit and illicit drug consumption, as well as human upbringing.
3) Insist on the children and the adolescents about the need to notify the school authorities or their parents of the existence of the problem.
4) Prohibit "hazing."
5) It is essential to eliminate violent and sexist content in the announcement sites.

6) Permission to use cellphones, cameras and devices of various natures must be controlled. These objects will only be allowed for academic activities.

REFERENCES

[1] Archer J. The nature of human aggression. *Int J Law Psychiatry* 2009; 32:202-8.

[2] Bowles S. Did war fare among ancestral hunter-gatherers affect the evolution of human social behaviors? *Science* 2009; 324:1293-8.

[3] Wrangham RW, Glowacki L. Intergroup aggression in chimpanzees and war in nomadic hunter-gatherers: Evaluating the chimpanzee model. *Hum Nat* 2012; 23:5-29.

[4] Fry DP, Söderberg P. Lethal aggression in mobile for ager bands and implications for the origins of war. *Science* 2013; 341:270-3.

[5] Martin DL, Harrod RP. Bioarchaeological contributions to the study of violence. *Am J Phys Anthropol.* 2015; 156 (Suppl. 59):116-45.

[6] *Informe sobre la situación mundial de la prevención de la violencia 2014.* Organización Mundial de la Salud (OMS). [*Report on the global situation of the prevention of violence 2014.* World Health Organization (WHO)]

[7] Olweus D. Bullying or peer abuse in school: Intervention and prevention. *Psychology, Law, Criminal Justice.* Oxford, UK, 1995; 248-263.

[8] Olweus D. School bullying: Development and some important challenges. *Ann Rev Clin Psychol* 2013; 9:751-80.

[9] Thornberg R, Thornberg UB, Alamaa R, Daud N. Children's conceptions of bullying and repeated conventional transgressions: moral, conventional, structuring and personal-choice reasoning. *Educ Psych* 2014; 36:1-17.

[10] Olweus D. Agression in the schools: Bullying and whipping boys. *Hemisphere.* Washington D.C. 1987.

[11] Olweus D. Bullying at school: basic facts and effects of a school based intervention program. *J Child Psychol Psyc*. 1994; 35:1171–90.

[12] *Student Report of Bullying and Ciber-Bullying: Results from the 2013 School Crime Supplement to the National Crime Victimization Survey*. WEB-tables. U.S. Department of education. April 2015. KCES 2015-056

[13] Craig W, Harel-Fisch Y, Fogel-Grinvald H, Dostaler S. A cross-national profile of bullying and victimization among adolescents in 40 countries. *Am J Public Health*2009; 54:216-224.

[14] Harel-Fisch Y, Walsh SD, Fogel-Grinvald H. Members of the HBSC Violence and Injury Prevention Focus Group. Negative school perceptions and involvement in school bullying: a universal relationship across 40 countries. *J Adolesc* 201; 34:639-52.

[15] Luxenberg H, Limber SP, Olweus D. *Bullying in U.S. schools: 2013 status report*. Center City, MN: Hazelden Foundation; 2014.

[16] Thornberg R and Jungert T. Callous-unemotional traits, harm-effect moral reasoning, and bullying among Swedish children. *Child Youth Care Forum* 2017; 46:559-575.

[17] Weng X, Chui WH and Liu Liu. Bullying behaviors among macanese adolescents—association with psychosocial variables. *Int J Environ Res Public Health*2017; 14:887.

[18] Sarková S, Sigmundová D, Kalman M. National time trends in bullying among adolescents in the Czech Republic from 1994 a2014. *Cent Eur J Public Health* 2017; 25 (Suppl 1): S32–S35

[19] Ybarra ML, Mitchell KJ, Wolak J. Examining characteristics and associated distress related to internet harassment: findings from these cond youth internet safety survey. *Pediatrics* 2006; 118:e1169-77.

[20] Smith PK, Mahdavi J, Carvalho M. Cyberbullying: Its nature and impact in secondary school pupils. *J Child Psychol Psyc* 2008; 49:376-85.

[21] Grigg D W. Cyber-aggression: Definition and concept of cyberbullying. *Aust J Guid Couns*. 2010; 20:143-156.

[22] Aoyama I, Saxon TF, Fearon DD. Internalizing problems among cyberbullying victims and moderator effects of friendship quality. *Multicultural Ed Technology* J 2011; 5:92-105.

[23] Berne S, Frisén A, Schultze-Krunbholz A. Cyber-bullying assessment instruments: A systematic review. *Aggress Violent Beh* 2013; 18:320-334.

[24] Betts LR and Spenser KA. Developing the cyber victimization experiences and cyberbullying behaviors scales. *J Genet Psychol* 2017; 10:1-18.

[25] Loredo Abdalá A, Perea Martínez A, López Navarrete GE. "Bullying": acoso escolar. La violencia entre iguales. Problemática real entre adolescentes. ["Bullying" school bullying. The violence between equals. Real problem among teenagers] *Acta Pediatr Mex* 2008; 29:210-214.

[26] Gómez Nashiki A. Bullying: El poder de la violencia. Una perspectiva cualitativa sobre acosadores y victimas en escuelas primarias de Colima. [Bullying: The power of violence. A qualitative perspective on bullies and victims in elementary schools in Colima] *Revista Mexicana de Investigación Educativa* 2013; 18: 839-870.

[27] Estudio sobre violencia entre pares (Bullying) en las escuelas de nivel básico en Mexico. [Study on peer violence (Bullying) in elementary schools in Mexico] *Programa Operativo Annual* ceameg@congreso.gob.mx. 2011.

[28] Juvonen J, Graham S, Schuster MA. Bullying among young adolescents: the strong, the weak, and the troubled. *Pediatrics* 2003; 112:1231-1237.

[29] Due P, Holstein BE, Lynch J. Bullying and symptoms among school-aged children: International comparative cross sectional study in 28 countries. *Eur J Public Health* 2005;15:128-132.

[30] Loredo Abdalá A. Navarro-Ampudia P. Maltrato entre pares o acoso escolar (bullying) En: Loredo Abdalá Matrato Infantil: gravedad y prevención. [*Maltreatment between peers or schoolchildren (bullying)* In: Loredo Abdalá *Child maternity: severity and prevention*] Editores de Textos Mexicanos. 2017 pp.71-91. Mexico.

[31] Williams K, Chambers M, Logan S, Robinson D. Association of common health symptoms with bullying in primary schoolchildren. *Br Med J* 1996;313:17-19.

[32] Nansel TR, Craig W, Overpeck M. Cross-national consistency in the relationship between bullying behaviors and psychosocial adjustment. *Arch Pediatr Adolesc Med* 2004; 158:730-736.

[33] Arseneault L, Walsh E, Trzesniewski K. Bullying victimization uniquely contributes to adjustment problems in young children: A nationally representative cohort study. *Pediatrics* 2006; 118:130-138.

[34] Spriggs AL, Lannotti RJ, Nansel TR, Haynie DL. Adolescents bullying involvement and perceived family, peer and school relations: commonalities and difference across race/ethnicity. *J Adolesc Health* 2007; 41:238-93.

[35] Rhee S, Lee SY, Jung SH. Ethnic differences in bullying victimization and psychological distress: A test of an ecological model. *J Adolescence* 2017, 1st Ed.

[36] Tippett N, Wolke D, Platt L. Ethnicity and bullying involvement in a national UK youth sample. *J Adolesc* 2013; 36:639-49.

[37] Kim YS, Koh YJ, Leventhal BL. Prevalence of school bullying in Korean middle school students. *Arch Pediatr* 2004; 158:737-41.

[38] BaldrysC, Winkel FW. Direct and vicarious victimization at school and at home as risk factors for suicidal cognition among Italian adolescents. *J Adolescence* 2003; 26:703e-716.

[39] Lambe LJ, Craig WM. Bullying involvement and adolescent substance use: A multi-level investigation of individual and neighborhood risk factors. *Drug Alcohol Depen* 2017; 178:461-468.

[40] Chung HL, Steinberg L. Relations between neighborhood factors, parenting behaviors, peer deviance, and delinquency among serious juvenile offenders. *Dev Psychol* 2006; 42:319-331.

[41] Kwan MP. The uncertain geographic context problem. *Ann Assoc Am Geogr* 2012; 102:958-968.

[42] Hong JS, Davis JP, Sterzing PR. A conceptual frame work for understanding the association between school bullying victimization and substance misuse. *Am J Ortho Psychiatr* 2014; 84:696-710.

[43] Rivers I. Morbidity among by standers of bullying behavior at school: concepts, concerns, and clinical/research issues. *Int J Adolesc Med Health*. 2011; 24:11-16.

[44] Kim MJ, Catalano RF, Haggerty KP, Abbott RD. Bullying at elementary school and problem behavior in young adulthood: a study of bullying, violence and substance use from age 11 to age 21. *Crim Behav Ment Health* 2011; 21:136-144.

[45] Thornberg R, Wänström L, Hong J S, Espelage DL. Classroom relationship qualities and social-cognitive correlates of defending and passive by standing in school bullying in Sweden: A multi-level analysis. *J School Psychol* 2017; 63:49-62.

[46] Bender D, Losel F. Bullying at school as a predictor of delinquency, violence and other anti-social behavior in adulthood. *Crim Behav Ment Heal,* 2011; 21:99-106.

[47] Bevilacqua L, Shackleton N, Hale D. The role of family and school-level factors in bullying and cyberbullying: a cross- sectional study. *BMC Pediatrics* 2017; 17:2-10.

[48] Srabstein J, McCarter R, Shao C, Huang Z. Morbidities associated with bullying behaviors in adolescents. *Int J Adolesc Med Health* 2006; 18:587-596.

[49] Sourander A, Jensen P, Rönning JA. Childhood bullies and victims and their risk of criminality in late adolescence: The Finnish from a Boy to a Man study. *Arch Pediatr Adolesc Med*. 2007; 161:546-552.

[50] Joffre Velásquez VH, García Maldonado G, Saldívar González AH, Martínez Perales G, Lin Ochoa D. Bullying in junior high school students: general characteristics and associated risk factors. *Bol Med Hosp Infant Mex* 2011; 68:177-185.

[51] Gini G, Pozzoli T. Bullied children and Psychosomatic Problems: A Metanalysis. *Pediatrics* 2013; 132:720-729.

[52] Kaltiala-Heino R, Rimpela M, Rantanen P. Bullying at school–an indicator of adolescents at risk for mental disorders. *J Adolescence* 2000; 23:661-674.

[53] Simckes MS, Simonetti JA, Moreno MA. Access to a loaded gun without adult permission and school-based bullying. *J Adolescent Health* 2017: 1-6.

[54] Klomek AB, Kleinman M, Altschuler E. High school bullying as a risk for later depression and suicidality. *Suicide Life Threat Behav* 2011; 41:501-516.

[55] Tharp-Taylor S, Haviland A, D'Amico EJ. Victimization from mental and physical bullying and substance use in early adolescence. *Addict Behav* 2009; 34:561-567.

[56] Bang YR, Park JH. Psychiatric disorders and suicide attempts among adolescents victimized by school bullying. *Australas Psychiatry*2017: 25:376-380.

[57] Hale R, Fox CL, Murray M. As a parent you become a tiger: Parents talking about bullying at school. *J Child Fam Stud* 2017; 26:2000-2015.

[58] Loredo Abdalá A, Trueba Llera NY y Navarro-Ampudia P. Propuesta de un programa para la prevenciòn del acoso escolar o maltrato entre pares (bullying) En: Loredo Abdalá *Maltrato Infantil: gravedad y prevención.* [*Proposal of a program for the prevention of bullying or bullying*] Editores de Textos Mexicanos. 2017, 93-101.

[59] Ttofi MM, Farrington DP. Effectiveness of school- based programs to reduce bullying: a systematic and meta-analytic review. *J Exp Criminol* 2011; 7:27-56.

[60] Seltzer S, Menoch M, Chen CH. Opportunistic screening for exposure to bullying in the pediatric emergency department. *Global Pediatric Health* 2017; 4:1-6.

[61] Amara G. Violencia intrafamiliar. En: Dulanto Gutiérrez E (ed.). *La Familia. Un espacio de encuentro y crecimiento para todos.* [Intrafamiliar violence. In: Dulanto Gutiérrez E (ed). *The family. A meeting and growth space for all*] Mexico: Editores de Textos Mexicanos, 2004:413-429.

[62] Díaz Huertas JA, Casado Flores J. Programas de prevención del maltrato infantil. En Loredo Abdalá A (ed.). *Maltrato en el niño.* [*Programs for the prevention of child abuse.* In: Loredo Abdalá A

(ed.) *Abuse in the child*] Mexico: McGraw-Hill Interamericana, 2001: 99-116.

[63] Mateos JMR. Violencia, salud infantojuvenil y calidad de vida En: Loredo Abdalá A (ed.). Maltrato en el niño. [*Violence, child and youth health and quality of life* In: Loredo Abdalá A (ed.). *Abuse in the child*] Mexico, McGraw-Hill Interamericana, 2001:43-62.

[64] Cuervo-Martínez A. Pautas de crianza y desarrollo socio-afectivo en la infancia. [Parenting guidelines and socio-affective development in childhood] *Revista Diversitas Perspectivas en Psicología* 2010; 6: 111-121.

Chapter 5

RITUALISM:
A COMPLEX FORM OF CHILD ABUSE

Arturo Loredo Abdalá[1,], Adriana Monroy Villafuerte[1]*
and Hugo Juárez Olguín[2]

[1]Centro de Estudios Avanzados sobre Maltrato Infantil-Prevención del
Instituto Nacional de Pediatría (CEAMI-P-INP),
Ciudad de Mexico, Mexico
[2]Laboratorio de Farmacología, Instituto Nacional de Pediatría,
Facultad de Medicina, Universidad Nacional Autónoma de Mexico,
Ciudad de Mexico, Mexico

ABSTRACT

Ritualism is considered a religious threat, which can generate physical, psychological and sexual abuse to the victims, most of them children. This type of violence evolved with the advance of time, beginning with religious fanaticism, witch hunts, change to religious sacrifices or exposure to children in unsafe situations or places of risk, as well as the risk of death by denying blood transfusions. The doctor and

---

[*] Corresponding Author Email: cainm_inp@hotmail.com.

any professional who is in contact with the children must consider this type of violence; that would enable him to offer comprehensive management.

It is necessary that the medical community and the society in general be on alert because the children are at high risk of being physically, sexually or psychologically abused by adults, including their parents, who under a religious fanaticism violate the rights of children. Because of the complexities in the diagnosis and the resulting denunciation, there is no clear mechanism to fully attend these children and young people. However, it is the responsibility of doctors, jurists and sociologists to design an algorithm that allows the rescue of the victims and prevent them from suffering damage. This chapter analyzes the risks of religious fanaticism and how it can affect to children.

Keywords: fanaticism, psychological abuse, ritualism, Satanism, sexual abuse

INTRODUCTION

A medical, social and legal problem of humanity that affects children and adolescents is currently known as Child Abuse (CA) [1]. In this entity, there are four predominating basic forms: physical abuse (PA), sexual abuse (SA), psychological abuse (PsA) and negligence (NE). Nevertheless, there are also little-known or little-considered situations where children and adolescents are victims of one or several types of aggression that have been pin-pointed but have not been well studied and, therefore, not diffused. Examples of them are satanic ritualism, ethnic abuse, children in situation of war, street children and peer abuse or bullying [2].

Ritualism constitutes a relative novelty of CA pathology. In this chapter, various forms of such a singular form of aggression in the children are presented. Its study would help the doctors and other professionals, whose work swivels around the children, to better understand this form of CA. The return of magical thought (MT) in the last years of the past century, in which science has advanced so extraordinarily, constitute a social phenomenon so surprising, that it forces us to reflect on the need to know what is currently happening. MT was the first way of human thinking and was born as a response to his sh. It was as a solution to all his doubts and an explanation to the existing unknowns [3].

As the primitive man did not know the cause of everything that occurred around him, he sought for an explanation and created responsible spirits for each phenomenon. In this way, the Animism as a religion, which is still professed by numerous towns on earth, was born [3]. Later, there was the emergence of the term Multiple Souls believed to guide man to One Soul and from there, to the existence of God [3]. This was how ancient civilizations (Sumerian, Egyptian, Chinese, Indian) and the American Prehispanic civilizations created multiple gods [3]. In the third century AD, with Christian ideas, Celio Aureliano, who dedicated to studying the mentally ill people, proposed that a special type of demon could appear in form of a man and sexually possesses a woman or women and seduces the men and in this way, Demonology is born [3].

The evil spirits of the primitive communities were replaced by the Christian demon, which, at that time, dominated the world. It was a time when Greek thoughts were forgotten. These ideas of demoniac possession spread all through the Middle Age and in the Renaissance were in full swing. It was in the Sixteenth and Seventeenth centuries that the belief claimed its greatest number of victims [3].

During that time, the mentally ill and epileptic patients, with their bizarre behaviors such as convulsive crisis and delusion, that particularly attracted the weird attention of the people, could only be the work of the demon, and therefore, had to be burned alive. In this way, the demented elderly women and hysteric ones were accused of witches having a pact with the devil and hence were also burned at the stake. The people love God but were much more afraid of the devil, and so, in the thirteenth century, the Holy Inquisition was born with the motive of persecuting the heretics and all crimes such as demonic possession and witchcraft that were against Christian faith. In the fifteenth century, two demonic German monks wrote an infamous book that became the bible of inquisitors to judge and castigate witchcraft. The book began by demonstrating that witchcraft exists and analyzed if the witch acted alone or required the help of a devil. Moreover, it presented articles stating that the devil could sexually possess women and if the product of a pregnancy was a work of Satan, the maternal womb was opened alive and both the child and mother were killed. This book was referred to have caused more death at stake in the sixteenth and seventeenth centuries than in the 1000 years that the Middle age lasted.

Spiritualism

In the eighteenth century, there used to appear groups of convulsing people on the tomb of a crazy clergyman, in Saint Medard cemetery, in Paris. These people believed in a supposed miracle of the tomb to cure people with this ailment and for the great scandal which they generated during such visit, the authorities were forced to close the cemetery. Nevertheless, with the cemetery closed, the believers continued to convulse outside and so the place became a convulsing epidemic center where all excesses were said.

In the eighteenth century, the demonology, persecution of witches and the burning of mentally ill people came to an end, mainly in German. After the end of demonology, people required other escapes for their anguish. It was then that Miss Fox's New Spiritualism was born in a little town in New York. This woman travelled to different neighborhoods in New York propagating the New Spiritualism. At the beginning of the century, spiritualism became a game for some people while others practiced it with conviction.

In the decade of the '60s of the twenty century, the book "The Return of the Witches" was published. This work marked the rebirth of magic in the Western countries. The people were fascinated and once again the practice of sorcery re-emerged. The Devil unleashed episodes of collective psychoses such as the Guyana massacre [3-5]. These collective psychoses were psycho-social phenomena triggered by the pathology of a single person and produced by contagion as in the time of Inquisition [3].

It is very probable that the investigations carried out by Jonker et al. in the Dutch Village of Oude Pekela in 1897 [6], in which 98 children from 4 to 11 years of age were attacked, and the study of Young et al. [7], who described the problem of 37 patients from 18 to 47 years old from different regions of the United States of America could have been what have aroused concern about this aspect of child abuse. These reports were initially taken lightly and their credibility was questioned in the absence of tangible findings by the local police.

The existence of recent information to this regard, has made use to conduct a review of the issue and thereby specify the current indications of this variant in violence against children.

GENERAL CONSIDERATIONS

The doctor and any professional who is in contact with the children must consider the information currently available on this CA variant in order to detect it and enrich the algorithm of action that would enable him to offer a comprehensive management.

The clinical spectrum of child abuse found by various researchers shows that children have been victims of sadism, perversity and other bizarre forms of aggression that are always associated with sexual abuse [8, 9]. Usually, the sadistic factor is characterized by introduction of sticks or objects in the vagina, anus or penis; witnessing the killing of children; dismembering them and sometimes fry them and eat [1-3, 10].

In the book "The Franklin Cover-up", the author exposes the elite network of crimes, satanic cults and child sexual abuses that spread through the elite groups until the highest level of power in societies of the first world [10]. In this book, Bonacci and other victims of Satanism describe these and other aberrant and criminal acts [10].

The offended creatures maintained in silence the tremendous aggression with its consequent sense of guilt and shame [11]. When they break the silence, they refer that the said acts occurred while their aggressors were under the influence of alcohol or some other drugs. Both the victims and their abusers dressed in unusual robes or clothes and wore masks during the session. In those acts, more than one child is involved and the parties were means to recruit more children. Pornography is often the typical feature of this type of action and it is found associated with satanic ritual that forms part of the religion. (Satan is the name of the supreme spirit of the devil and Satanism refers to the practices and rites pertaining to his worship).

The descriptions that some children have made include tortures and sacrifices of both animals and human beings, consumption of some parts of the body or drinking of the body fluids (blood, semen, urine), as well as burial ceremonies of these people [4, 5]. In this type of rituals, there is a union between religious, magical or supernatural aspects through which the aggressor or the group of aggressors infuse fear or terror to the children [11]. As an example, we could refer to the story of a survivor of Satanic Ritualism in Spain.

The Bar Spain Case

Satanic Ritual sacrifice declaration, relates Miguel Angel Mauro Ferreres: In Spain, a 16-year old boy who had missed from his house described that he was drugged by a social worker who took him to the Casa Bar España (Spanish Bar House) where he remained locked until he became 16 years old. The place had "Halloween" look. When he escaped from this home, he said that in addition to being drugged, he was a victim of sexual abuse. Also, apparently he witnessed how his companions, young abductees, were forced to shoot a firearm at the head of smaller children and the dead bodies were put at each of the tips of a Star of David. Likewise, he pointed out that the girls were drugged and raped. They were also threatened that if they denounce the acts, some of their companions would be killed. Kelly indicated that this activity has three variants [12]:

a.   The true cult which is when the sexual abuse forms part of the complete introduction of the child in the group.
b.   Pseudo-ritual which is when sexual abuse is the primary activity and ritual cults are secondary.

c. Psycho-pathologic ritual which is when the adults, mentally ill, abuse the children while using some rites of their religion.

There are several problems to understand in general this rare variety of aggression to the children. The first is the acceptance of a term that clearly defines the problem in question. For instance, some authors [13], prefer not to use the term "satanic" since it is apparently confusing and emotional. Thus, it is necessary to accept that not all ritualistic activities are spiritually motivated and that not all ritualistic actions are satanic.

To perform rites can be part of an excessive religiosity of a deranged mind or it can be a misunderstood aspect of sexual abuse. The motivation may not be indoctrination of a child to belong to a specific system but it serves to modify, control, manipulate or confuse the child. Also, it must be taken into consideration the possibility that not all the things the victim relates are true, but could be a consequence of a certain distorted or poorly conceived situation. In this regard, it is thought that perhaps something may be symbolic or "contaminated" and even false [14].

This was one of the problems which the police had in the Dutch case. The problem, therefore, is to determine the reality. Despite the existing difficulties, it is pertinent to keep in mind that in the United States, there are approximately 50,000 children assassinated in human sacrifice and that the "satanics" have taken over the children's day care centers [15]. Notwithstanding the above, there is no real evidence that this condition is a problem in some countries such as Canada, England or the Netherlands just to mention a few [15].

It has not been possible to completely precise the site (children's day care centers, colleges, some religious communities, etc.) where a child has more risk of being victim of the phenomenon.

Regarding the nurseries and centers where services for children's care are given, it is necessary to point out that more and more frequently it is insisted on the risk the children have of suffering various forms of abuse in these places [5, 12-16]. One of the least known and understood varieties is what we are presenting here, which has some characteristics that the reader should know:

a. Every day, there are more reports of cases where children are victims of sexual or physical abuse or both.
b. There are various perpetrators, including adult females, who try to create a religious environment in the children where they will suffer various types of aggression.
c. The children are threatened if they dare to relate what they lived [4].

On the other hand, the assaulted children have some other characteristics that make them more vulnerable [17]. Such characteristics are:

a. Living and suffering serious problems in their family.
b. Being children or adolescents that are frequently alone.
c. Having "desirable" aspects in their physical attributes.

For the aggressors to identify the chosen children, they are usually tattooed or are forced to use symbols such as a five-point star inside a circle with an inverted vertex, the eye of Horus (an eye inside a triangle); the nail of the middle finger or the little finger painted black or other type of tattoos that are hidden by the hair [18].

Some characteristics of the aggressor are:

a. Having been a victim of the same type of abuse in infancy.
b. Belonging to "Heavy Metal" bands.
c. Tendency to consume substances.

GROWING FANATISM

Although many professionals, including health professionals, view the cult activities with skepticism [14], the events that took place in Monte Carmelo, Waco Texas in the beginning of 1993, make us to consider the phenomenon seriously. In this place, 38 children that formed part of the

Davidiana Branch which was a sect that separated from Seventh-day Adeventist Church in 1934, were victims of this group of fanatics, who in their conviction that Christ had returned, were expecting the end of the world. The children were with the leader of the sect called David Koresh of 33 years old. This man had a great knowledge of the bible and great ability to convince anybody with his religious and sexual ideas. These children suffered physical and sexual abuses. Also, 17 of them died burned in the final episode of this sect [19].

An antecedent, almost similar to the above phenomenon, happened in Jonestown, Guyana, when American religious fanatics that belonged to the sect "The People's Temple" founded in California by Rev. J Jones of 42 years old, arrived in this place with 900 converts. As part of the group's activities, the methods used to "discipline children", were beatings with belts, iron buckles, logs; cold water baths; electric shocks and something that Jim Jones called "blue eyed monster" which he assumed when he was inflicting injury and terror to the converts during which he performed various sexual and ritual events in men, women and children [19]. In his book "The Children of Jonestown", Kenneth Wooden described the children in a dark room [20]. The later discovery of these and other acts gave rise to a collective suicide at the end of 1978 in which 287 children died by making them to drink a mixture of cyanide with Kool Aid, administered in some by their own mothers and in others by the nurses of the group [19].

We must also analyze the group known as "destructive sects", which uses in their functioning dynamics, unethical techniques of psychological manipulation in order to achieve their own benefits, causing physical and psychological damage to the members and to their families [21]. They are highly manipulative groups and constitute a threat for the children because:

a. They live under an absolutist ideology that dictates physical discipline and rejection of medical intervention.
b. They function as closed societies and sometimes, physically isolated, where it is difficulty to carry out researches on child abuse.

c. They use religious beliefs to justify their ideology and isolation nature.

HOW RITUALISM AFFECTS CHILDREN

The effects suffered by the children whose parents belong to certain religious communities include several prohibitions such as not transfusing or using blood or its derivatives, not accepting organ transplant and not using hormonal medicines, instead, they prefer to use their own substitutes as prayers and spiritual healing. Two clear examples of these practices are the Jehovah Witness and the sect known as Christian Science.

In a very controversial and polemic publication of the Jehovah Witness, children who preferred to die instead of receiving blood transfusion were declared "Heroes" [22]. Their photos appeared in the cover of the magazine titled "Youths who put God first".

At the National Institute of Pediatrics (Spanish acronym INP), it has been observed that transfusion of blood or its derivatives as well as organ transplant are prohibited in any patient whose parents are a member of Jehovah Witness. First, the medical problem and its treatment must be explained to them and if they agree, the child will be treated; otherwise, they have doctors who belong to their congregation that take charge of the problem of the child.

To counteract the practices such as prayers and spiritual healing used by the Christian Science and other groups in Ohio state, U.S.A, a law which abolished the exceptions of healing by faith was proclaimed in 1989 in the statutes on "Danger and Child Negligence" [23].

The damages which can be found in the children whose parents belong to different sects are multiple and varied and can range from small injuries to death [24]. Gaines et al. [25], interviewed 70 former members of sects in order to "determine the effects in their past and present state of health for having belonged to these groups". The study included the children and the following are some of the most relevant data:

a. 27% of the respondents said that the children were not vaccinated against childhood diseases.

b. 23% reported that the children did not get up to 8 hours of sleep in a day.

c. 60% commented that physical punishments to the children were permitted.

d. 13% said that in order to teach a lesson to the children, they were sometimes physically injured or physically incapacitated.

e. 13% mentioned that sometimes the physical punishment was such that it puts the life of the child at risk or required medical care.

f. 61% said that the families were encouraged to live together and share responsibilities.

g. Only 37% commented that the children were seen by a doctor when they were sick.

The American Academy of Pediatric has protested against the religious groups that under the banner of "Freedom of beliefs" commit all kind of abuses against small children [26]. In 1996, the official belief of the Church of Satan was announced in the United States. Its founder and first priest was Anton Szandor La Vey "The Black Pope". The doctrines of the church are contained in the satanic bible book "The Satanic Ritual and Complete Witch". The symbol of this church is the Baphomet seal, which is a circle enclosing the head of a goat in an inverted five-point star with a Hebrew letter in each of the end. Among their ceremonies we can highlight those dedicated to the admission of the adherents who swear to live in marriage to the Satan for their entire life. In their rituals, it is recommended to wave a human arm or leg in the air. They perform sacrifices of animals, rapes and including the murder of their own sons.

In Italy, a group of young people who had committed various crimes were denominated "la Bestiie di Santana" (The beast of Santana). These young people were studied by a group of forensic psychiatrics and the findings were that all the members of this satanic sect had a weak and immature personality, very low educational level and a degree of social disadvantage [27-28].

In their report, they commented on the need to explore the social and cultural response of the youths answer to Satanism, because, though statistically it seems to be a very rare phenomenon, it does have a very high criminal potential [29].

Defenders of Christ

The sect "Defenders of Christ" was founded by Ignacio Gonzalez de Arriba, a Spanish man, better known as "Maestro Fenix" who proclaimed himself as the reincarnation of Christ. It started to operate in Mexico in 2010, first in Coahuila and later in Nuevo Laredo, Tamaulipas. Through the internet, the organization had about four thousand followers from 80 countries. This sect induced their followers to practice incest, commit sexual abuse against children and organ trafficking.

The victims of the sect narrated that they were forced to eat viscera, practice polygamy and be subjected to confinements. A proof of this can be found in the denunciation made by one of the victims who reported that she was forced to stay whole days without eating, participate in orgies and eat raw animal viscera. And to perpetuate polygamy, he made one of his sons to see pornography, since childhood, in order to be prepared in such a practice when he became an adult. Also, forceful marriages with female minors were permitted and encouraged among the members of the sect as depicted in the marriage of an eleven-year old girl with a 40-year old man against her wish.

In January of 2013, three leaders and 20 members of the sect were arrested in Mexico. Later, some former members of the sect received help from Support Network for Victims of Sects [Spanish acronym: Red de Apoyo para Víctimas de Sectas (Ravics)]. People who detected fraud in the program sold by the sect created a website against it in which they warned the public on the dangers of the sect and its false promises [30].

Satanic Churches in the World

The development of the black mass, which is the main rite of the satanics, usually takes place in a completely enclosed ceremonial precinct decorated with an inverted cross, five-point star, a sword, communion wafer, a chalice full of liquor, several candles, a bell, a male goat, a woman dressed like a nun and another naked. The adepts enter the precinct dressed in black and with hood they invoke the name of Satan with prayers said in Latin, English and French. The rituals culminate in sexual orgies and with the aforementioned events [31]. Aleister Crowley together with La Vey is considered as the main inspirers of various currents of Satanists. His church, Astrum Argentum, founded in England, follows the doctrine of La Vey satanic Bible whose motto is "Exclude mercy, torture, kill and do not forgive anyone". This sect pays tribute to the devil, celebrating black mass, orgies and collective consumption of different drugs. His followers sacrifice animals and drink their blood as sexual stimulant and worship their spiritual leader that is tied to a cross. In New York, Robert Brown, a member of a satanic sect, murdered 10 people including children during a ritual and after extracting their hearts and blood, he ate and drank them [32].

The United States is a country with the largest number of sects. It was reported that during the service an average of 50,100 crimes per year, typified as ritual abuse, are carried out [33]. Currently, there are satanic temples in American cities such as San Francisco and Dallas that are open to public worship and are permitted by the government. England is the cradle of sects and some of them even have branches in Spain and Italy, two countries with also a significant number of them.

Sects in Internet

The satanic sects are listed in approximately 200 pages on the global internet network. In these pages, their followers made campaigns, form discussion groups, make descriptions, definitions, bibliographic recommendations, prayers as well as the most varied forms of worship to the Satan. There are also "guides" of satanic ceremony for beginners and sentences with specific pronunciation indications [33]. In Mexico, two well-organized sects are known and one of them also operates in the United States and France. In these sects, Lucifer is worshipped through the innovation of the dead. Also, sexual practices are characteristics of them and in the rituals they invoke their spirit. Their members must have tattoos with the number 666 on their chest. The chief priest ties black leather around the neck that presses the carotids, causing increased venous pressure and hypoxia and this makes him to see strange images interpreted as establishment of "contact" with the dead. Following this, he sacrifices a rooster and splashes the blood on a mirror and writes the name of the spirit of the dead invoked [34].

Adolfo de Jesus Constanza, leader of a sect that was murdered in 1989 for carrying out satanic narco acts. In those acts, 15 people were sacrificed and their bodies were found in Matamoros, Tamaulipas. In this city, two of his chapels were discovered while in Mexico city eight similar centers where there were vestiges of rituals such as alters with candles, vessels with human skulls, goat heads and chicken feathers. In Mexico, an important relationship between drug traffickers and Satanism has also been established.

In the coastal areas of Oaxaca, Chiapas, Tabasco and Guerrero the presence of satanic cults has been found, usually in people of low socioeconomic and cultural levels. In these zones a strong influence of the African rituals is conserved [33].

Pertinent to consider in at this point, apart from the ritual forms, are some practices of the "popular medicine" whose use can lead to some harm to the children. In our rural environment, it is very common to treat the sunken anterior fontanelle i.e., the "caved in soft spot" caused mainly by dehydration generated by vomiting and diarrhea by turning and keeping the child in an upside-down position. This measure which does not resolve the dehydration may provoke retinal and intracranial hemorrhage [35].

The Chamula community in the state of Chiapas, Mexico has a particular way of communicating with their "god". They drink "poch", a very strong local brandy prepared by them, in the worship ceremony of their god in a Catholic Temple and in which all the families participate. Usually, they get to the state of drunkenness during the prayer and burp loudly in order to eliminate the "bad spirits". In this action, children are involved, regardless of their age.

EXPECTATIONS

Given these written evidences, it is necessary that the medical community and the society in general be on alert because the children are at high risk of being physically, sexually or psychologically abused by adults, including their parents, who under a religious fanaticism violate the rights of children. Because of the complexities in the diagnosis and the resulting denunciation, there is no clear mechanism to fully attend these children and young people. However, it is the responsibility of doctors, jurists and sociologists to design an algorithm that allows the rescue of the victims and prevent them from suffering damage.

REFERENCES

[1]   Loredo Abdalá A,Trejo Hernandez J, Bustos Valenzuela V. Maltrato al menor: Consideraciones clínicas sobre maltrato físico, agresión sexual, deprivación emocional. [Child abuse: Clinical considerations about physical abuse, sexual aggression, emotional deprivation] *Gac Méd Méx* 1999;135: 611-620.

[2]   Loredo Abdala A. Maltrato en Niños y Adolescentes. [Abuse in children and adolescents] *Editores de textos mexicanos* 2004; 397.

[3]   Jiménez Olivares E. El retorno del pensamiento mágico y demonología. [The return of magical thinking and demonology] *Rev Fac-Med UNAM* 1985; 28:58-61.

[4]   Finkelhor D. Williams L. *Nursery crismes. Sexual abuse in day care.* London: Sage, 1988.

[5]   Cartwright G. The innocent and the damned, *Texas Monthly* 1994; 22:100-118.

[6]   Jonker F, Jonker Bakker P. Experiences With ritualist child sexual abuse. A case study from the Netherlands, *Child Abuse Neglect* 1991; 15:191-196.

[7]   Young WC. Sachs RGJR. Patients reporting ritual abuse in childhood: a clinical syndrome. Report of 37 cases. *Child Abuse Neglect* 1991; 15:181-189.

[8]   Jones DP. Ritualism and child sexual abuse. *Child Abuse Neglect* 1991; 15:163-170.

[9]   Mascareñas J, Mascareñas CO. Un estudio psicoanalítico sobre la relación lider -feligresia en la iglesia de La Luz del Mundo. [A psychoanalytic study on the leading relationship -feligresia in the church of La Luz del Mundo] *Revista Académica para el Estudio de las Regiones* 1997; 1:85-114.

[10] The Franklin. *Cover-up: Child abuse, satanism and murder in Nebraska-John W. de Camps,* AWT. 1992; 411.

[11] Escalante P. El abuso sexual y el uso simbólico del concepto religioso del "Padre". [Sexual abuse and the symbolic use of the religious concept of the "Father"] *Revista Académica para el Estudio de las Religiones* 1997; 1:130-140.

[12] Kelly SJ. Ritualistic abuse: a law enforcement view of perspective. *Child Abuse Neglect* 1991; 15:171-173.

[13] Lanning KV. Ritual abuse; a law enforcement view of perspective. *Child Abuse Neglect* 1991; 15:171-173.

[14] Jeffrey VS. The dangers of moral panics. *Skeptic* 1995; 3:44-51.

[15] Putman FW. The satanic ritual controversy. *Child Abuse Neglect* 1991; 15:175-9.

[16] Kelly SJ, Brant R. Sexual abuse of children in day care canters. *Child Abuse Neglect* 1993; 17:71-89.

[17] Johnson CF. Constricting bands: manifestation of possible child abuse. *Child Pediatr* 1988; 27:439-444.

[18] Johnson CF. Inflicted injury versus accidental injury. *Pediatr Clin North Am* 1990; 4:791-814.

[19] Singer MT, Lalich J. *Cults in our midst,* San Francisco: Jossey-Bass Publishers, 1995.

[20] Wooden K. *The children of jones town.* New York; McGraw-Hill, 1985.

[21] Ederly J. Sectas destructivas; definiciones y metodología de análisis. [Destructive sects; definitions and analysis methodology] *Revista Académica para el Estudio de las Religiones* 1997; 1:1-25.

[22] Bottons BL, Diviak KR, Davis SL. Jurors' reactions to satanic ritual abuse allegations. *Child Abuse Neglect* 1997; 9:845-859.

[23] Korbin JE. The cross-cultural contest of child abuse and neglect. In: Kempe HC, Helfer RE. (eds), *stress and child abuse in the battered child.* 3th ed. Chicago; University of Chicago Press, 1980; 21-36.

[24] Markowitz A, Halperin DA. Cults and children. The abuse of the young. *Cultic Studies J* 1984; 1:143-155.

[25] Gines MI. The effects of cult membership on the health status of adults and children. *Health values: Achieving High Level Wellness* 1984; 8:13-17.

[26] Committee on bioethics. Religious exemptions from child abuse status. *Pediatrics* 1988; 81:169-171.

[27] Birkhoff J, Candelli C, Zoreli S, Lategola D. Carabellese F. The "Bestiie di Santana" murders. *J Forensic Sci* 2013; 58:1660-5.

[28] Hendren RL, Strasturger VC. Rock music and music videos. *Adolescent Med* 1993; 4:577-78.

[29] Sjöberg RL. Witch persecutions and torture: Comment on Alison and Alison. *Am Psychol* 2017; 72:703-704.

[30] Perlado M. Incesto, abuso infantil y tráfico de órganos, otras prácticas de la secta. [Incest, child abuse and organ trafficking, other practices of the sect] *Hemerosectas 2013;* Retrieved from https://www.hemerosectas.org/defensores-cristo-19/]

[31] Scherer IM, Vera R. Satanismo y exorcismo, Prácticas frecuentes en Mexico. [Satanism and Exorcism, Frequent Practices in Mexico] *Proceso* 1997; 1064:28-33.

[32]   Scherer IM. La lucha entre el bien y el mal por internet. [The struggle between good and evil on the internet] *Proceso* 1997; 1064:32.

[33]   Scherer IM. Misas negras, crímenes, drogas, orgias y el endiosamiento del ego en las sectas demoniacas. [Black Masses, Crimes, Drugs, orgies and the deification of the ego in demonic sects] *Proceso* 1997; 1064:31.

[34]   Scherer IM, Vera R. El satanismo es casi una moda. [Satanism is almost a fad] *Proceso* 1997; 1064:29-30.

[35]   Cuarnaschelli J, Lee J. Fallen fontanelle. A variant 9 of the battered child syndrome. *JAMA* 1972; 222:1545-1547.

In: Child Abuse: Harm and Solutions   ISBN: 978-1-53614-271-6
Editors: Arturo Loredo Abdalá et al. © 2018 Nova Science Publishers, Inc.

Chapter 6

SEXUAL ABUSE:
CLINICAL AND PREVENTIVE ASPECTS

Gloria Elena López Navarrete[1,],*
Nancy Jordán González[1] and Arturo Loredo Abdalá[2]
[1]Departamento de Seguimiento Pediátrico,
Instituto Nacional de Perinatología, Ciudad de Mexico, Mexico
[2]Centro de Estudios Avanzados sobre Maltrato Infantil-Prevención
del Instituto Nacional de Pediatría (CEAMI-P-INP),
Ciudad de Mexico, Mexico

ABSTRACT

The National Center for Child Abuse and Neglect conceptualized
sexual abuse (SA) in children as "a contact or interaction between a child
and an adult, when the adult (aggressor) uses the child to sexually
stimulate himself/herself or another person." It can also be perpetrated by
a person under the age of 18, when he/she is significantly older than the
child (victim) or when the aggressor is in a position of power or control
over the child." The adult may use acts of violence, threat, surprise, deceit
or seduction to ensure the participation of the victim in a sexual context

* Corresponding Author Email: glopez29@yahoo.com.

taking advantage of the victim's inability to consent because of the age, difference in power or the nature of the relationship.

Sexual abuse is estimated to occur in 11% of women and in 2% of men. Children are more often abused by people they know than by strangers. The abuse in children impacts on their health in adult life. It can generate mental illnesses and even metabolic diseases given the constant exposure of stress. Hence, its prevention becomes essential. This chapter reviews the sexual abuse in children as part of child abuse and the impact on their health.

Keywords: aggressor, incest, rape, sexual abuse, sexual harassment

INTRODUCTION

Sexual abuse (SA) is a global problem of epidemic proportion that affects children of all ages, races, social status and cultural aspects [1].

It is one of the forms of abuse with greater under-registry due to various causes among which are:

a) Lack of consistent or universally accepted definition that facilitates its full identification.
b) Lack of economic resources to maintain systems for case reporting and handling.

A fundamental factor that should be highlighted is the secrecy or "conspiracy of silence" that so often surrounds the cases, mainly because the psychosocial effects are traumatic for the victim and for the inability of young children or children with disabilities to express such abuse or differentiate inappropriate behaviors from correct ones. It is common that the perpetrators of SA are parents, close relatives, friends or people on whom the child depends and for that the child feels ashamed or guilty about it or to express it. Parents or caregivers often feel outraged or become upset when the child does not tell them what is happening; thus, adopting an inquisitive behavior with the child which, far from helping, aggravates the problem [1-3].

EPIDEMIOLOGY

In 2014 in the United States of America, an estimated 702,000 victims of child abuse were reported. Out of this number, 8.2% were SA. The prevalence depends on the population, the definitions of abuse and the study designs. Recently, SA is estimated to occur in 11% of women and in 2% of men when it comes to aggression by unrelated peers. Nevertheless, when aggression by peers or strangers is included in the questionnaires, this figure increases, particularly in the group of adolescents. Children are more often abused by people they know than by strangers [4].

According to the data of the United Nations (UN), four children suffer SA every minute in Latin America. It is found in some population surveys of women, report of SA before 15 years of age. For example, in Guatemala such report was found in 4.7% while it was 7.8% in Honduras [5]. Mexico occupies the first place among the countries of the Organization for Economic Cooperation and Development (OECD) in SA, physical violence and homicides of children under 14 years. It is reported that in Mexico around 4.5 million children are victims of SA of which only 2.0 percent of the cases are known at the time of abuse [6].

DEFINITION

Different definitions of this phenomenon have been described. The National Center for Child Abuse and Neglect conceptualizes SA in children as: "The contact or interaction between a child and an adult, when the adult (aggressor) uses the child to sexually stimulate himself/herself or the child or another person. It can also be perpetrated by a person under the age of 18, when he/she is significantly older than the child (victim) or when the aggressor is in a position of power or control over the child" [3]. In the '70s, Schecter and cols. referred to SA as that activity in which children or adolescents who had not understood the biological and psychological bases of a sexual act are involved and therefore, cannot grant rational consent to the adults [3].

Other definitions mention the different components in the form of interaction between the victim and the perpetrator, before and during the aggression. Olamendi points to this act as, "the practice by an individual that involves physical or visual contact or both which leads to committing act of violence, threat, surprise, deceit or seduction to ensure the participation of a person in a sexual context taking advantage of the victim's inability to consent because of the age, difference in power or the nature of the relationship" [3].

SA is generally defined as any sexual activity (including vaginal/anal penetration, oro-genital contact, genital-genital contact, touching and exposition to pornography or prostitution) that involves a child who is unable to give his/her consent.

The topics on the comprehension and especially on the prevention of violence in childhood have become, in recent years, the responsibilities of the public sector. In 2016, the product of a joint effort of different world organizations brought forth 7 strategies to end all forms of violence against children, and among them, child sexual abuse [7].

CLASSIFICATION

The classification of SA is based on several aspects:

1. Physical contact between the aggressor and the victim.

SA with physical contact comprises all the forms in which the aggressor touches the child and these include, among others, the touching of any body part of the child, anal and/or vaginal penetration, oral sex and the use of the child for the aggressor's excitation.

2. The mechanism of the aggression.

This can be:

    a)   Incest

    b)   Rape

    c)   Sexual harassment, induction and promotion of prostitution.

3.   The place where the aggression was perpetrated.

    a)   Intra-familiar SA.

This sexual abuse occurs when a family member is the perpetrator of the aggression. Usually, incest is the most common form. Among the factors that favor it are: the absence of the mother, cohabitation with the stepfather or stepmother, family disintegration and a child with disability [3]. The intra-family category includes incest in all its forms as well as SA by any member of the family even if the person has no legal family link with the victim [2]. It has been pointed out that the risk of intra-family SA is five times greater at homes where the child is under the tutelage of stepfather or stepmother when compared with homes where the child lives with the biological parents. The same magnitude of risk is observed in homes where the child lives with alcoholics or drug addicts, in families where there is a conflict between the parents, in families with violence (indifference, anger, fights, separated and divorce) or families where the woman has submissive attitude toward the couple and becomes a passive aggressor on ignoring the phenomenon or even favors it [8].

    b)   Extra-family SA

This is when the abuse is perpetrated outside the family: schools, nurseries, churches, recreation centers and other meeting places including on public roads [3].

THE DYNAMICS OF SEXUAL ABUSE

The dynamic in which SA occurs as well as the consequences are influenced by various factors such as the age of the victim, the level of development and the relationship with the perpetrator [3].

In the case of preschoolers, their communication possibilities are limited and this can make it difficult for them to articulate their stress. Children, in general, are very curious. They seek for the attention and love of older ones and respect the authority. Automatically, there is a difference in power between a child and an adult since the child depends on the adult for support, upbringing and guidance. The children usually trust in adults, particularly those close to them, in such a way that they do not question their intuition on whether something may not be good or well. This power and trust can be used by the adult to perpetrate sexual abuse or exploitation. The perpetrator can also use fear or deceit to continue the abuse and maintain the secrecy. In this way, children can be seen as potential victims [4].

In the case of abuse within the home, it is seen as a family responsibility in which the pathological relationship between adults is manifested in the attitude of the father (or whoever is the aggressor) of seeking sexual gratification in the child, and in one way or the other, depicts the passive participation of the wife or other members of the family. Also, there is a controversy in this dynamic, since some professionals indicate that SA is the responsibility of only the perpetrator, usually a male adult. These professionals refer that SA results from the impossibility of the perpetrator to control his sexual impulses or to establish appropriate adult relationships. Such a perpetrator is pedophile [2].

It has been reported in different papers that children with developmental disabilities have a particularly higher risk of being subjects of any form of abuse than their peers without disabilities, due to their physical and cognitive limitations and although, it is referred to in different observational studies to be always beclouded with the scarce evidence of specific association with SA [8, 9].

In adolescents, the risk is greater in the girls. Adolescence is an age in which the children sought for independence and want to be accepted by others, experiment new relationships and ways to interact with others. As a result, adolescents may be at risk of being sexually exploited and most of the time without taking into consideration that such exploitation can be a consequence of their actions [4]. The use of some substances consumed voluntarily or by deception among the adolescents facilitated the perpetration of SA. Substances like Rohypnol (flunitrazapam), a potent benzodiazepine, also known as the rape drug; hydroxybutrate family (HBF) and ketamine cause sedation and amnesia in few minutes that can last for hours. When taken in high doses, these substances can be life-threatening due to respiratory depression [10].

Clinicians should bear in mind that there is no association between SA, race and economic level. Aggression has not been associated with educational level or civil status. In fact, no specific profile leading to aggression has been shown. Aggressors may or may not have a history of having lived SA or having any psychiatric pathology. However, antisocial behaviors have been shown in some aggressors. They may be hostile or depressed individual, have a pre-existing mental illness, criminal record or tendency to use drugs [4].

DIAGNOSIS AND MANAGEMENT

Sexual abuse can have diverse expressions in clinical setting. No symptom or isolated behavior is absolutely associated with SA, but some sexual behaviors can be very suggestive [4].

In practice, SA is detected or can be suspected in different ways:

1. in routine medical checkup,
2. during the treatment of an illness other than abuse,
3. at the request of the parents of a child on suspicion of being sexually abused,

4. at the request of a legal authority or social worker as part of a judicial process or in the emergency room when a patient has a reference of having suffered such an aggression.

Given the complexity in making the diagnosis and in giving appropriate management to the cases, a wide knowledge of the problem and its methodical, discreet, professional and ethical studies by an interdisciplinary group are required [3].

In most of the cases, children do not reveal their history of abuse. It is until the parents notice some abnormalities that they interrogate the child in a direct manner. Only 20% of the cases are discovered the same day they occur, 50% after one month of its occurrence and 32% after 6 months. Moreover, in most of the cases, the child has been a victim in more than one occasion, thus making it difficult to determine the time that has elapsed since the beginning of the phenomenon [1, 3].

CLINICAL MANIFESTATIONS

It is important to know and recognize some behaviors related to child sexuality that may or may not be normal. The expected behaviors in smaller children are the touching of their genitals and the breasts of their mother. In bigger children, it is common to observe behaviors such as playing the doctor, asking some questions about sexuality and when they observe some television programs with explicit sex, while children from 2 to 6 years old do not show sexual knowledge of the adults and generally do not manifest curiosity or play games about it [11].

Sexual game is defined as unsophisticated acts involving the genitals such as observation or touching between children who are not more than 4 years of age difference and in the absence of bribes or deceit. Preschoolers rarely describe sexual acts or insert objects in their genitals or make attempts to engage in explicit sexual acts with another child. In contrast, children who have been sexually abused tend to exhibit sexual behaviors (Table 1) [11].

Table 1. Worrying sexual behaviors

Repeated insertion of an object into the anus or the vagina.
Inappropriate sexual knowledge for the age.
The child asks to be touched, caressed, kissed etc. on his/her genitals
Sexual games that involve one or more of the following behaviors:
- Oral-genital contact
- Anal-genital contact
- Genital-genital contact
- Digital penetration of vagina or anus
- Penetration of the vagina or anus with any object
- If it occurs between child with more than 4 years of age difference.
- If there is the use of force, deceit or trick.
Frequent or compulsive masturbation.
The form of speaking or the language used during this behavior.

Modified from: Sapp and Vandeven 2005 [1].

Other non-sexual manifestations to consider after ruling out some disorders are:

1. Functional disorder: sleep disorder (insomnia, nightmares), enuresis, encopresis and appetite disorder.
2. Emotional problems: these include depression; anxiety; withdrawal (avoiding certain people or places); isolation from friends and family; evidence of abuse or sexual discomforts in their drawings, games or fantasies; regression behaviors; lack of emotional control (aggressiveness) and phobias.
3. Cognitive development problems such as delay in speaking, attention deficit and low academic performance [3].

The most common clinical manifestation of SA is a positive story. Suspect of sexual abuse can be based exclusively on the child's accounts, since children cannot invent these allegations and it is very important that parents, physicians and other adults believe them. The details of the child's account vary depending on the age and level of language development.

Children of 3 or 4 years can make a simple but credible declaration that somcone touched his/her genitals [2].

In some cases, the abuse is directly denounced by one of the parents who may be found in a situation of significant anguish, annoyance or anger. In such case, the interview should be aimed at calming the parents and clarifying the situation. When the presentation of the case is done indirectly by requesting care for any non-specific symptom or behavioral disorder, the interview should be directed to detect a possible SA. In either of the cases, it is important to explore the opinion of the parents and the type of information they have [2].

Throughout the interview and all contact with the child, the decision to speak and not about the abuse must be respected. For the child, it is a conflict to reveal a secret of this nature, especially if the abuse happened long ago. The child may feel that he/she can cause problem with this action, and sometimes fears that it will affect, alter or end the relationship that he/she usually have with the perpetrator. The child must be informed the importance of what he/she has confessed and highlight the bad action of the aggressor [2].

The clinical manifestations of SA can appear in the short, medium or long term after the event has occurred. This may be due to an isolated event or repeated abuse. The manifestation will depend on the age or maturity of the child [2]. The temporality of the act is fundamental to establish the approach to adopt, particularly with regard to the search of physical findings and forensic evidence, which will be more feasible to identify in the first 72 hours. Nevertheless, about 96% of the evaluations in the cases of SA have revealed genitalia of normal characteristics since in majority of these cases, there are no vaginal or anal penetrations. In all the cases, it is necessary to obtain a careful and complete medical history. If weeks or months have passed after the aggression, the examination will only be performed if there are symptoms of sexually transmitted diseases (STD), injuries or bleeding [1].

The physical examination of a child who had suffered SA must be complete and not only in the genital or anal area. It must be performed only once except for medical reasons when there are injuries, active bleeding or surgical intervention. Care must be taken not to produce additional trauma. Before doing the examination, the child must be explained what it consists and why it is necessary to do it and in the presence of a companion. The examination should be started from the extra-genital area searching in all the body, the presence of any type of injuries [3, 7].

In boys, the anatomy is constant throughout their childhood except for the size of the penis, the testicles and the appearance of pubic hair in adolescents. The presence of bites, excoriations in the penis must be evaluated. In chronic sexual abuse, the examination can reveal even less data. During the revision, sustained erection can be observed which speaks of an erotic over-stimulation [3].

In the case of girls, a sufficient knowledge is required to evaluate the normal and abnormal characteristics of their body in different stages of development [3, 12]. The examination must be done placing the girl in lithotomy position. In pubescents and adolescents, the examination is also done in dorsal decubitus with the thigh flexed and the heels resting on the table. The examination must include: pubic hair, major and minor lips, clitoris, peri-urethral tissue and vaginal introitus, the determination of sexual maturity status and detailed description of injuries. To check the vaginal introitus, the internal face of the major lip should be held with the thumb and the external face with the indexes and slightly pulled towards the front and outside.

Another technique consists of placing the two index fingers and middle finger on the major lips and separating them laterally and downward. In both sexes, the evaluation of the anal region must be made, verifying the sphincter tone and the characteristics of the mucosa [3,4].

All the patients with a history of penetration and contact with the secretions of the aggressor or lesions must receive a prophylactic treatment for the most STD in the first 72 hours. If more time has elapsed between the aggression and its discovery, confirmatory tests for such infections must be performed and based on the results, determine the appropriate treatment (Table 2). In this period of time, anti-conceptive treatment should be administered to the adolescent if she is in reproductive age [7].

Table 2. Prophylactic treatment for sexually transmitted infections (STI)

Infection to prevent	Therapeutic scheme
Gonorrhea Syphilis	Intramuscular ceftriaxone <40 kg: 125 mg single dose >40 kg 250 mg single dose
Chlamydia	Azithromycin via oral <40 kg: 20 mg/kg Single Dose (Maximum dose 1 gr) >40 kg: 1 g single dose
Trichomoniasis and Bacterial Vaginosis	Tinidazole or metronidazole oral via <40 kg: 50 mg/kg single dose >40 kg: 2 g single dose
HIV*	Zidovudine 240 mg/sc^2/day every 12 hrs for 30 days. Do not exceed doses of 200 mg every 6 hrs. Lamivudine 4mg/kg/dose every 12 hrs for 30 days. Do not exceed doses of 150 mg in each administration. Lopinavir/Ritonavir. Children of 15 to 40 kg: 10m mg/k of Lopinavir and 2.5 mg/kg of Ritonavir every 12 hrs. The maximum dose in a child with more than 40kg of weight is: 400mg of Lopinavir and 100 mg of Ritonavir every 12 hrs.
HBV	Hepatitis B vaccine if the patient was not previously vaccinated and the result of AgsHB is negative.
HPV	Administrate HPV vaccine based on the scheme according to the age.

*Offer non-professional postexposureprophylalxis considering current treatment guidelines and the clinical scenario.

Modified from Finkel and Giardano 2015, (7).

MEDIUM AND LONG TERM CONSEQUENCES

Exposure to stress increases the individual risk for various physical and mental problems throughout life, including obesity; decreased immune response; limitations in brain development; physical problems (allergy, diabetes, arthritis, asthma, bronchitis, arterial hypertension and ulcer);

neurobehavioral and cognitive symptoms; and emotional and behavioral problems [13].

SA has been repeatedly associated with high risks of developing obesity compared to unexposed population, including when other covariates or comorbidities that can potentially influence sociodemographic, educational, food insecurity, reduced consumption of fruits and vegetables; and physical activity have been adjusted [14].

Within the neurological modifications secondary to severe abuse, disequilibrium of the hypothalamic-pituitary-adrenal (HPA) axis has been described. This may be manifested by the elevated secretion of glucocorticoids that initiates the activation of central corticotropin-releasing factor (CRF) in the hypothalamus, with the stimulation of monoaminergic cells and limbic structures which leads to the clinical expression of behavioral, autonomic and neuroendocrine changes that usually accompany the chronic activation of a stressful stimulus. Cortisol, on the other hand, promotes the differentiations of adipocyte precursors and stimulates lipogenesis in the presence of insulin; reorganizes energy deposits in a central rather than peripheral distribution in the form of abdominal fat and increases the risk of cardiovascular diseases [15]. Some studies have shown higher rates in the history of abuse, especially of sexual and physical abuse, in samples of patients diagnosed with compulsive eating disorder than in the control groups, and comparable numbers in patients with nervous bulimia [16].

SA has been associated with problems in alcoholic consumption, sleep disorder, irritability or anger, lack of concentration, hypersensitivity and exaggerated response, as well as symptoms of post-traumatic stress [17]. In both genders, a greater anxiety of being abandoned and psychological stress have been observed. In boys, there is a greater tendency to self-injury, suicidal thoughts, up to 10 times more risk of planning suicide and attempting against their life. In the case of girls, there is a feeling of guilty, isolation and depression [18, 19].

PREVENTION

All prevention programs should be designed taking into account the opportunity to start, as soon as possible and within the family, communication between the children and the family members on affective-sexual education that promotes self-care. A framework of promotional approach on good treatment of the children in all its contexts (family, school, sports, recreational, religious), directed not only to this form of child abuse but also to other forms, should be indicated and must be applied in all the levels of prevention [20].

Primary Prevention

It refers to any type of information directed at raising the awareness of the children on sexuality, increasing their knowledge about it and providing guidelines for positive relationship and self-protection. It includes working with "population of childrenat risk" (i.e., people who due to different circumstances have a higher possibility of suffering SA) such as institutionalized children, children with physical or cognitive disabilities, children who remain alone for a long time or are in the care of other people, children from unstructured families where there is violence among the family members, children from families in a situation of extreme poverty or overcrowding and children living in families where there have been experiences of sexual abuse [21].

Secondary Prevention

They are the cases where SA has been presented and efforts are being made to avoid its repetitions. There are actions that would permit the child to identify circumstances of risk, give him/her the tools that will permit him/her to repel dangerous approaches of a possible aggressor or the opportunity to look for help as well as actions that would keep the child away from scenes where the abuse is committed or from the aggressor. Such actions include the separation of the aggressor from the child by detaining the aggressor in order to comply with a court order; prohibition of the aggressor, by the order of an authority or the family of the child, from having contact again with the child, both inside and outside the home; take the child to the home of another relative and keep him/her in custody of this relative; and keep the child under the custody of an official institution or non-governmental organization indicated by responsible authorities [21].

Tertiary Prevention

This form of prevention consists of therapeutic actions directed to:

1. Attention to or limitation in the appearance of sequels.
2. Psychological impact which the event could have at short and long term.
3. Achieve maximum development of the individual in all the areas.
4. Reduce, as much as possible, the presence of complications.
5. Achieve that the victim has an adequate quality of life.

It is important to point out the possibility of limiting the transgenerational replication of SA actions as an aggressor by the victim at some point in his/her life. For this, the people must be aware of these realities and all the professionals that face this form of child abuse should act in a comprehensive manner, through physical and psycho-emotional follow-up of the victims in order to avoid the replication of the phenomenon [22-24].

In recent years, the role of parents and their involvement in the prevention programs, in innovate ways, that would permit the improvement of parenting practices against SA and mitigate the behaviors that may increase a child's risk of suffering it have been highlighted. Parents can play a crucial role as protectors of their children in two ways:

directly; by strengthening external barriers through supervision, participation and communication and indirectly; by promoting competences, well-being and self-esteem of their children that can make them less likely target of abuse and more capable of responding appropriately to the threat or being able to disclose it when it occurs [20].

REFERENCES

[1]   Sapp MV, Vandeven AM. Update on childhood sexual abuse. *Curr Opin Pediatr* 2005; 17:258-264.

[2]   Ludwig S. Abuso sexual, manejo en la emergencia pediátrica. [Sexual abuse, management in the pediatric emergency] *Arch Pediatr Urug* 2001; 72:545-554.

[3]   Perea MA. Loredo Abdalá A, Monroy VA, Guicho AE. Abuso sexual: Del silencio ignominioso a una realidad estigmatizante. En: Loredo Abdalá A. Maltrato en niños y adolescentes. [Sexual abuse: from ignominious silenceto a stigmatizing reality. In: Loredo Abdalá A. *Abuse in children and adolescents*] Editores de Textos Mexicanos, 2004.

[4]   Chiesa A, Goldson E. Child Sexual Abuse. *Pediatr Rev* 2017; 38:105-118.

[5]   Bottoms BL, Peter LC, Hagene MA, Epstein TRA, Wiley CE, Reynolds AG. Abuse characteristics and individual differences related to disclosing childhood sexual, physical, and emotional abuse and witnessed domestic violence. *J Interpers Violence.* 2016; 31:1308-1339.

[6]   Organización Panamericana de la Salud. INSPIRE. *Siete estrategias para poner fin a la violencia contra los niños y las niñas.* [*Seven strategies to end violence against children*] Washington D.C., PAHO, 2017.

[7]   Finkel M. Giardino A. Evaluación médica del abuso sexual infantil. Una guía de práctica. Academia Americana de Pediatría. [*Medical*

evaluation of child sexual abuse. A practice guide American Academy of Pediatrics] 3rd edition, Bogota Col. 2015.

[8] Winters N, Langer L, Geniets A. Physical, psychological, sexual, and systemic abuse of children with disabilities in East Africa: Mapping the evidence. *PLoS One* 2017; 12:e0184541.

[9] Jones L, Bellis MA, Wood S, Hughes K, McCoy E. Prevalence and risk of violence against children with disabilities: A systematic review and meta-analysis of observational studies. *Lancet* 2012; 380:899-907.

[10] Blackwood CL. Sexual assault. *Clin Fam Prac* 2005; 7:139-51.

[11] Jonson CF. Child maltreatment: recognition, reporting and risk. *Pediatr Int* 2002; 44:554-60.

[12] Adams JA, Kellogg ND, Farst KJ, NS Harper, Palusci VJ. Updated guidelines for the medical assessment and care of children who may have been sexually abused. *J Pediatr Adolesc Gynecol* 2016; 29: 81-7.

[13] Scheneiderman JU, Mennen FE, Negriff S, Trickett PK. Overweight and obesity among maltreated young adolescents. *Child Abuse Neglect* 2012; 36:370-8.

[14] Burke NJ, Hellma JL, Scott BG, Weems CF, Carrion VG. The impact of adverse childhood experiences on an urban pediatric population. *Child Abuse Neglect* 2011; 35:408-13.

[15] Brito DB, Castro FR, Domínguez CS, Cabrera de León A. Psicoendocrinoneurología de la obesidad. [Psychoendocrino-neurology of obesity] *Rev Esp Obes* 2007; 5:204-25.

[16] Gustafson TB, Sarwer DB. Childhood sexual abuse and obesity. *Obes Rev* 2004; 5:129-35.

[17] Smith KZ, Smith PH, Grekin ER. Childhood sexual abuse, distress, and alcohol-related problems: Moderation by drinking to cope. *Psychol Addict Behav* 2014; 28:532-7.

[18] Sigurdardottir S, Halldorsdottir S, Bender SS. Consequences of childhood sexual abuse for health and well-being: gender similarities and differences. *Scand J Public Health* 2014; 42:278-86.

[19] Hillis SD, Mercy JA, Saul JR. The enduring impact of violence against children. *Psychol Health Med* 2016; 16:1-13.

[20] Rudolph J, Zimmer-Gembeck MJ, Shanley DC, Hawkins R. Child Sexual Abuse Prevention Opportunities: Parenting, Programs, and the Reduction of Risk. *Child Maltreat* 2017:1077559517729479.

[21] Villanueva CH. Abuso sexual infantil o juvenil. En: Loredo AA. Maltrato infantil: gravedad y prevención. [Child or juvenile sexual abuse. In: Loredo AA. Child abuse: severity and prevention] First edition. *Editores de Textos Mexicanos*, 2017, 35-8.

[22] Bartlett JD, Chie KotakeCh, Fauth R M, Easterbrooks A. Intergenerational transmission of child abuse and neglect: Do maltreatment type, perpetrator, and substantiation status matter?. *Child Abuse Neglect* 2017; 63:84-94.

[23] Voncina MM, Milovancevic MP, Maravic VM, Tosevski DL. Time line of Intergenerational Child Maltreatment: The Mind-Brain-Body Interplay. *Curr Psychiat Rep* 2017; 19:50.

[24] Leve LD, Khurana A, Reich EB. Intergenerational transmission of maltreatment: A multilevel examination. *Dev Psychopathol* 2015; 27:1429-1442.

In: Child Abuse: Harm and Solutions   ISBN: 978-1-53614-271-6
Editors: Arturo Loredo Abdalá et al. © 2018 Nova Science Publishers, Inc.

Chapter 7

PARENTAL ALIENATION SYNDROME: A GROWING PHENOMENON

Arturo Loredo Abdalá[1,], Juan Alan Román Olmos[1]*
and Hugo Juárez Olguín[2]

[1]Centro de Estudios Avanzados sobre Maltrato Infantil-Prevención del
Instituto Nacional de Pediatría (CEAMI-P-INP),
Ciudad de Mexico, Mexico
[2]Laboratorio de Farmacología, Instituto Nacional de Pediatría, Facultad
de Medicina, Universidad Nacional Autónoma de Mexico,
Ciudad de Mexico, Mexico

ABSTRACT

Parental alienation syndrome(PAS) is described as a mental illness in
which a child is involved in the separation or violent divorce of the
parents by psychologically manipulating him or her to be strongly
associated with a parent (alienator) and to reject the relationship with the
other parent (alienated) without legitimate justification. The child could
be a victim of one or several types of child abuse such as sexual abuse,
psychological abuse and neglect in the course of a separation and divorce

* Corresponding Author Email: cainm_inp@hotmail.com.

of the parents. The magnitude of the child's problems can be associated with the type of separation, the age and gender of the child and the predominating inclination of the child's relationship (mother-child or father-child). Usually, there is an increase in emotional manifestations of the child such as depression, anxiety and aggression. Therefore, it is pertinent to consider the age of the child and the physical, intellectual, emotional and economic capacity of the parents to always ensure the best interests of the child. In this chapter we will discuss how the parents' divorce or separation affects the mental, emotional and physical health of the children in such a family.

Keywords: alienator, marriage, neglect, parental alienation syndrome, separation and divorce

INTRODUCTION

As has been repeatedly stated in this book, the reader must be informed that in addition to the four basic forms of Child Abuse (CA), there are other forms that subtly affect children and teenagers which are worthy of reckoning by pediatricians, paramedical staff, teachers and lawyers who act or interact with people of this age group. The awareness of these subtle modalities of abuse would, undoubtedly, help the professionals to properly diagnose them and at a given moment, establish prevention strategies.

In this chapter, we will exhaustively delve into the clinical, social and legal data pertaining to Parental Alienation Syndrome (PAS) [1-3] spotlighting the strategies that must be employed in other to take accurate decisions on the custody of the child or children that would ensure their best interest.

HISTORICAL CONCEPT

The family is the fundamental cell of the society and constitutes the basic social institution [4-6]. The social and economic transformations that have occurred in the families of Mexico and in general Latin America, have been the main elements in the current conformation of the roles of the father, the mother, the grandparents, the stepfathers and the children. These modifications become very evident when the parents of a child or a teenager separate or divorce, especially when such a change in the family occurs violently.

Faced with this situation, it is advisable that parents ensure the best interests of their children. However, the bitter point is that immersed in the separation or divorce problem, parents always fall short of fulfilling this assurance and this generates a terrible conflict between them and their children. Consequently, various physical, emotional, educational and moral problems ensue in the family. In this scenario parental alienation syndrome (PAS) can present [7-8]. It is very probable that from the initial remarks of Reich in 1949 [9], and mainly those of Gardner in 1985 [10-12], who described parental alienation as a syndrome, the study of this pathology has been developed in different countries of the world, with the objective of specifying the clinical picture of the victims as well as the various interventions that parents, doctors and jurists must make to specify a comprehensive care for each case.

In Mexico and in some Ibero-American countries, editorial efforts have been made in order to inform the professional community involved in handling this problem, about the various implications the phenomenon can have [13-14].

PARENTAL SEPARATION: EPIDEMIOLOGICAL FACTS

Parental separation is a serious problem worldwide. The figures coming from epidemiological records depict its alarming nature and will serve as a preamble to understand the seriousness of the problem. Due to the magnitude of the problem in the world of today, a vast space is needed to fully compile the epidemiological issues of its frequency. However, because of lack of such a space, only some records of this phenomenon in the world are mentioned in this topic.

European marriage registry showed that in 2011, there were about 2,100,000 marriages. Close to 986,000 of these marriages ended in divorce and almost half (500,000) involved children. Moreover, between 1965 and 2011, the record of violent divorce rose to 150% [15-16] in this continent.

In the US, the marriage: divorce frequency in the year 2000 was 8.2:4 for every 1000 people. In 2009, the marriage rate fell to 6.8 and in 2014, it slightly increased to 6.9 marriages, a figure that remained the same in 2015. On the contrary, the divorce rate in this country has been decreasing over the years. In 2015, it decreased to 3.1 with respect to the year 2000. In 2010, it was reported that approximately 740,000 children and teenagers were victims of PAS (Table 1) [17].

In Mexico, the situation of parental separation has an increasing trend since the year2000. In this year, the rate of divorce: marriage figure was 7 divorces for every 100 marriages. In 2010 and 2013, it was 15 and 19 respectively for every 100 marriages. The trend continued to soar up in such a way that in 2016 the number of divorces has increased by 136.4% with respect to the year 2000.

Table 1. Number of divorces in the United States

2000	2003	2006	2009	2012	2014[1]	2015[1]
944 000	927 000	872 000	840 000	851 000	813 862	800 909

[1]Excluding data from California, Georgia, Hawaii, Indiana, and Minnesota.
Source: CDC/NCHS National Vital Statistics System.

Table 2. Number of divorces in Mexico

1993	1997	2001	2004	2012	2013	2015
32 483	40 792	55 370	67 575	99 509	108 727	123 883

Source: INEGI/Statistics/Population, Households and Housing/Nuptiality/Divorces/ Relationship divorces-marriages, 1980 to 2013; ENOE 2016.

DIVORCE AND CHILDREN

In Mexico, the involvement of children in divorce cases is worrisome. In 2015, 88.5% of divorce cases were judicial i.e., a judge intervened to end the conjugal partnership. In 61.3% of these cases, there was an involvement of children under 18 years. A breakdown of this involvement showed that in 30.5%, there was one child involved, two in 22.3% and three in 8.5% of the cases. Table 2 shows the evolution of divorce from 1993-2015 in Mexico [18].

IMPACT ON FAMILIES AND CHILDREN

Probably one of the most important characteristics of divorcing families is the significant decrease in the level of their economic capacity, which is expressed with insufficient monetary income to cover part of the basic needs [16, 19]. This situation drags along some psychological adjustment problems such as depression and aggressive behavior; some health problems including overweight; low academic level and socio-emotional failure [20]. With the passage of time, the parental separation begins to affect the family members, especially the teenagers and adolescents in the family. It was estimated that approximately 19% of the teenagers and adolescents in a divorcing family has a problem due to the separation. Among these problems, emotional manifestations such as depression, anxiety and aggression can be reckoned. Obviously, all the problems are associated with the type of separation; the age and gender of the child; and the inclination of the child's relationship (mother-child or father-child) that predominates [21-22].

DEFINITION OF PARENTAL ALIENATION SYNDROME (PAS)

Richard Gardner defined PAS in 1985 as the "set of symptoms that result from the process of divorce characterized by one of the parents transforming the conscience of his or her child with the aim of preventing, hindering or destroying the bond of the child with the other parent" [11, 23-24].

Other authors such as Johnston KJB in the year 2001 defined it as "Someone who expresses anger, hatred, rejection and/or fear towards a parent in a significantly disproportionate way" [25]. Bernet et al., described PAS as a mental illness in which a child involved in the separation or violent divorce of their parents strongly allied with a parent (alienator) and rejects the relationship with the other parent (alienated) without legitimate justification [17]. The definition of American Psychiatric Association's Diagnostic and Statistical Manual of Mental Disorder (DSM-V), published in 2013, is based primarily on the definition of Bernet et al. [26].

TRIGGERING FACTOR

As already mentioned, the problem can be triggered when the parents separate without mutual consent (violent divorce) therefore, one of the parents struggles, apparently, for the custody of the children in order to retain or get the benefits achieved during the marriage.

For pediatricians, general doctors, social workers, mental health professionals and lawyers who attend or interact with children and adolescents in this situation, the paramount point is to count with a clear knowledge of the situation that favors the formation of the family or its loss, and its consequences.

The civil or religious marriage, so characteristic of Latin American societies, has brought into limelight three prevailing situations in today's marriage:

a. Real predominance of couples in free union.
b. Official marriage decline in the last 10 years has gone up to 19%.
c. The ascending curve of separations or divorces.

In parental separation situation, family members may present various emotional and/or behavioral problems, whose severity will depend mainly on the age, gender, moral education and the sociocultural level. Depending on the type of divorce, the problems can occur during the process of separation or time after. However, sometimes the separation can be beneficial when it is perceivable the possibility of conjugal violence and that the girls, boys and teenagers in the family can be direct or indirect victims of it [27-29].

CONTROVERSIES

PAS is a syndrome that has not been fully accepted in the mental health and legal fields. However, DSM-V, (Diagnostic and Statistical Manual of Mental Disorders) published in 2013 indirectly included the term or at least, its basic significances in this publication. In its section titled "Conditions that can be a focus of clinical attention", it refers to the patterns of relationship of the parents or caregivers of their daughters or sons which have a significant impact on their mental health [26].

In the light of these controversies, some researchers coined up other related syndromes such as:

a. The Syndrome of Allegation of Sexual Abuse in Divorce (false accusations to obtain custody of children) [27, 29-30].
b. The Medea Syndrome (murder of the children in revenge on the couple wanting to separate or divorce)
c. The Malice Syndrome (evil actions aimed at committing a crime)

PAS SUSPICTION CONDITIONS

The predominant situations where PAS can be suspected are:

a. When the problem develops within a family that is in a phase of violent emotional or legal breakdown with the involvement of not only the couple and the children, but also the family of the other parent.

b. When a parent (usually the guardian or custodian of the child or children) predisposes, by various strategies, the child or children against the other parent and his or her extended family. Sometimes this predisposition reaches an extreme and the child or children are alienated by strongly allying with the alienating parent [31].

c. There is an alienating parent (alienator).

d. There is an alienated parent.

e. There is an alienated daughter or son.

f. The minor usually develops genitourinary, gastrointestinal, dermatological and neurological problems.

THE GRAVITY OF THE PROBLEM

Taking into consideration the different clinical manifestations that have been observed in the cases of PAS, some authors have described three degrees of this syndrome:

a. *Mild.* It almost goes unnoticed because the denial that the alienated parent is not with his or her child is occasional and probably unimportant. There is little or no interruption in the visitation of the alienated parent.

b. *Moderate.* It is characterized by a greater and more frequent restriction of visitation of the parent who does not have guardianship or custody of the child. In this case, the alienating parent usually comes up with a series of pretexts in the character that the boy or girl is sick, he or she has a lot of homework, the child is presenting exams the next day or that he or she is going to his or her swimming, ballet or karate class, etc. Coincidentally, all the commitments sprout up when the alienated parent wants to schedule a visit.

c. *Serious*. Apart from conglomerating the symptoms mentioned above, severe cases of PAS go beyond to include a very complex and an extraordinarily serious situation involving the accusation of the alienated parent of sexual abuse or other forms of child abuse (CA) in one of the children by the alienating parent.

In severe PAS situation, three conclusions can be made:

a. It establishes the complete rupture of the bond that could still exist between the parents and their respective families.
b. There is a need for professional interventions (pediatrician, gynecologist, psychiatrist or lawyer) to determine if sexual abuse or another form of CA actually occurred in any of the children. To establish this diagnosis is usually very complicated because there is usually no physical evidence since too much time has elapsed.
c. There is always the possibility of an exaggerated intentional deformation of the truth. Therefore, it is usually very difficult and exhausting to discover which part is true and which is invented.

CLINICAL PICTURE DURING THE EVOLUTION OF THE PROCESS

PAS is fraught with some set of clinical manifestations shown in the child or children of the separating or divorced parents. Usually, the girl or boy begins to manifest unusual behavior, which most of the time has a sudden onset [32]. The most important observations in these children are:

a. Manifestations of anxiety, depression or distress.

b. Sudden onset of sleep disturbance such as: night terrors, nightmares, can't fall asleep, doesn't want to go to sleep or wet the bed when he had overcome this stage of disturbance.

c. Manifestations of some nutritional problems such as not wanting to eat, becoming prissy on what to eat, not finishing what the mother offers him or her and preferring to consume "junk" products.

d. Radical changes in behavior at home, at school and in the neighborhood. The child's self-esteem diminishes. He or she becomes introverted, isolated and does not want to play with his friends.

e. The child begins to show feelings of helplessness when he or she is with the absent parent.

f. He or she begins to show rejection towards the "alienated" parent and his family. This behavior worsens with the passage of time and the couple's conflict becomes more acute.

g. The child develops and expresses a learning strategy to avoid the targeted parent. He or she manipulates or resolves conflicts always at his or her convenience and at the convenience of the "alienator" progenitor.

EMOTIONAL MODIFICATIONS AND BEHAVIOR DURING SEPARATION

Professionals involved in situations of separation or violent divorce should be alert to detect varying degrees of loyalty and disloyalty of the child or teenager with one of the parents, depending on the situation of "alienator" or "alienated". These manifestations of the minor are expressed in different ways such as:

a. Loyal support to the alienating parent.

b. Accepts the lies of the alienator in order not to be with the alienated parent.
c. Rejects the family of the alienated parent.
d. Insults and does not want to be with the alienated parent.
e. In an extreme degree of the problem, the child accepts and maintains the position that he or she has been a victim of sexual abuse or other forms of child abuse.

It is convenient to keep in mind the DSM-V criteria that, in general, substitute the suspicion criteria established by Gardner (Table 3).

There are other clinical manifestations that professionals in this matter should consider:

a) Girls, boys or teenagers may manifest varying degrees of loyalty or disloyalty with either parent.
b) In this way, they initiate and develop diverse degrees of alliance that are manifested in various ways such as frank support to the alienating parent, acceptance of the lies coined up in order not to be with the alienated parent and rejection of the family of the latter as well as directly expressing insults to and rejection of the alienated parent. In an extreme case, the child supports the information of being a victim of sexual abuse by the alienated parent.
c) Generally, the child shows no guilt for his or her alienating behavior developing an idealization towards the alienating parent and in some cases, agrees with the separation of the parents.

Table 3. DSM-V diagnostic criteria for parental alienation syndrome

A.	In the context of the child. The involvement of the child takes place mostly in a violent divorce of the parents. The boy or girl is strongly associated with one of the parents and rejects the other parent, without a justification.
B.	The girl or boy manifests any of the following behaviors: Persistent refusal or denigration of a parent. Through a persistent criticism, the child develops a frivolous, absurd and weak relationship against the alienated parent.

C.	The girl or boy manifests two or more of the following behaviors:
	1. Lack of affective ambivalence towards parental figures.
	2. Appearance of the phenomenon of "independent thinker".
	3. Automatic support to the beloved parent in any circumstance.
	4. Absence of guilt in the child, manifested by his or her expression of rejection.
	5. Apparition in the story of the child of borrowed or forged scenarios that he or she had not lived and cannot remember.
	6. The extent of rejection includes the family or environment of the rejected or alienated parent.
D.	The minimum duration of the problem or phenomenon is two months.
E.	The disturbance causes distress or clinically significant deterioration in the child's social, academic and occupational performance or other areas he or she participates.
F.	The refusal of the child to have contact with the rejected parent has no legitimate justification. However, in this situation, it is necessary to rule out any form of Child Abuse that might be a cause of rejection of the alienated parent by the child.

Taken from American Psychiatric Association [26].

This establishes a degree of pathological hatred - from a child to a parent, a condition that will obviously affect the minor's mental and physical health.

The situation becomes more critical when one parent accuses the other of sexually assaulting the child. In this way, a consideration of whether the problem is medical or legal comes into play. At this time of the problem, the legal authority that deals with the case can request the intervention of a specialist doctor or an institution that would determine a probable phenomenon of child sexual abuse (CSA) so as to clarify the truth.

It is very convenient that legal specialists, pediatricians, mental health professionals and social workers determine the veracity of the probable CSA and if it was a factor that triggered the divorce or separation. To establish the veracity of this, the version of what the child said and the behavior must be thoroughly considered. It must be borne in mind that a child who has actually suffered sexual abuse may present the following situations:

a) The alienated child is afraid that by reporting the assault, the parents will separate or divorce.

b) The child is afraid of being left alone with the alienating parent.

c) The child exhibits a degree of tranquility for being away or removed from the aggressor parent.

Table 4. Real situation of child sexual abuse

a. The act is revealed by the girl or boy.
b. The victim reveals some characteristic information.
c. The girl or boy describes, by their own words, the possible event of sexual abuse.
d. Usually during their story, he or she rectifies his or her words or sentences.
e. It's possible that the minor presents feelings of guilt or shame.
f. The parent cares more for the welfare of the child than for the punishment of the abuser.

Table 5.Common situation of a false accusation of CSA

a. CSA act is revealed by the alienator parent during the process of violent separation or divorce.
b. The story focuses exclusively on the possible event of CSA.
c. The minor describes the Accumulation Swing Index (ASI) chart with adult vocabulary, with great detail and is automated.
d. The girl or boy doesn't show feelings of guilt or shame.
e. The accusatory parent (alienator) cares more for the punishment of the abuser (alienated) than for the welfare of the victim.

In case the findings of the experts are devoid of any act of sexual abuse, a real case of parental alienation will be established. On the contrary, the sexual abuse, usually chronic, might be the reason for the separation of the parents [13]. Table 4 shows the main characteristics revealed by girls and boys who have truly been victims of Sexual Abuse or who are lying and making a false accusation of CSA. Table 5 shows the false exposure of CSA.

The knowledge of the elements presented in Tables 4 and 5 will allow the professionals to establish with precision specific diagnosis of CSA. In this task, it is proposed the intervention of a multidisciplinary team constituted by:

a) Medical professionals composed of a pediatrician, a gynecologist or a family doctor with extensive knowledge of the subject. The main objective is to confirm or rule out physical damage by CSA. In this process it is very convenient to remember that 85-90% of CSA cases are touching, caresses, oral sex and pornography; and none of these situations leaves a physical print. In the case of vaginal or anal penetration, no more than 48-72 hours of the event should elapse to perform the physical examination.

b) The intervention of the Social Worker is necessary in order to work in the obtention of useful information by interviewing relatives, neighbors or teachers of the victim.

c) A mental health professional (psychiatrist or psychologist) experienced in the field of pediatric medicine will try to determine the human behavior of the people involved in the problem and especially the victim.

d) The intervention of the competent legal authority (Family Judge) is required. Ideally, this responsibility should fall on a lawyer expert in the subject. He is responsible for making the best decision for the child, the accused and the rest of the family. It should be borne in mind that a diagnostic error harms the minor, the family and the possible aggressor in variable degree and severity.

Once the precise diagnosis of CSA is established, the following action strategies are proposed.

a) The minor must receive attention on his mental health to detect and contain the emotional manifestations already described, in the short, medium or long term.

b) Both parents must be cared for in a similar way.

c) The girl or boy should be monitored by a pediatrician experienced in the subject to assess the physical growth, neurological and emotional development and the behavior as well as the school evolution without forgetting the proper handling of immunizations, food, recreation and sports activity.

d) As long as the girl or boy stays longer with the alienating custodian, the later has an advantageous situation to increase the rejection of the child for the other parent. Therefore, a prolonged period of custody can aggravate the father-mother-child relationship.

e) The responsible legal authority must make a correct decision about which parent should have custody of the child.

f) Considering the age of the children, it is of paramount importance to determine the physical, intellectual, emotional and economic capacity of the custodian parent in order to ensure the best interests of the child.

g) The authority must be attentive to the changes of address of the parents, mainly of the alienator.

h) Remember that the physical, psycho-emotional and behavioral alterations of girls, boys and teenagers are mostly related to inadequate management of the rupture.

When the parents are separated or divorced, the child may be the victim of one or several types of child abuse such as physical abuse, sexual abuse, psychological abuse and neglect. Therefore, the pediatrician must be aware of the presence of clinical data that are suggestive of this pathology [33].

Finally, this responsibility not only falls on the doctor; the legal authority must guarantee that the Rights of the Minor are fulfilled to avoid physical, emotional and moral damages. Worthy to mention is the fact that the consequences of a child suffering adverse experiences in the first years of life makes him or her vulnerable to develop depression, addiction to licit and illicit drugs as well as tendency to suicide in his or her adult life [34-35].

All the aforementioned situations must be considered in the integral attention of each case, in order not to regret, years later, the problems already mentioned. The characterization of the problem is crucial bearing in mind that if there is a break in a couple, there should not be a break in the family [36].

It should be noted that depression, addictions, alteration in the self-esteem and confidence of the child in other people in in his or her adult life are the major consequences this problem can generate in the lives of children or teenagers as well as the possibility of CSA replication in their children [37-38]. Parents also suffer from various emotional problems and these can sometimes contribute to suicide [39-41].

REFERENCES

[1]   Aguilar Cuenca JM. *Síndrome de Alienación Parental: Hijos Manipulados por un Cónyuge para Odiar al Otro.* [*Parental alienation syndrome: children manipulated by a spouse to hate the other*] Córdoba, España, Almuzara. 2004.

[2]   Bolaños I. El síndrome de alienación parental. Descripción y abordajes psico-legales. [Parental alienation syndrome. Description and psycho-legal approaches] *Psicopatología Clínica, Legal y Forense.* 2002; 2-3:25-45.

[3]   Segura C, Gil MJ, Sepúlveda MA. El Síndrome de Alienación Parental: Una forma de Maltrato Infantil. [Parental alienation syndrome: a form of child abuse] *Cuad Med Forense* 2006; 12:43-44.

[4]   Leñero Otero L. Mitos y realidades de la familia en Mexico. En: Dulanto Gutiérrez E. *La familia.* [Myths and realities of the family in Mexico. In: Dulanto Gutiérrez E. *The family*] Editores de Textos Mexicanos. Mexico. 2004, 93-109.

[5]   Salazar Rojas D. *Familia, economía, pobreza y quiebre cultural en Latinoamérica.* [*Family, economy, poverty and cultural breakdown in Latin America*] Ciudad de Mexico, 2007.

[6]   Dulanto Gutiérrez E. *La familia.* [*The family*] Editores de Textos Mexicanos. Mexico 2004, 119-126.

[7]   Arce R, Fariña F, Seijo D. Razonamientos judiciales en procesos de separación. [Judicial reasoning in separation processes] *Psicothema* 2005; 17:57-63.

[8]   Granados F. Lo irracional en el conflicto familiar. [The irrational in family conflicto] *Actualidad Civil* 1987; 35:2087-2095.

[9]   Reich W. *Character analysis*. En: Farrar, Straus and Giroux. 3er. Ed. New York 1949.

[10] Garner RA. Recent trends in divorce and custody litigation. *Acad Forum* 1985; 29:3-7.

[11] Garner RA. *The parental alienation sindrome: A guide for mental health and legal professionals*. Cresskill NJ. 2ª. Ed. Creative Therapeutics.

[12] Vilalta Suárez RJ. Descripción del Síndrome de Alienación Parental en una muestra forense. [Description of the Parental Alienation Syndrome in a forensic simple] *Psicothema* 2011; 23:636-641.

[13] Tejedor A. El síndrome de alienación parental. Una forma de maltrato. [The parental alienation syndrome. a form of abuse] *Ed EOS*, 2006. 3rd Editores de Mexico, 2015; 1-156.

[14] Loredo Abdalá A. Síndrome de Alienación parental: una triste realidad vigente. En: Loredo Abdalá A. *Maltrato Infantil: gravedad y prevención*. [Parental Alienation Syndrome: a sad reality in force. In: Loredo Abdalá A. *Child abuse: Severity and prevention*] Editores de Textos Mexicanos. Mexico. 2017, 55-70.

[15] Marriage and Divorce Statistics. *EUROSTAT* (2015). Available at: http://ec.europa.eu/eurostat/statistics-explained/index.php/Marriage_ and_divorce_statistics.

[16] Seijo D, Fariña F, Corras T, Novo M, Arce R. Estimating the epidemiology and quantifying the damages of parental separation in children and adolescents. *Front Psychol* 2016; 7:1611.

[17] Bernet W, Galahau B, Baker W, Morrison SL. Parental alienation, DSM-V and ICD-11. *Am J Fam Ther* 2010; 38:76-187.

[18] Fuente: *INEGI/Estadística/Población, Hogares y Vivienda/ Nupcialidad/Divorcios/Relación divorcios-matrimonios, 1980 a 2013*; ENOE 2016. [Source: *INEGI/Statistics/Population, Households and Housing/Nuptiality/Divorces/Relationship divorces-marriages, 1980 to 2013*] ENOE 2016.

[19] McLoyd V, Mistry R S, Hardaway CR. Poverty and children's development. In: *Societal contexts of child development: pathways of influence and implications for practice and policy*. ET Gershoff, RS Mistry, DA Crosby eds, New York, NY: Oxford University Press 2014; 109-124.

[20] Garner RA, Sauber SR, Lorandos D. *The international handbook of parental alienation síndrome: Conceptual, clinical and legal considerations*. Springfield IL Charles C. Thomas 2006.

[21] Andre K. Parent alienation syndrome. *Ann Am Psychother Assoc* 2004; 7:7-11.

[22] Darnall D. The psychosocil treatment of parental alienation. Child *Adoles Pschiatric Clin N Am* 2011; 3:479-494.

[23] Gardner RA. *The objective diagnosis of minimal brain dysfunction*. New Jersey, USA: Creative Therapeutics. 1979.

[24] Gardner RA. Recent trends in divorce and custody litigation. *Academy Forum* 1985; 29:3-7.

[25] Johnston KJB Jr: The alienated child: a reformulation of parental alienation syndrome. *Fam Court Rev* 2001; 39:249-66.

[26] American Psychiatric Association. *Diagnostic and Statistical Manual Disorders, Fifth Edition*. Arlington, VA: American Psychiatry Association. 2013.

[27] Turkat I. Divorce related malicious mother syndrome. *J Fam Violence* 1995; 10:253-264.

[28] LowensteinL. Parent alienation syndrome: a two step approach toward a solution. *Contemp Fam Ther* 1998; 29:505-520.

[29] Kelly JB, Johnston JR. The alienated child: A reformulation of parental alienation syndrome. *Family Court Review* 2001; 39:249-265.

[30] González Trujillo CJ. *Síndrome de Alienación parental: lazos rotos, corazones desgarrados. Intervención psicoeducativa.* [*Parental alienation syndrome: broken ties, torn hearts. Psycho educational intervention*] Mexico. Ediciones de Laurel, 2014.

[31] Bone J, Walsh M. Parental alienation syndrome: How to detect it and what to do about it. *The Florida Bar Journal* 1999; 73:44-48.

[32] Zicavo Martínez N. La alienación parental y el proceso de la padrectomía. [Parental alienation and the process of fatherctomy] *Rev Cubana Psicol* 2008: 57-62.

[33] Loredo Abdalá A. *Maltrato Infantil En Maltrato Infantil: gravedad y prevención.* [*Child Abuse In Child Abuse: seriousness and prevention*] Mexico. Editores de Textos Mexicanos. 2017.

[34] Merrick M, Ports K, Ford D, Afifi T, Gershoff E, Grogan-Kaylor A. Unpacking the impact of adverse childhood experiences on adult mental health. *Child Abuse Neglect* 2017; 69:10-19.

[35] Casas Muñoz A. Conocer y ejercer los derechos de niñas, niños y adolescentes para respetarlos y educarlos con responsabilidad. En: Loredo Abdalá A. *Maltrato Infantil: gravedad y prevención.* [Know and exercise the rights of children and adolescents to respect them and educate them with responsibility. In: Loredo Abdalá A. *Child abuse: severity and prevention*] Editores de Textos Mexicanos, 2017, 265-278.

[36] Martinón JM, Fariña F, Corras T, Seijo D, Souto A, Novo M. Impacto de la ruptura de los progenitores en el estado de salud física de los hijos. [Impact of the breakdown of the parents in the physical health status of the children] *Eur J Educ Psychol* 2016; 10:9-14.

[37] Baker A. The long term effects of parental alienation on adult children: a qualitative research study. *Am J Fam Ther* 2005; 33:289-302.

[38] Baker AJ. Adult children of parental alienation syndrome: Breaking the ties that bind. *J Can Acad Child Adolesc Psychiatry*. New York: Norton, 2008.

[39] Leo Sher, Parental Alienation and Suicide in Men. *Psychiatria Danubina* 2015; 27:288-289.

[40] Bernet W, Baker AJ, Verrocchio MC. Symptom Checklist- 90-Revised scores in adult children exposed to alienating behaviors: an Italian sample. *J Forensic Sci* 2015; 60:357-362.

[41] Black MM, Walker SP, Fernald LCH, Andersen CT. Advancing early childhood development: from science to scale 1 early childhood development coming of age: Science through the life course. *Lancet* 2017; 389:77-90.

In: Child Abuse: Harm and Solutions   ISBN: 978-1-53614-271-6
Editors: Arturo Loredo Abdalá et al. © 2018 Nova Science Publishers, Inc.

Chapter 8

CHILD ABUSE AND ITS IMPACTS ON THE PREVALENCE OF PREGNANCY IN ADOLESCENCE: PREVENTION STRATEGIES

Arturo Perea Martínez[1],*, Arturo Loredo Abdalá[2]
and Hugo Juárez Olguín[3]

[1]Clínica de Adolescentes. Instituto Nacional de Pediatría.
Ciudad de Mexico, Mexico
[2]Centro de Estudios Avanzados sobre Maltrato Infantil-Prevención
del Instituto Nacional de Pediatría (CEAMI-P-INP),
Ciudad de Mexico, Mexico.
[3]Laboratorio de Farmacología, Instituto Nacional de Pediatría.
Facultad de Medicina, Universidad Nacional Autónoma de Mexico,
Ciudad de Mexico, Mexico

---

* Corresponding Author Email: clinicaadolecentes.inp@hotmail.com.

ABSTRACT

Pregnancy in adolescents is a gestational process that occurs in the life stage of a girl who has not completely concluded her biopsychosocial growth and development. According to its administrative record, a gestation that occurs between 10 and 19 years of age should be considered as teen pregnancy. Its impact is reflected on the health, education, life project, social and cultural relations of the girl as well as on her and her family economy. Being an adolescent mother or father is usually fraught with and/or re-enforces, without social distinction, a series of associated conditions of vulnerability.

The processes of professionalization and adaptation, of education, health, communication and of other conditions that may serve as a vehicle for the application of preventive strategies to prevent the phenomenon are extremely necessary. The results obtained presume a partial success in the prevention of unwanted pregnancies in this stage of life thus, re-enforcing the achievements which can be obtained with additional strategies.

Due to the multifactorial nature of its genesis, teen pregnancy will have an individual expression. Generally, the magnitude of the impacts depends on the circumstances of the person, the couple, the family and the society as well as on the demographic circumstances of each country and its different regions. Hence, a general approach with an individual flexibility is required when dealing with teen pregnancy. This chapter reviews teen pregnancy, its predisposing factors and its prevention.

Keywords: child abuse, immaturity, sexual abuse, teen pregnancy, unwanted pregnancy

BACKGROUND

1. Teen Pregnancy. Global Rate

The World Health Organization (WHO) remarks that the phenomenon of teen pregnancy has gotten to a situation that warrants its consideration as a public health problem. Its impacts on prevalence, biological health and psychosocial well-being of the communities are reflected in some figures described below [1]:

(a) Annually, there are around 16 million births of babies born to women aged 15 to 19 years. In addition, there are about 1 million births from girls under 15 years, most of them from low and middle income countries.

(b) At worldwide level, complications during pregnancy are the leading cause of death among girls aged 15 to 19 years.

(c) Every year, about 3 million girls under 15 to 19 years undergo dangerous abortions.

(d) Babies born to teenage mothers face a significantly higher risk of dying than those born to women aged 20 to 24 years.

(e) In low and middle income countries, complications arising from teen pregnancy and the birth of a baby from a girl under 19 years old are the leading cause of death in this age group.

(f) The neonatal mortality of babies born to mothers from 15 to 19 years is 50% higher when compared with those born to older mothers.

(g) Adolescent mothers (10 to 19 years) face higher risks of eclampsia, puerperal endometritis and systemic infection than women aged 20 to 24 years, and the babies born to adolescent mothers face higher risks of low birth weight, premature delivery and severe neonatal conditions than those born to women between 20 and 24 years old.

(h) Newborns of adolescent mothers have a higher prevalence of low birth weight.

2. Child Abuse. Global Rate

In 2013, a meta-analytic study on the global prevalence of child abuse, conducted by Stoltenberg et al., put the occurrence of child abuse at 22.6%, a value that overpassed by twice the previous reference of the 20th century in which the World Health Organization indicated an approximate figure of 10% [2].

CHILD ABUSE AS A PREGNANCY RISK FACTOR
IN ADOLESCENCE

In 2014, Jenkins et al., conducted a meta-analytic study that included pregnant women under 20 years of age. In this study, they investigated, in general terms, the relationship between the different forms of violence suffered in childhood by the population under study with the prevalence of pregnancy in adolescence. In 38 studies with a total of 75,300 individuals, they found that the risk of adolescent pregnancy was associated with sexual and physical abuses, determining an odd ratio (OR) of 2.06 (CI 95%: 1.75 − 2.38) and of 1.48 (CI 95%: 1.24 − 1.76) respectively for each abuse. On the other hand and in significant form, the value of OR increased substantively to 3.83 (CI 95%: 2.96 − 4.97) when both forms of abuse coexists. In contrast to the above, the risk of sexual abuse was not significantly different with negligence and emotional abuse forms with OR of 1.01 and 1.29 respectively. The authors concluded that both sexual and physical abuses are directly related to the risk of teen pregnancy, while social negligence and emotional abuse do not show this association. In particular and in some regions of the world, sexual abuse in childhood, as one of the different expressions of violence against a minor, reaches variable prevalence. In a study conducted by Levine et al., (2017), it is shown that one in every five adults included in their research accepted having suffered sexual abuse in her childhood, a phenomenon that was associated, in her future life, with higher rates of depression, alcohol consumption and risky sexual behaviors. On the other hand, Boyer et al., in a study carried out in Washington, investigated the prevalence of sexual abuse and its relation with pregnancy rate in adolescents and found that 2 in every 3 pregnant adolescents had suffered sexual aggression in their childhood. In their report, it was indicated that the victims showed a greater consumption of alcohol and other drugs, risky sexual behaviors including a lower acceptance to the use of contraceptives [3]. In 1994, Stevens et al., agreed that a history of sexual abuse in childhood is related to a higher rate of teen pregnancy [4].

Jenni Noll et al., (2009), performed a meta-analytic study comprising of 21 studies in which they demonstrated the clear association between the history of childhood sexual abuse and greater prevalence of teen pregnancy. These authors establish an Odds ratio of 2.21 with a confidence interval of 1.94 – 2.51 [5].

PREGNANCY IN ADOLESCENTS: A RISK OF SOCIAL AND PSYCHIATRIC MEDICAL PATHOLOGIES

Pregnancy in adolescents is a gestational process that occurs in a life stage when a girl has not completely concluded her biopsychosocial growth and development. It is considered as a teen pregnancy any gestation that occurs between 10 and 19 years of age. Its impact is reflected on health, education, life project, social and cultural relations, and on the economy among others. Being an adolescent mother or father is usually fraught with and/or re-enforces, without social distinction, a series of conditions of vulnerability associated with: a) lack of preparation for this new responsibility, b) loss of the opportunity for the characteristic development typical in this stage, c) lack of preparation for the adoption of traditional gender roles and d) the loss of experiences and acquisition of knowledge typical of adolescence. Early motherhood or fatherhood tends to have serious negative effects on the children of the adolescent parents and in the latter, exposes them to adverse conditions that hinder and slow down their development. In addition and as in all pregnancies, there is an increase in the nutritional requirements of a pregnant adolescent and this must be covered, otherwise, she will be subjected to the risk of developing one or several nutritional deficiencies that will generate impact for the binomial. Congenital malformations, prematurity, maternal and infant mortality, family disintegration, social dysfunction, recurrent pregnancies, violence against the infant and the mother are just some of the direct and indirect consequences of gestational undernutrition.

Among the interventions that have proven to be effective in reducing teen pregnancy are:

1. Integral education in sexuality in schools.
2. Health services and friendly clinics for the adolescents.
3. Adequate and effective contraceptive supplies to adolescents.
4. Direct interventions in the media.
5. Social policies for school retention and for labor insertion.

The processes of professionalization and adaptation of the education, health, communication and other systems that serve as a vehicle for the application of preventive strategies for the phenomenon are necessary. So far, the results obtained presume a partial success in the prevention of unwanted pregnancies in this stage of life thus, re-enforcing the achievements which can be obtained with additional strategies [6-8].

TEEN PREGNANCY IN MEXICO

Adolescent pregnancy in Mexico is a phenomenon that has regained importance in recent years. The current fertility rate reaches 77 births per 1,000 adolescents aged 15 to 19 years thus, placing it in the first place among the countries that conform the Organization for Economic Cooperation and Development (OECD) [9].

In Mexico, 23% of the adolescents begin their sexual life between 12 and 19 years old. Moreover, it was found that 15% of men and 33% of women did not use any contraceptive method in their first sexual intercourse. The result of the above is the occurrence of approximately 350 to 400 thousand births in girls under 19 years of age.

In response to this circumstance, the Mexican Government developed the National Strategy for the Prevention of Pregnancy in Adolescents (ENAPEA by its Spanish acronym) which agglomerates the actions of the 16 Federal Government agencies and the participation of civil society organizations, international organizations and academic experts on the subject.

The general objective of ENAPEA is to reduce the number of teen pregnancies in Mexico with absolute respect to the human rights, particularly sexual and reproductive rights. Its primordial goal is to bring down teen pregnancy and then aspire to zero births in girls aged 10 to 14 years, as well as to decrease by 50% the specific fertility rate of adolescents aged 15 to 19 years by the year 2030 [7,8,10-11].

THE SOCIAL CIRCUMSTANCE

Most pregnancies in girls under 19 years old occur in biologically mature women, so the repercussions on the state of health of the mother and her baby depend more on environmental factors such as family function and health, access to health services, competent professionals to attend the process, human development index, individual socioeconomic circumstance and contexts, gender equity, the level of education of those involved, the existence of care programs, among others. Teen pregnancy will potentially affect the actors and their families in their health, education, life project, social and cultural relations and their economy. Parenthood in adolescence is frequently associated with a series of vulnerable conditions such as absence of preparations for this new responsibility, loss of the opportunity to acquire the developments typical in this stage, lack of preparation to adopt the traditional gender roles and the loss of experiences and acquisition of knowledge typical of adolescence. Early motherhood and fatherhood often have serious negative effects on the children of adolescents, exposing them to adverse conditions that hinder their development.

Because the genesis is multifactorial, teen pregnancy will have an individual, couple, family and societal expressions. Moreover, it will also be considered in the context of each country and of its regional and demographic circumstances. Therefore, it requires a general approach with an individual flexibility when dealing with this phenomenon. In Mexico for example, the National Strategy for the Prevention of Pregnancy in Adolescents describes in its introduction the prevailing circumstance in the country which is summarized below:

(a) Of the total population in Mexico, around 20 to 22 million are between 10 and 19 years old, that is, are teenagers.

(b) Women aged between 10 and 19 years old constitute the largest age group among women in childbearing age.

(c) The decrease in fertility in adolescents is less than in other age groups. This is attributed to low use of contraceptives in this group of population where it was found that only 37.6% of the adolescents used a method of contraceptives in their first sexual intercourse and 45% one method in their last sexual intercourse and in both cases, the methods used are mainly those with little effectiveness. This situation is aggravated when we consider that the percentage of the adolescent population who have become sexually active has increased.

(d) As was reported by ENSANUT at national level, the proportion of the population aged 12 to 19 that have started their sexual life went up from 15% in 2006 to 23% in 2012.

(e) At the national level, according to the available data from the last demographic survey of 2009, the average age for the onset of sexual life in women aged 15 to 19 is 15.9 years.

(f) As a result of these trends, the percentage of births from teenage mothers also increased from 15.6% to 18.7% between 2003 and 2012.

(g) In Mexico, an important fact is the increase of pregnancies in the population under 15 from 1,933 in 2003 to 10,924 in 2012, and that this group is associated with increased maternal-fetal morbidity and mortality. In fact, maternal mortality in the age group of 10 to 14 years is 58.8 per 100,000 live births compared to 33 per 100,000 live births of the group of 15 to 19 years of age.

(h) The percentage of deceased children from women of 12 years and over by age group, in 125 municipalities with high and 125 municipalities with low Human Development Index (HDI), indicates that the higher is the HDI, the lower is the number of deceased children, except in the group of women under 14 years of age whose percentage is similar regardless of the level of HDI.

EARLY PREGNANCY AND ADOLESCENCE

For practical purposes, all pregnancies in children under 14 should be considered as early pregnancy and potentially, they are as a result of sexual abuse. It can be said that pregnancy in adolescents directly indicates the social and psychological state of a population that affect the well-being of the gestating dyad. If this statement is accepted, then, the process that will be established as a prevention program of the phenomenon should go beyond aspects like promotional actions that only enrich sexual and reproductive health to a multi-sectorial system that facilitates the acculturation of the topic and permit responsible and free learning of sexuality in this stage of life [9,11-13].

PREGNANCY IN ADOLESCENTS IN THE UNITED STATES OF AMERICA

In the United States of America, although an improvement has been registered, the rates of pregnancy in adolescents continued to be an important problem. The prevention of teen pregnancy was identified by the Center for Diseases Control and Prevention as one of its top six priorities. In the Teen Pregnancy Prevention Program, a strategy was designed to improve the professionalization of the members of the health team and other sectors in the field of sex education and contraception, and to optimize sex education to the population and permeate the usefulness and safety of long-acting oral contraceptives (LAOC) showing their efficacy in reducing birth rate among adolescents. In the case of pregnant adolescents, the strategies for their care, monitoring and prenatal attention were improved thus, reducing the perinatal risk for the binomial. The system also includes care for adolescents in the postpartum period, encouragement and support to breastfeed, control of depression and access to reliable contraceptives to avoid the repetition of unwanted pregnancy [14].

The Phenomenon of Pregnancy in Adolescents.
Associated Factors

Stern in 1997 and later Menkes indicated, with precision, the circumstances and the impact of this problem in public health. The first distinguished that about 450,000 pregnancies in adolescents would constitute a big problem in perspective and would involve a multi-sectorial analysis of the causes and possible containment strategies. In his revision, he clearly distinguished the importance of attaching adolescents to school environment as an crucial factor of prevention and protection [15,16]. In his report, Stern states the following: "will it be that many of the problems that lead to teen pregnancy and in turn, the problems which this leads to are derived by the way in which premarital sex has been assessed and, particularly, sanctioned adolescent sexuality?" Negative assessment of the exercise of sexuality before union could be justified in the context of a society in which sexuality and reproduction were almost inextricably linked, as a result of the relatively short period between the onset of fertile age and the union, and of a function almost exclusive of a woman as a wife and mother. But over the time, this justification is becoming less and less valid, because as these conditions change, options for women increase and the period between sexual maturation and family formation is extended, during which it is necessary to re-enforce the preparation of young people for the prevention of unwanted pregnancies and inconveniences. The negative sanction hinders access to information, education and preparation to exercise sexuality in a pleasant and responsible manner, in such a way that a large part of the problem lies in the way adults qualify the phenomenon and in the way social institutes – the family, school, religious institutions, health sector, etcetera – interpret and manage it" [15].

On the other hand, Menkes and Suarez highlighted the following points in their research on the phenomenon and causality of teen pregnancy [16]:

The results indicate that teen pregnancy in Mexico responds primarily to a social context. The statistical model directly relates teen pregnancy to conjugal union, age and educational level. The alternatives of female development seem to be one of the most important aspects related to this topic. The authors also report that although in general, teen pregnancy is associated with fewer educational opportunities, knowledge and use of contraceptive methods is still very limited in adolescents in the different social contexts, especially in regard to first sexual relationship. An important point is the lack of knowledge of condom among those women who have already had sexual relationship, a circumstance that leads to other consequences such as the recent growth in sexually transmitted infections, among others. Other findings that strongly and clearly relate the low level of female education with less knowledge and use of contraceptive methods are less planning in the first sexual relationship and an earlier age at the first sexual intercourse which makes women less schooled more vulnerable to pregnancy and sexually transmitted diseases. According to the results of these authors, gender inequality and other sociocultural aspects related with conditions of inequality of women are aggravated by the context of poverty and lack of opportunities. Finally, it is distinguished that the level of knowledge of students in the junior and high schools on the biology of reproduction is low. The knowledge generated is suggested as a starting point to evaluate the educational contents that are taught in the public schools of the country [16].

Recently, Reyna Samano evaluated the family and individual context of adolescents before, during and after pregnancy [17]. Although derived from a non-representative sample, the results obtained highlight the following findings that coincide with what are observed in the clinical practice and which are also reiterated by other authors:

(a) The pregnant teenagers had a family history of teen pregnancy.

(b) The girls revealed feelings of repression, loneliness and indifference toward their parents, situations that led them to practice unprotected sex and probably without fear of pregnancy.

(c) Almost everyone said that they were looking for love outside the family, which revealed a scenario of limited communication and unsatisfactory relationship within the family.

(d) After pregnancy, communication between the girls and their parents improved but worsened with their partners. As a result, these teenagers felt as they were before they become pregnant.

(e) The teenagers said that they would make their situation work for their child's sake and regretted having dropped out of school and became pregnant so young.

The authors of this study analyzed and concluded the following points about teenage pregnancy:

It is crucial to know and understand the importance of communication between parents and children at early stage of life as a vehicle of prevention of pregnancy in adolescence and their consequences and to make the general population aware of the scholastic, economic and psychosocial impact of living the phenomenon [15].

RECURRENT ADOLESCENT PREGNANCY

A study carried out in Georgia, USA examined the determinants for teen pregnancy recurrence in a focused group. The findings indicate that repeated motherhood is associated with poor parent-child relationship, conflicting support for the roles that teenage mothers are expected to fulfill, limited social pressures for effective parenthood and limited access for social services for all members of the family. Teenage mothers mentioned the alienation of their mothers and the difficulty of talking about sexual matters. Mothers of pregnant teenagers expressed anger toward their daughters. Both the teenage mothers and their mothers believe that the first birth should have been delayed. The mothers and the grandmothers differ in their thoughts on the responsibilities of having children. Many grandmothers take care of their grandchildren. The fathers were proud of the pregnancy, but less eager to provide support to their children. The schools did not provide a replacement subject for the lost classes, but the programs for teenage mothers and children of teenage mothers had a supportive environment. The adolescents believe that health education should be centered on understanding the risks [18].

Repeating involuntary conceptions could result in emotional, psychological and educational damage for young women, often with lasting consequences for their life possibilities. Unfortunately, systematic review studies reveal that the strategies currently developed to prevent the repetition of teen pregnancy are not yet successful [19].

In addition, it is of vital importance that adolescents are motivated in the family environment so that they can continue their studies. There is an urgent need to implement measures that compensate educational inequality and strengthen the strategies aimed at teenage mothers and pregnant adolescents that promote their school performance through scholarships and day care programs. Many of the problems inherent to adolescence are related to lack of affection and support.

The Mexican Academy of Pediatrics A.C. has privileged among its line of work the following strategies aimed at health professionals and the general population: a) to bring all sectors involved in the phenomenon to work, b) to raise the level of knowledge on the topic, c) to facilitate education on sexual and reproductive responsibility, d) to include in the official basic table of drugs, the prescription of contraception and use of reversible long-acting contraceptives, e) to timely detect and care pregnant adolescent couples and f) to enrich their context and provide them with the instruments that would allow them, in their roles as young parents, to respond to this challenge.

In view of the above objectives and in an effort to prevent teen pregnancy, the Academy emitted the following recommendations [20]:

1. Academic and infrastructural development for the comprehensive care of adolescents.
2. Multi-sectorial professionalization in the knowledge of adolescents, their growth and development, and the diseases that affect them.
3. Permanent programs in the sectors involved in the care of adolescents.
4. Provide sexual education from early stages of development based on scientific information that will facilitate healthy behaviors from newborn to late adolescence and also to include the parents, teachers and the community through courses, workshops, fairs, congresses, plays etc.
5. The education of sexuality should not be punitive, sinful or referenced in the myths and beliefs. Sexuality should be considered healthy, pleasant, responsible and as one of the conditions to achieve happiness.
6. The education of sexuality contained in the institutional programs of sexual and reproductive health must include the men, taking into account the different masculinities of youth cultures, with perspective of equity, gender and existing roles in our culture.
7. All programs aimed at the adolescent group should be based on the promotion of life skills, among which we can highlight - in terms of sexual and reproductive health – self-esteem, assertive communication and decision-making.
8. Essential condition to facilitate human development and responsible decision-making in sexuality is the preparation of a life plan, which should include personal project; universal, cultural and family values; human rights and ecological conscience. All these are indispensable elements of the holistic model of attention to the adolescents.
9. Promote, as a right, the full exercise of sexuality through dissemination of human rights, and sexual and reproductive rights of adolescents.

10. Being consistent with the previous recommendations, one of the objectives of the entire program should be to postpone the age at which a woman has her first child, not the age of first intercourse, through abstinence as the only recourse, since this is against healthy, free and responsible exercise of sexuality.

11. The subjects of sexual education should include topics of pleasant and healthy exercise of sexuality such as human sexual response, gender identity, eroticism, etc. and not only topics of problems as abortion, sexual transmitted and coital infections, rape, etc.

12. Educate and promote contraception. Facilitate Access to and availability of information and resources. Take a long-acting reversible contraceptive as a useful recourse.

13. To have highly professionalized services for the detection and care of pregnant adolescents couples. Take care of their nutrition and integral well-being during the process.

14. Establish education and care programs for teenage parents, facilitating the understanding, learning and development of skills to exercise their responsibility to the fullest.

15. Reintegrate the pregnant and adolescent mother in the family, school, work and any other that corresponds to each case.

EXPECTATIONS AND RECOMMENDATIONS FOR CHILD ABUSE-ASSOCIATED ADOLESCENT PREGNANCY

The coincidence of these recommendations with those generated by Teen Pregnancy Prevention (TPP) Program, designed through the work of different organizations, government and public institutions, in the United States of America, since 2010; which, in a reiterated manner, establish the importance of applying at least the following actions [21-22]:

1. Professionalization of health services for the care of the adolescents. Establish institutions for the exclusive attention of the

adolescent population, involving professionals of various sectors, especially the health sector, that are competent and convinced on the importance of serving this part of the population in a special way. Professionals with sufficient experience and academic preparation that would enrich the profile of the adolescents and their families, applying the importance of a healthy upbringing, generating skills and competencies in all its members, and facilitating the strategies to confront individual and group challenges. In nutshell, professionals who are capable of providing support, necessary for the adolescents and others, to develop families with resilience and solvency of resources for everyday life.

2. Sex education from early stage of life.

   To establish early sex educational process that transmits clear, concrete and understandable knowledge in accordance with the stage of life in which it is being disseminated. Such sex education will allow the recognition of sexual coexistence as a free right, pleasant and human, and susceptible to result in unexpected pregnancy or in a sexually transmitted infection.

3. Promoting individual competencies.

4. Delay pregnancy but not sexual life.

REFERENCES

[1]   World Health Organization. *Adolescent Pregnancy*. WHO. 2018.

[2]   Stoltenborgh, M; Bakermans-Kranenburg, MJ; van Ijzendoorn, MH; Alink, LR. Cultural-geographical differences in the occurrence of child physical abuse? A meta-analysis of global prevalence. *Int J Psychol*, 2013, 48, 81-94.

[3]   Boyer, D; Fine, D. Sexual abuse as a factor in adolescent pregnancy and child maltreatment. *Fam Plann Perspect*, 1992, 24, 4-11.

[4]   Stevens, SC; Reichert, S. Sexual abuse, adolescent pregnancy and child abuse. *Arch Pediatr Adolesc Med*, 1994, 14, 23-27.

[5] Noll, JG; Sherrk, CE; Putnam, KT. Childhod sexual abuse and adolescent pregnancy: A meta-analytic update. *J Pediatr Psychol*, 2009, 34, 366-78.

[6] Loredo Abdalá, A; Vargas Campuzano, E; Casas Muñoz, A; González Corona, J; Gutiérrez Leyva, CJ. Adolescent pregnancy: its causes and repercussions in the dyad. *Rev Med Inst Mex Seguro Soc*, 2017, 55, 223-229.

[7] Jiménez González, A; Granados Cosme, JA; Rosales Flores, RA. Adolescense pregnancy in a marginalized rural community in Mexico. *Salud Pública Mex*, 2017, 59, 11-18.

[8] López, LM; Bernholc, A; Chen, M; Tolley, EE. School-based interventions for improving contraceptive use in adolescents. *Cochrane Database Syst Rev*, 2016.

[9] López, Brito. Mexico, primer lugar en embarazos en adolescentes. *Mensaje Politico*. [Mexico: first place in teenagers' pregnant. Mensaje Politico] 2017.

[10] Mmari, K; Sabherwal, S. A review of risk and protective factors for adolescent sexual and reproductive health in developing countries: an update. *J Adolesc Health*, 2013, 53, 5652-72.

[11] Secretaria de Salud, Estrategia Nacional para la Prevención del Embarazo en Adolescentes, *SALUD*. 2017. [Health secretary. National Strategy for the Prevention of Teenage Pregnancy] 2017.

[12] Instituto Nacional de las Mujeres, Estrategia Nacional para la Prevención del Embarazo en Adolescentes. *SALUD*. 2017. [National Institute of Women, National Strategy for the Prevention of Pregnancy in Adolescents] SALUD, 2017.

[13] Estrada, F; Campero, L; Suárez López, L; Vara-Salazar, E; González-Chávez, G. Knowledge about pregnancy risk and self-efficacy in adolescent males: parental support and school factors. *Salud Publica Mex*, 2017, 59, 556-65.

[14] McCracken, KA; Loveless, M. Teen pregnancy: an update. *Curr Opin Obstet Gynecol*, 2014, 26, 355-9.

[15] Stern, C. El embarazo en la adolescencia como problema público: una visión crítica. [Adolescent pregnancy as a public problem: A critical visión] *Salud Pública de Mexico*, 1997, 39, 137-143.

[16] Menkes, C; Suárez, L. Sexualidad y embarazo adolescente en Mexico. [Sexuality and teen pregnancy in Mexico] *Papeles de Población* No. 35 2003, CIEAP/UAEM. Universidad Nacional Autónoma de Mexico/Instituto de Salud Pública de Mexico.

[17] Sámano, R; Martínez Rojano, H; Robichaux, D; Rodríguez Ventura, AL; Sánchez Jiménez, B; de la Luz Hoyuela, M; Godínez, E;Segovia, S. Family context and individual situation of teens before, during and after pregnancy in Mexico City. *BMC Pregnancy Childbirth*, 2017, 17, 382.

[18] Aslam, RW; Hendry, M; Stand, A; Carter, B; Charles, JM; Craine, N; et al. Intervention now to eliminate repeat unintended pregnancy in teenagers (INTERUPT): A systematic review of intervention effectiveness and cost-effectiveness, and qualitative and realist synthesis of implementation factors and user engagement. *BMC Med*, 2017, 15,155.

[19] Charles, JM; Rycroft-Malone, J; Aslam, R; Hendry, M; Pasterfield, D; Whitaker, R. Reducing repeat pregnancies in adolescence: applying realist principles as part of a mixed-methods systematic review to explore what Works, for whom, how and under what circumstances. *BMC Pregnancy Childbirth*, 2016, 16, 271.

[20] Eréndira, Sequeiros; Fernández, Paredes; Mendoza, Rojas. Embarazo en adolescentes: problema de salud persistente. [Pregnancy in adolescents: persistent health problem] *Acad Num*, 2. 2016].

[21] Kagawa, RMC; Deardorff, J; García, GA; Knauer, HA; Schnaas, L; Neufedl, LM; Fernald, LCH. Effects of a parenting program among women who began childbearing as adolescents and young adults. *J Adolesc Health*, 2017, 61, 634-41.

[22] Dorrell, LD. A future at risk: children having children. Adolescent parenting; Adolescent pregnancy. *Cognitive Development Clearing House* 1994, 67, 224-7.

In: Child Abuse: Harm and Solutions   ISBN: 978-1-53614-271-6
Editors: Arturo Loredo Abdalá et al. © 2018 Nova Science Publishers, Inc.

Chapter 9

CHILD ABUSE: NUTRITIONAL ASSOCIATION IN CHILDREN AND ADOLESCENTS

Verónica Martín Martín[1,], Marcelino Esparza Aguilar[2]
and Arturo Loredo Abdalá[3]*
[1]Subdirección de Investigación Médica,
Instituto Nacional de Pediatría (INP)
[2]Departamento de Investigación en Epidemiología, INP
[3]Centro de Estudios Avanzados sobre Maltrato Infantil-Prevención del
Instituto Nacional de Pediatría (CEAMI-P-INP),
Ciudad de Mexico, Mexico

ABSTRACT

Child abuse (CA) in any of its modalities – physical abuse (PA), child sexual abuse (SA), psychological/emotional abuse (PsA/EA) and negligence (NE) – can have immediate and lifelong negative repercussions on the physical and mental health of the child or adolescent. CA is a factor that strongly contributes in the development of malnutrition (MN) which can be expressed like undernutrition (UNT),

* Corresponding Author Email: veromar27@yahoo.com.

stunting, overweight and obesity. The presence of any of the aforementioned manifestations may be the physical expression of any of the forms of CA. In this chapter we will review the relationship between childhood abuse and eating disorder, as well as the impact on adulthood.

Keywords: eating disorders, malnutrition, overweight, obesity, stunting, undernutrition

INTRODUCTION

Child abuse (CA) in all its categories – physical abuse (PA), child sexual abuse (SA), psychological/emotional abuse (PsA/EA) and negligence (NE) – can have immediate and lifelong negative effects on the physical and mental health of children and adolescents [1, 2]. Such repercussions are of variable degree and severity and the consequences can involve other areas that are not necessarily the characteristics of a particular form of CA.

Child abuse is a factor that contributes to malnutrition (MN), i.e., undernutrition (UNT), overweight and obesity (OO) and stunting (S) and for that, all CA forms involve a complex interaction of medical and psycho-social factors [1, 2]. In the presence of *MN* evidence, CA can be present in any of the four forms (PA, SA, PsA/EA or NE) either individually or combined [3].

EPIDEMIOLOGY

The incidence and prevalence, both of CA and MN, are variable. This is because these two epidemiological measurements of CA and MN depend much on the medical, legal and social definitions of the population studied. In addition, the socio-demographic factors of a child such as age, sex, birth condition, type of CA, its chronicity and intensity, as well as the "uses and customs" of the population influence in these definitions. Given these many variables in the epidemiological studies that analyze and estimate

CA and MN, it is necessary that physicians or professionals who attend a possible victim of CA individualize each case and personalize their attention.

ETIOPATHOGENESIS

Malnutrition (MN) in children or adolescents who are victims of aggression can be a manifestation within the wide range of clinical expressions of CA. Among the causes of MN are the failure to provide a diet that meets the nutritional, emotional and social needs of a child; and the psychological repercussions that alter his/her eating behavior, thereby affecting his/her growth and development.

The history of CA in a child and the emotional consequence (such as feeling of guilt, low self-esteem, anxiety and depression), as well as the habitual barrier in talking about CA experience, particularly SA, influence in the development of Disordered Eating Behaviors (DEB) and of Eating Disorders (ED), a situation which can lead to any of the forms of MN such as undernutrition, including stunting, overweight or obesity [4, 5].

UNDERNUTRITION

Among the characteristics of undernutrition (UNT) is the loss of fat and lean tissue that is manifested by wasting, which represents acute undernutrition that in its moderate to severe degree confers greater risk of morbidity and death. A clinical finding of undernutrition which has been traditionally related to CA is failure to thrive commonly determined by less increase in weight, height or both in children less than 3 years of age. This stage of life is marked by accelerated growth and development, hence any act of negligence or harm can affect the nutritional status, giving rise to non-organic or psychosocial types of FTT [6].

Worldwide report on the prevalence of wasting in children under 5 years is 8.0%. In high-income countries, it is 1.7% and in Latin America, 1.4% [7]. In Mexico, the prevalence of this clinical expression has been reported in 1.6% [8]. In the United States, the prevalence of FTT due to medical or psychosocial cause is between 5 – 10%. In most of the cases (90%), no underlying medical cause can be found [9, 10].

In a study carried out by the Integral Care of the Abused Child Clinic of National Institute of Pediatrics (Spanish acronym CAINM-INP), Mexico City on 84 children under 12 years of age who were victims of physical abuse (PA), one in five (18%) presented moderate or severe wasting [4]. In children who are victims of factitious disorder imposed on another (formerly Munchaussen syndrome by proxy), it has been described that anorexia or FTT are falsified or induced in up to 25% of them [11].

It has been shown that the difficulties in the interaction mother or caregive-child have relation with UNT. In a comparative study of two groups of children in the first three years of life, consisting of a group with normal development (n = 211) and the other with diagnosis of feeding disorder and FTT (n = 122), dysfunctional patterns were identified in the mother-child interaction during feeding in later group. The mothers in this group were found to be in a state of anxiety, depression and hostility while the children showed anxiety/depression, somatic complaints and aggressive behavior [12].

In a longitudinal study conducted by Cravioto et al. it was found that children from mothers with lesser scores in verbal communication and in expression of affection towards their child significantly presented higher frequency of severe undernutrition [13]. In addition to this, the physical appearance of a child, the cry, anorexia or the voracity to eat can cause tension in the parents or caregiver and this propitiates PA. Ramos Galvan in a study of undernourished children pointed out that 77% of the mothers were "violent and irascible" and that 52% showed evident dysthymia [14]. Some reports mentioned undernutrition as a characteristic mainly of abandonment [15].

STUNTING

The most frequent cause of stunting (S) for a given age is the accumulated negative effects of undernutrition over time. Stunting for a given age is an indicator of chronic undernutrition [16].

The prevalence of stunting in children under 5 years of age is estimated in 25.7%, comprising of 13.4% in Latin America and 7.2% in high income countries [7]. In Mexico, it is reported in 13.6% [8].

Association between Stunting and CA

In a cross-sectional study of 84 girls and boys under 12 years of age who had suffered PA, it was found that one third of them (31%) had stunting. In girls under 5 years of age, the frequency was 48% [4]. With respect to stunting, both normal growth and development can be impeded by repercussions of negligence due to the prolonged periods of lack of attention and care, which in turn lead to nutritional deficiencies [17, 18].

Regarding the participating mechanisms that affect growth, alterations in the axis of growth hormone, thyroid stimulating hormone (TSH) and in the hypothalamus-pituitary-adrenal axis have been proposed since the decade of sixties of the last century [19]. Powell et al. studied the pituitary and suprarenal reserves of a group of 10 patients who were victims of affective deprivation and observed that 6 of them had decreased secretion of growth hormone and corticotropin. The levels of these hormones were corrected when the abuse suffered by these people disappeared [20]. Loredo Abdala et al. studied the basal concentration of growth, thyroid and cortisol hormones in plasma of 16 patients who were victims of PA in the acute phase of the aggression. In the initial evaluation, these hormones were elevated and after 15 days of hospitalization, they became normalized [21]. These results contrast with those of Powell Blizzard et al. [22] who reported that in the absence of undernutrition in children older than 3 years of age, the concentrations of growth hormone were low but not so in undernourished children less than this age where the levels of growth hormone were normal.

Skuse et al. [23] studied the body mass index (BMI) and family stress in children with stunting and reported low levels of growth hormone and the association of hyperphagia and polydipsia. When the stressful conditions in the family subsided, growth hormone levels returned to normal. Patton et al. [24] also supported the notion that depressed states can affect the functions of cerebral cortex and hypothalamus, and that due to the connections with the pituitary gland, the release of growth hormone is modified. Again the theory holds that by improving the living conditions within the family nucleus and those of the abused child, the levels of the above mentioned hormones became normal and this circumvents the alterations in the physical growth of the victims.

OVERWEIGHT AND OBESITY

Obesity is a complex and multifactorial disease, characterized by excess body fat, and which is associated with increased risk of chronic degenerative diseases and death.

The worldwide prevalence of overweight/obesity (OO) in children and adolescents under 20 years of age is 23.8% in boys and 22.6% in girls. In underdeveloped countries, the prevalence is 13.4% in girls and 12.9% in boys [25]. The interesting thing about this information is that CA may be contributing in the development of this medical-social condition.

Association between Overweight/Obesity and CA

Presently, the manifestation of malnutrition (MN) described to be more related to CA is OO (especially on the cases of severe CA) and SA. Nevertheless, most of the studies indicate that this effect is found in adulthood. A recent meta-analysis revealed that CA was associated with an increased risk of developing obesity during the course of life however, the association was not significant in children and adolescents [26]. Among the investigations that have shown relations of OO in children under 18 years of age is a study conducted in adolescent girls, aged between 12 and 17 years, who were admitted in a psychiatric hospital due to adverse childhood experiences. The study revealed that girls who were sexually abused had a risk of suffering obesity two times higher than those without this aggression [27].

In a cohort study of women who were followed up until 22 and 29 years of age, it was found that those with a history of severe PA before 11 years of age had weight gain of 740 g/m² in adulthood and those who suffered severe EA had an increase in weight of 850 g/m². When this involved two forms of CA, including SA, the increase in weight was 1 kg/m² [28]. Likewise, another cohort study showed that girls and adolescents who suffered from severe SA and PA had greater risk of presenting obesity and central adiposity in adulthood [29].

A meta-analysis of 22 cohort studies found a relationship in the four forms of CA (PA, SA, NE and PsA) with obesity in adulthood, concluding that when CA was severe, the association with obesity was stronger [30]. In another meta-analysis of observational studies conducted in seven different countries, higher risk of obesity in adulthood was found when there were histories of CA in general and for each specific type (PsA, SA, PA). This association showed dose-response effect with the severity of CA [31].

In a prospective cohort study, peer abuse, aged 7-11 years, had a positive association with obesity in women and central adiposity in men and women in the fifth decade of life [32].

The possible mechanisms to explain the different associations between CA and obesity come from some psycodynamic theories, without conclusive hard evidence, but which assure that the women victims of childhood sexual abuse (CSA) develop overweight or obesity as a defense mechanism to avoid future CSA attack [33].

From the physiological point of view, it has been suggested that chronic stress or poor coping of stressful situations are associated with mild hypercortisolemia that is related with prolonged activation of sympathetic nervous system, which in turn could favor abdominal adiposity [4, 31].

EATING DISORDERS AND DISORDERED EATING BEHAVIORS

Another group of nosological entities that should be considered in the presence of MN are Eating Disorders (ED) and Disordered Eating Behaviors (DEB) that have a well-described relationship with CA.

ED, such as anorexia nervosa (AN), bulimia nervosa (BN) and Binge Eating Disorder (BED) are psychiatric conditions whose diagnoses require the identification of specific clinical criteria (compiled in the most recent revision, DMS-5).

On the other hand, DEB is characteristic behaviors of ED, but do not strictly comply with their clinical criteria, and so, can differ depending on the author that investigates, defines and denominates them. Usually, both eating problems occur in adolescence or youth [34-36].

In the English literature, in adolescents of a community, the accumulated ED prevalence in an 8-year follow-up was 13.1%, according to DSM-5 criteria. The frequencies by type of disorder were: AN 0.8%, BN 2.6%, BED 3.0%, atypical anorexia nervosa 2.8%, sub-threshold-BN 4.4%, sub-threshold-BED 3.6% and purging disorder (PD) 3.4% [37]. In a cohort of 999 women followed up between 14 and 24 years of age, the incidence of accumulated bulimic syndrome or anorexic syndrome (complying with 2 criteria of DMS-IV for AN or BN) was 7.2% [38, 39].

Association between DEB and CA

In a study of adolescents with history of adverse experiences in childhood, those who suffered SA had three times the risk of presenting extreme weight loss behavior (EWLB). In the same study, it was found that adolescents who had lived domestic violence, engaged in excessive exercises to lose weight 2.5 times more frequently [27].

A meta-analysis of 32 observational studies involving 14,169 participants, with ages between 14 and 65, showed that the history of CA was positively related with ED. SA, PA and EA were associated with BN and BED while PA was associated with AN [34]. A similar meta-analysis report that included women of different ages with a history of childhood SA, found an association between childhood SA with BN and AN in women. When there was severe childhood SA (raping), it was only related with BN [40].

In another study, the history of both childhood poly-victimization and exposure to violence as CA and peer abuse, were risks factors to present DEB in young adults between 18-24 years [41]. In Mexican adolescent girls from 15 to 19 years old, the criticism given by the parents, brothers and sisters on the weight and figure in the last 3 years is directly related to DEB, even when the criticism had the same frequency in the different groups of BMI [42].

From a psychodynamic perspective and according to Feinholz, in adolescent, the body and the food become, at the same time, depositories and means to relieve depression, anxiety, tension and aggressiveness, whether by stopping to eat or eating in excess [43].

BREAST FEEDING (BF)

The history of CA (PA, EA and especially SA) in the mothers predisposes to the cessation of breast feeding (BF) before 4 months of age [44]. BF creates a better affective bond and favors a lower risk of CA as demonstrated by a 15-year prospective study in which the occurrence of abuse by the mother, particularly negligence, increased as the duration of breast feeding decreased. The probability of negligence was 3.8 times higher in non-breastfed children than in those breast fed for 4 or more months. In the studies of meta-analysis, it was confirmed that BF is a factor that reduces the risk of overweight and obesity both in childhood and in adolescence [45-47].

In table 1, the relationship of CA with undernutrition (UN) and the problems of eating behavior can be observed.

Table 1. Relationship between types of Child Abuse and the effects on nutrition and eating behavior reported in the literature

History of/Cause	Effect/Consequence
Physical abuse	Wasting and stunting in under 5 years old.
Psychological abuse	Disordered Eating Behavior (DEB) in women from 15 to 19 years old.
Sexual abuse	Obesity in girls from 12 to 17 years old
Severe sexual abuse	Anorexia nervosa and bulimia nervosa in any age group
Severe sexual and physical abuses	Obesity and central adiposity in adults
Sexual, physical and emotional abuses	Bulimia Nervosa and Binge Eating Disorder in individuals from 14 to 65 years old
Physical, emotional and sexual abuses during childhood	Cessation of breastfeeding before the child is 4 months old
Severe physical, emotional and sexual abuses between 9 and 14 years old	Greater weight gain from 22 to 24 years
Physical, sexual and psychological abuses, negligence and severe child abuse	Obesity in adult age
Psychological, sexual, and physical abuses and severe child abuse	Obesity in adults
Factitious disorder imposed on another (formerly-known as Munchaunsen syndrome by proxy)	Failure to thrive in children under 3 years old.
Peer abuse	Obesity and central adiposity in men and women at 45 years of age
Peer abuse and violence	Disordered eating symptoms (DES) in people from 18 to 24 years old
Domestic violence	Extreme weight loss behavior (EWLB) in girls from 12 to 17 years old
Intimate partner violence	Low birth weight and premature newborn
Maternal breastfeeding longer than 4 months	Lesser risk of negligence from 0 to 15 years of age

CLINICAL APPROACH

In the face of a girl, boy or an adolescent with clinical manifestation of malnutrition (MN) which is suspected by the physicians or other professionals attending or interacting with the child as being or has been caused by CA, then it is obligatory to carry out a comprehensive diagnosis of the problem. In general terms, within the medical-nutritional factors, it is necessary to identify if there is any growth and development alterations; incomplete, unbalanced or inadequate diet for his/her growth stage and health conditions; and if there is altered feeding behavior disorder as well as if there is any sickness that is the cause of or contributes to the MN.

ANAMNESIS

To this end, the clinical assessment implies the knowledge of the child's eating situation, even before birth, specify the habitual diet of the child by dietary recall and by the food frequency, the dietary habits and schedules of the child and of his/her family, with whom does the child eats, his/her eating behavior as well as physical activity and sleeping habits, and the perinatal and first year of life histories.

It is essential to specify the socio-demographic variables such as family income; educational level and age of the parents; the type of family; the number of family members; the house space availability for the people living in it; detection of psychosocial risk factors (poverty, food insecurity, overcrowding, ignorance in child upbringing); any disease in the mother or any member of the family (depression or anxiety in the mother; and the abuse of licit and illicit substances or domestic violence).

Physical Examination

It is also essential to carry out a complete anthropometric evaluation (weight, stature, cephalic perimeter and body mass index compared with specific percentile curves as the World Health Organization (WHO), Centers for Disease Control and Prevention (CDC) or those corresponding to specific cases e.g., premature, Down syndrome, Turner or Prader Willi syndrome. Likewise, it is very important to correlate the child's somatometry with that of the parents.

LABORATORY

Where necessary or possible, laboratory and/or imaging studies should be performed. There are biochemical indicators of nutritional deficiency such as hemoglobin, hematocrit, vitamin D, iron and zinc that have been associated with CA suspect [48].

DIFFERENTIAL DIAGNOSIS

These evaluations will facilitate to establish if there is MN either by the clinical, anthropometrical, biochemical or cabinet manifestations and will directly reveal the nutritional information of the child. The multidisciplinary care team, ideally integrated by medical (pediatrics or general physicians), nutritional, social work, psychological and nursing areas, have to identify the medical, socioeconomic or psycho-social causes in the CA associated MN or the association of poverty, ignorance or customs and habits.

PREVENTION OF MN IN CA CASES

Once the diagnosis of CA is established, a multidisciplinary strategy must be developed to avoid the replication of the damage. From a nutritional perspective, any risk in this area must be prevented or any alteration already established must be corrected. The parents or caregivers are responsible of "What, When and How" to provide food and the children decide how much they eat. Breastfeeding should be favored and promoted. It is necessary to establish sleep schedules in a calm environment, promote physical activity through games and sports, and fix a specific and constant participation in the house chores according to the age, growth stage, and physical and intellectual capacity [49].

Finally, communication with the multidisciplinary team must be in place to strengthen the actions of each team member for the child and the family and to ensure that the actions have a positive effect.

REFERENCES

[1]   Gilbert, R, Widom, CS, Browne, K, Fergusson, D, Webb, E, Janson, S. Burden and consequences of child maltreatment in high-income countries. *Lancet* 2009; 373:68-81.

[2]   Harper, NS. Neglect: failure to thrive and obesity. *Pediatr. Clin. North Am.* 2014; 61:937-597.

[3]   Finkelhor, D, Turner, HA, Shattuck, A, Hamby, SL. Violence, crime, and abuse exposure in a national sample of children and youth. *JAMA Pediatr.* 2013; 167:614-21.

[4]   Martín-Martín, V, Loredo-Abdalá, A. Nutritional status in children victims of physical and sexual abuse. *Rev. Invest. Clin.* 2010; 62:524-31.

[5]   Rosen, DS. American Academy of Pediatrics Committee on Adolescence. Identification and management of eating disorders in children and adolescents. *Pediatrics* 2010; 126:1240-53.

[6]   Goh, LH, How, CH, Ng, KH. Failure to thrive in babies and toddlers. *Singapore Med. J.* 2016; 57:287 91.

[7]   Black, RE, Victora, CG, Walker, SP, Bhutta, ZA, Christian, P, de Onis, M, Ezzati, M, Grantham-McGregor, S, Katz, J, Martorell, R, Uauy, R; Maternal and Child Nutrition Study Group. Maternal and Child Nutrition 1 Maternal and child undernutrition and overweight in low-income and middle-income countries. *Lancet* 2013; 382:427-51.

[8]   Gutiérrez, JP, Rivera-Dommarco, J, Shamah-Levy, T, Villalpando-Hernández, S, Franco, A, Cuevas-Nasu, L, Romero-Martínez, M, Hernández-Ávila, M. *National survey of health and nutrition 2012. Cuernavaca*, Mexico: National Institute of Public Health (MX), 2012.

[9]   Rabago, J, Marra, K, Allmendinger, N, Shur, N. The clinical geneticist and the evaluation of failure to thrive versus failure to feed. *Am. J. Med. Genet .C. Semin. Med. Genet.* 2015; 169:337-48.

[10]   Homan, GJ. Failure to Thrive: A Practical Guide. *American Family Physician.* 2016; 94:295-299.

[11]   Mash, C, Frazier, T, Nowacki, A, Worley, S, Goldfarb, J. Development of a risk-stratification tool for medical child abuse in failure to thrive. *Pediatrics* 2011; 128:1467-73.

[12]   Ammanti, M, Ambruzzi, AM, Lucarelli, L, Cimino, S, D′Olimpio, F. Malnutrition and dysfunctional mother-child feeding interactions: clinical and research implications. *J. Am. Coll. Nutr.* 2004; 23:259-71.

[13]   Scrimshaw, NS. *Nutrition and Agricultural Development.* New York: Springer; c1976. Chapter 3, Microenvironmental Factors in Severe Protein-Calorie Malnutrition; p. 25-35.

[14]   Ramos Galván, R. Malnutrition, a component of the social deprivation syndrome. *Gac. Med. Mex.* 1966; 96:929-45.

[15]   Stavrianos, C, Stavrianou, D, Stavrianou, I, Kafas, P. Nutritional child neglect: a review. *Internet. J. Forensic Sci.* 2008; 4:1-7.

[16]   Mehta, NM, Corkins, MR, Lyman, B, Malone, A, Goday, PS, Carney, LN, Monczka, JL, Plogsted, SW, Schwenk, WF. American

Society for Parenteral and Enteral Nutrition board of directors. Defining pediatric malnutrition: a paradigm shift toward etiology-related definitions. *J. Parenter. Enteral. Nutr.* 2013; 37:460-481.

[17] Olivan, G. Catch-up growth assessment in long-term physically neglected and emotionally abused preschool age male children. *Child Abuse Neglect.* 2003; 27:103-108.

[18] Harper, NS. Neglect: failure to thrive and obesity. *Pediatr. Clin. North Am.* 2014; 61:937-57.

[19] Johnson, DE, Gunnar, MR. IV. Growth failure in institutionalized children. *Monogr. Soc. Res. Child Dev.* 2011; 76:92-126.

[20] Powell, GE, Brasel, JA. Emotional deprivation and growth retardation simulating idiopathic hypopituitarism. *N. Engl. Med. J.* 1967; 276:1271-1278.

[21] Loredo, AA, Cornejo, BJ, Ulloa, AA. Endocrine behavior in the acute phase of aggression. *Bol. Med. Hosp. Infant. Mex.* 1989; 45: 272-276.

[22] Bizzard, RM. Plasma somatomedin activity in children with growth disturbances. In. Raiti S (ed). *Advances in human growth hormone research.* Bethesda: National Institutes of Health 1973:124.

[23] Skuse, D, Albanase, A, Stanhope, R, Gilmor, J, Voss, L. A new stress-related syndrome of growth failure and hyperfagia in children, associated with reversibility of growth hormone insufficiency. *Lancet* 1996; 348:353-358.

[24] Patton, RJ, Garner, LI. Influence de L entourage familial sur la crossanc: le syndrome de "maternal deprivation." *Ann. Endocrinol.* 1961; 22:713-716.

[25] Ng, M, Fleming, T, Robinson, M, Thomson, B, Graetz, N, Margono, C, Mullany, EC, Biryukov, S, Abbafati, C, Abera, SF, Abraham, JP, Abu-Rmeileh, NM, Achoki, T, AlBuhairan, FS, Alemu ZA, Alfonso R, Ali MK, Ali R, Guzman NA, Ammar W, Anwari P, Banerjee A, Barquera S, Basu S, Bennett DA, Bhutta Z, Blore, J, Cabral, N, Nonato, IC, Chang, JC, Chowdhury, R, Courville, KJ, Criqui, MH, Cundiff, DK, Dabhadkar, KC, Dandona, L, Davis, A, Dayama, A, Dharmaratne, SD, Ding, EL, Durrani, AM, Esteghamati, A,

Farzadfar, F, Fay, DF, Feigin, VL, Flaxman, A, Forouzanfar, MH, Goto, Λ, Green, MΛ, Gupta, R, Hafezi Nejad, N, Hankey, GJ, Harewood, HC, Havmoeller, R, Hay, S, Hernandez, L, Husseini, A, Idrisov, BT, Ikeda, N, Islami, F, Jahangir, E, Jassal, SK, Jee, SH, Jeffreys, M, Jonas, JB, Kabagambe, EK, Khalifa, SE, Kengne, AP, Khader, YS, Khang, YH, Kim, D, Kimokoti, RW, Kinge, JM, Kokubo, Y, Kosen, S, Kwan, G, Lai, T, Leinsalu, M, Li, Y, Liang, X, Liu, S, Logroscino, G, Lotufo, PA, Lu, Y, Ma, J, Mainoo, NK, Mensah, GA, Merriman, TR, Mokdad, AH, Moschandreas, J, Naghavi, M, Naheed, A, Nand, D, Narayan, KM, Nelson, EL, Neuhouser, ML, Nisar, MI, Ohkubo, T, Oti, SO, Pedroza, A, Prabhakaran, D, Roy, N, Sampson, U, Seo, H, Sepanlou, SG, Shibuya, K, Shiri, R, Shiue, I, Singh, GM, Singh, JA, Skirbekk, V, Stapelberg, NJ, Sturua, L, Sykes, BL, Tobias, M, Tran, BX, Trasande, L, Toyoshima, H, van de Vijver, S, Vasankari, TJ, Veerman, JL, Velasquz-Melendez, G, Vlassov, VV, Vollset, SE, Vos, T, Wang, C, Wang, X, Weiderpass, E, Werdecker, A, Wright, JL, Yang, YC, Yatsuya, H, Yoon, J, Yoon, SJ, Zhao, Y, Zhou, M, Zhu, S, Lopez, AD, Murray, CJ, Gakidou, E. Global, regional, and national prevalence of overweight and obesity in children and adults during 1980-2013: a systematic analysis for the Global Burden of Disease Study 2013. *Lancet* 2014; 384:766-81.

[26] Danese, A1, Tan, M. Childhood maltreatment and obesity: systematic review and meta-analysis. *Mol. Psychiatry* 2014; 19:544-54.

[27] Isohookana, R, Marttunen, M, Hakko, H, Riipinen, P, Riala, K. The impact of adverse childhood experiences on obesity and unhealthy weight control behaviors among adolescents. *Compr. Psychiatry* 2016; 71:17-24.

[28] Mason, SM, MacLehose, RF, Katz-Wise, SL, Austin, SB, Neumark-Sztainer, D, Harlow, BL, Rich-Edwards, JW. Childhood abuse victimization, stress-related eating, and weight status in young women. *Ann. Epidemiol.* 2015; 25:760-66.

[29] Boynton-Jarrett, R, Rosenberg, L, Palmer, JR, Boggs, DA, Wise, LA. Child and adolescent abuse in relation to obesity in adulthood: the Black Women's Health Study. *Pediatrics* 2012; 130:245-53.

[30] Wang, Y, Wu, B, Yang, H, Song, X. The effect of childhood abuse on the risk of adult obesity. *Ann. Clin. Psychiatr.* 2015; 27:175-84.

[31] Hemmingsson, E, Johansson, K, Reynisdottir, S. Effects of childhood abuse on adult obesity: a systematic review and meta-analysis. *Obes. Rev.* 2014; 15:882-93.

[32] Takizawa, R, Danese, A, Maughan, B, Arseneault, L. Bullying victimization in childhood predicts inflammation and obesity at mid-life: a five-decade birth cohort study. *Psychol. Med.* 2015; 45:2705-11

[33] Felitti, VJ. Childhood sexual abuse, depression and family dysfunction in adult obese patients: a case control study. *South Med. J.* 1993; 86:732-6.

[34] Caslini, M, Bartoli, F, Crocamo, C, Dakanalis, A, Clerici, M, Carrà, G. Disentangling the association between child abuse and eating disorders: a systematic review and meta-analysis. *Psychosom. Med.* 2016; 78:79-90.

[35] Stice, EL, Marti, CN, Spoor, S, Presnell, K, Shaw, H. Dissonance and healthy weight eating disorder prevention programs: long-term effects from a randomized efficacy trial. *J. Consult. Clin. Psychol.* 2008; 76:329-40.

[36] American Psychiatric Association. *Diagnostic and statistical manual of mental disorders. 5th Ed.* Washington (DC): American Psychiatric Publishing; 2013. 991 p.

[37] Stice, E, Marti, CN, Rohde, P. Prevalence, incidence, impairment, and course of the proposed dsm-5 eating disorder diagnoses in an 8-year prospective community study of young women. *J. Abnorm. Psychol.* 2013; 122:445-457.

[38] American Psychiatric Association. *Diagnostic and Statistical Manual of Mental Disorders: DSM-IV.* Arlington, VA: American Psychiatric Publishing; 1994.

[39] Sanci, L, Coffey, C, Olsson, C, Reid, S, Carlin, JB, Patton, G. Childhood sexual abuse and eating disorders in females: findings from the Victorian Adolescent Health Cohort Study. *Arch. Pediatr. Adolesc. Med.* 2008; 162:261-7.

[40] Chen, LP, Murad, MH, Paras, ML, Colbenson, KM, Sattler, AL, Goranson, EN, Elamin, MB, Seime, RJ, Shinozaki, G, Prokop, LJ, Zirakzadeh, A. Sexual abuse and lifetime diagnosis of psychiatric disorders: systematic review and meta-analysis. *Mayo Clin. Proc.* 2010; 85:618-29.

[41] Hassellea, AJ, Howella, KH, Dormoisa, M, Miller-Graff, LE. The influence of childhood polyvictimization on disordered eating symptoms in emerging adulthood. *Child Abuse Neglect.* 2017; 68:55-64.

[42] Unikel-Santocini, C, Martín-Martín, V, Juárez-García, F, González-Forteza, C, Nuño-Gutiérrez, B. Disordered eating behavior and body weight and shape relatives' criticism in overweight and obese 15 to 19-year old females. *J. Health Psychol.* 2013; 18:75-85.

[43] Feinholz, D. Adolescence. *Cuad. Nutr.* 1997; 20:59.

[44] Sørbø, MF, Lukasse, M, Brantsæter, AL, Grimstad, H. Past and recent abuse is associated with early cessation of breast feeding: results from a large prospective cohort in Norway. *BMJ Open* 2015; 5:e009240.

[45] Strathearn, L, Mamun, AA, Najman, JM, O'Callaghan, MJ. Does breastfeeding protect against substantiated child abuse and neglect? A 15-year cohort study. *Pediatrics* 2009; 123:483-93.

[46] Aguilar Cordero, MJ, Sánchez López, AM, Madrid Baños, N, Mur Villar, N, Expósito Ruiz, M, Hermoso Rodríguez, E. Breastfeeding for the prevention of overweight and obesity in children and teenagers; systematic review. *Nutr. Hosp.* 2014; 31:606-20.

[47] Jing, Yan, Lin, Liu, Yun, Zhu, Guowei, Huang, Peizhong, Peter Wang. The association between breastfeeding and childhood obesity: a meta-analysis. *BMC Public Health* 2014; 14:1267.

[48] Harper, E, Ekvall, S, Ekvall, V, Pan, W. Chapter 16. The Nutritional Status of Children with Suspected Abuse. In: Atroshi F, editor. Pharmacology and Nutritional Intervention in the Treatment of Disease. London: *Intec*; c2014. p. 327-336.

[49] Satter, EM. *Child of mine. Feeding with love and good sense.* Palo Alto. Bull. Publishing Co, 1986.

In: Child Abuse: Harm and Solutions   ISBN: 978-1-53614-271-6
Editors: Arturo Loredo Abdalá et al. © 2018 Nova Science Publishers, Inc.

Chapter 10

NEGLIGENCE: A SERIOUS VARIETY OF CHILD ABUSE

Arturo Loredo Abdalá, Mónica Rodríguez González and Abigail Casas Muñoz[1]*

Clínica de Atención al Niño Maltratado del Instituto Nacional
de Pediatría, Col Cuicuilco, Ciudad de Mexico,
(CAINM INP-UNAM), Mexico

ABSTRACT

Negligence is recognized as the most frequent form of Child Abuse (CA), but because of its clinical and social complexity, it is the CA most difficult to establish an accurate diagnosis, integral care and registration. It is defined as: the failure of a relative or a caregiver of a child to cover his needs for food, clothing, protection, medical care or to supervise his health, education, safety and to protect him from everyday dangers.

The basic expression of this form of CA is intentional action of the primary caregiver aimed at not covering in an adequate way the victim of fundamental biopsychosocial needs. The affectations of negligence can be social, emotional and economic. The effect on cognitive function can

---
* Corresponding Author Email: cainm_inp@hotmail.com.

range from variable degree of neurodevelopmental delay to an affectation of variable degree in school or academic performance. The emotional involvement occurs approximately 80% of them, some mental health affectations such as anxiety and depression. It is clear that CA requires the implementation of a series of preventive strategies of moral, family, social and governmental nature, whose orientation will depend on the specific form in question. This chapter tells us about the psychological, emotional and physical damage caused in children by parents' lack of attention.

Keywords: Medical negligence, negligence, negligence in supervision, parents' lack of attention

INTRODUCTION

In the last 2 – 3 decades, child abuse (CA) has been accepted worldwide as a serious pathology. Such acceptance is due mainly to the consequence of its presence in almost all the countries of the world, the magnitude of the physical and emotional injuries suffered by the victim and the social and economic impacts on the family and the community [1, 2]. Despite its morbidity and mortality, there is a sub-registry of the cases because they are not correctly diagnosed and/or because the situations leading to no acceptance of this pathology, in all its magnitude, are not denounced [3-5].

FREQUENCY

It is very difficult to specify the frequency of CA due to the variability and complexity of the problem. In some industrialized countries, it is probably possible to know the prevalence of some CA modalities, but in most developing societies, CA knowledge is very precarious. In the USA, as a representative of the first world countries, a case of CA is reported every ten seconds and at least four deaths per days a result of some kind of abuse are registered [6]. And despite this, it is estimated that only 50% of the cases are officially recognized [7]. In England, a global frequency of 1.5% is reported, while in Canada, 2.15% is reported and in Australia, 3.34% [3].

In Mexico, the figures are little reliable, although it is likely that 1 in every 10 children is a victim of child abuse and only 1 in every 100 cases is attended [8].

However, due to the clinical and social studies carried out in this pathology and its legal consequences, CA has been depicted as a medical, social and legal problem [9-12].

BASIC CONCEPTS

It must be understood that CA is a very complex problem because it is laden with biological-social and legal involvements on the part of the victim and his family and these result in the victim's attention being very complicated [3, 13-14].

On the other hand, this pathology is often not managed under an international nomenclature. For this, the International Classification of Disease (ICD-10) must be used [15].

Based on this, the pathology is classified and registered as Child Abuse (CA) and its four major forms are: physical abuse, sexual abuse, psychological abuse and negligence.

NEGLIGENCE

Negligence (Ng) is recognized as the most frequent form of CA, but because of its clinical and social complexity, it is the CA most difficult to establish an accurate diagnosis, integral care and registration [16]. The world organizations (The United Nation Organization, through the World Health Organization), defined Ng in a similar way. It is considered as a multidimensional problem that requires multifaceted and urgent management [17]. Likewise, it is accepted that Ng has the same weight of impact in the physical and emotional health of the victim as serious as that observed in other forms of CA [18-19].

The Pan Americana Health Organization defined Ng as "deprivation of basic needs that would guarantee a child a normal biopsycho-affective development when there is an evident possibility to provide food, education, health or care" [20].

In the United State of America, American Samoa, Puerto Rico and the Virgin Islands; Ng is defined as: the failure of a relative or a caregiver of a child to cover his needs for food, clothing, protection, medical care or to supervise his health, education, safety and to protect him from everyday dangers [21].

The Colombian association called "Afecto" used the definition of Polansky which defined Ng as "a condition in which a caregiver responsible for a child, deliberately or by extraordinary negligence, allows the child to experience avoidable suffering and/or fails to provide one or more ingredients generally considered as essential, for the adequate physical, intellectual and emotional development of the people" [22-23]. The Medical College of Peru declared as Ng "… an abuse by omission, in which safeguarding the health, safety and welfare of a child is forsaken. Its extreme expression is abandonment and this can be physical, medical, emotional, affective and/or educational" [24].

In Mexico, the National Human Rights Commission consider that Ng is "… the repeated failure to provide a child with the minimum standard food, clothing, medical attention, safety and to satisfy his physical and emotional needs".

From a legal perspective, Ng has been defined as "…an illicit act characterized by the omission in the care, protection and help to the people of younger age which by its nature constitutes a crime" [25-27]. When a child or an adolescent is a victim of a crime, the provisions of the General Law of Victims and others should be applied [28]. Likewise, within the Integral Model of Attention to Victims, an involvement of other institutions are required in order to implement a close surveillance of Ng cases in a framework of multidisciplinary attention [29].

NEGLIGENCE ATTITUDE

Negligence can also be manifested when the parents or guardians of a child portray passive attitude and permit that other people act violently against the child in their custody. Similarly, overprotection and absence of promoting behavioral norms in the children should also be considered as Ng.

Faced with this reality, it is indispensable to emphasize and disseminate the basic clinical and social aspects of Ng, its differential diagnosis with abandonment, laziness, social negligence, etc. as well as the legal problem which this form of CA implies. In this way, professionals that attend and/or interact with children or adolescents can more easily establish a diagnostic suspicion, and later make a precise diagnosis, develop an integral attention and finally establish the pertinent record for the case.

Table 1 shows the basic characteristics of four conditions that must necessarily be a cause for differential diagnosis.

Table 1. definitions of the main differential diagnosis of Negligence

Terms	Definition
Social Negligence:	Term proposed and used by the authors to express lack of care or attention to a child as a result of poverty.
Abandonment:	To leave a child or an adolescent alone in the house when going away without providing a care to him/her or being worried of what may happen.
Dissertation:	Utterly forsake or desert a child or an adolescent without a shelter or anything to cover his/her need. To leave someone without any protection.
Slovenliness or laziness:	Lack of effort or care to perform a task. It is the desire to abandon what one has.

Mexican Academy of Language. Spanish Dictionary.

CLASSIFICATION

To detect cases of this form of CA, it is essential that health personnel (medical doctors, nurses, social workers, psychologists and nutritionists), teachers and caregivers or relatives who are in contact with people in this age group know that this problem can be suspected only when we bear in mind that Ng is the least clear of all CA forms and is often immersed in the other forms of CA and could occur in all socioeconomic, cultural, religious and/or educational levels [30-32].

The basic expression of this form of CA is intentional action of the primary caregiver aimed at not covering in an adequate way the victim´s fundamental biopsychosocial needs [20, 33]. The affectations of Ng can be classified into five sub-groups and each sub-group into sub-categories as follows:

- – Negligence in the care of the child
- – Environmental negligence
- – Medical negligence
- – Educational negligence
- – Negligence in supervision

Negligence in the Care

a. It is the failure to provide a child with the necessary food that will permit him to cover his or her needs and nutritional requirements or that such provision is abjectly of very poor quality. The clinical expression could be low weight and height for his/her age, overweight or obesity and anemia.

b. Failure to provide adequate personal hygiene
    The expression of this may be dirty physical aspect, lack of bathing, kinky and uncombed hairs, overgrown nails and dirty

teeth. The child stinks or stenches and may have harmful wildlife like lice, nits, bedbugs, fleas, etc.

c. Failure to wear appropriate clothing

The child does not have convenient or enough clothes (dresses, pants, sweaters, jackets, shoes and uniforms) to cover the environmental vigor (cold, heat, humidity) according to the age and sex. The garments are dirty, torn and old.

Environmental Negligence

The house is not safe to protect the child from the environment hazards (cold, heat, humidity). It does not have the necessary hygiene and required space. It is unsafe and does not have the required fences, windows, doors or bars.

Medical Negligence

Medical surveillance of the child either healthy or sick is not adequate and sufficient. The immunization program is not complete.

There is no adequate supervision of the growth as well as adequate protection against accidents, and during sickness and recovery, an adequate care is lacking.

Educational Negligence

The child does not go to school or college according to the age and sex. Frequently, the school assistance is inconsistent and most of the time arrives late.

The learning at school and homework completion are not checked and monitored. The school uniform or clothes are dirty, torn or old or the school uniform may be missing.

Negligence in Supervision

There is negligence in the supervision of the daily activities of the child at home. The child can stay alone or be under the supervision of an older brother or sister (children-parents). The physical and emotional stimulation for gross and fine motor as well as social adaptive and language developments are lacking. The child has no adequate bond or attachment with the mother and the father.

All these alterations will give rise to the manifestations of physical damage; deterioration of physical aspect; detriment of clothing, emotional expression, school performance and social behavior among other alterations (Table 2).

Table 2. Clinical, social and school manifestations of Negligence

Heading	Clinical data
Physical expression	Variable degree of malnutrition, overweight or obesity, growth arrest, short stature, decreased cephalic perimeter.
Physical aspect	Failure in neatness, poor body and dental hygiene, dirty hair and long nails.
Clothing	Uncared clothes; old and ripped, usually in inadequate hygienic conditions, inappropriate for the weather, age and sex.
Emotional expression	Withdrawal, apathy, shyness, anguish, indifference to the surrounding, suicidal ideation, enuresis, encopresis.
Development	Neurodevelopmental delay, low performance at school, addiction to "licit and illicit drugs".
Pathological Backgrounds	Repeated accidents, delay in medical attention request, poor adherence to treatment.
Lack of record	Birth certificate, vaccination card, school credentials.
Comorbidity	Clinical data of other child abuse forms.

SEVERITY LEVELS

The severity of Ng has been classified into mild, moderate and severe.

Mild: It is when a child suffers a negligence which does not cause him or her any physical or emotional problem that alters his/her social life.

Moderate: There is no physical damage but it can be the direct cause for rejection at school, by the neighborhood peers, sports team, etc.

Severe: In this situation, the victim can present different physical injuries as well as delay in intellectual development. Hence, he or she requires specific attention and treatment.

Obviously, each case must be individually contextualized and in this action, the family, school and social environment must always be considered (Table 3).

DIFFERENTIAL DIAGNOSIS

In the presence of some of these manifestations, health professionals are obliged to rule out that such manifestations are not the product of fundamental consequence of some of the "social adversities" such as poverty, ignorance, inadequate educative and/or disciplinary strategies, parenting models or some pediatric conditions that can cause similar clinical picture [31-35].

The consequences of poverty and ignorance clearly indicate the presence of "social negligence" and the government and/or some people in the civil society are principally responsible for their existence. Other consequences of these two socioeconomic factors are loss of values or misunderstanding of them in the family, school, church and/or parenting profiles and models.

Finally, the existence of chronic pediatric disease, in the presence of inadequate diagnosis and/or treatment can also condition the clinical expression of demeanor, overweight, obesity or short stature as well as low self-esteem, depression and distress [36-39].

**Table 3. Acronym for initial recommended approach in a patient
with suspected child abuse**

Do not issue hasty judgment
Socioeconomic and cultural status of the patient
Generate objective evaluation
Limit value judgments
Investigate other varieties or patterns of abuse
Win the trust of the primary caregivers
Extreme search for reasons
List and name risk factors
Record the grounds of the case in writing
invite multidisciplinary team
Assist the relatives to facilitate the objective

If the possibility of an intention of not caring or inadequately caring a specific child or adolescent is established, its precise diagnosis is a priority in order to start as soon as possible a comprehensive care to the victim, an action that will prevent further physical and emotional damage [40].

Finally, in this situation, it is always necessary to consider the predominant family and environmental characteristics as well as the damage in the growth and development of the victim in the short, medium and long term.

For its prevention, the implementation of useful protective measures in this age group is required [20].

SOCIAL, EMOTIONAL AND ECONOMIC IMPACTS

A facet that has been little considered in the medical and paramedical environment is the difficulty to quantitatively establish the social, emotional and economic impacts that are generated by the care of a person who has been a victim of Ng in the family and/or in the society in general [41].

Analyzing the medico-social impacts that the children and adolescents suffered or have suffered by being victims of Ng, we have that: a) these children have 1.5 times more probability of consuming licit drugs such as alcohol or tobacco and illicit drugs in adult life, b) the risk of being pregnant at teenage or adolescent age is higher than 50% and c) the risk of committing crime is up to 25% [42-44]. The effect on cognitive function can range from variable degree of neurodevelopmental delay to an affectation of variable degree in school or academic performance [45-48].

A late effect is that in their young adulthood, approximately 80% of them can develop some mental health affectations such as anxiety, depression, behavioral disorder, aggressiveness, decreased academic performance, school absenteeism and problem with the authorities [49-52].

In order to know or specify the economic cost required for the comprehensive care of victims of CA, the estimate varies according to what was published in the first world countries or in the developing countries. Similarly, it should be taken into account the direct cost of care (mainly consult, hospitalization, surgical intervention, and laboratory and cabinet studies) and/or indirect care (medicines, food, rehabilitation, special education and long-term follow-up). There is no study that specifically indicates the cost required to attend this form of CA. Nevertheless, the published figures allow us to establish an idea of how economically high it is to care for CA victims [53-54].

PREVENTION

It is clear that CA requires the implementation of a series of preventive strategies of moral, family, social and governmental nature, whose orientation will depend on the specific form in question.

WHO promotes and insists on the development and assessment of CA prevention programs. Nevertheless, it has not been proven that any of them has a worldwide real effectiveness and this may be owed to the diversity in the clinical manifestations of CA and socio-family and cultural contexts of the people that make it impossible to equalize the populations, especially in the context of "social diversities" [56].

Based on this, it is insisted that the public health policies should include a section of orientation from a medical, psychological, epidemiological, sociological, criminological, educational and economic perspective for preventive purposes. Only with the alliance of all these disciplines could negligence and any form of CA be reduced.

CONCLUSION

Although in the last three or four decades, there has been a growing interest in the recognition of CA in any of its four forms in Mexico, it is important to accept that little progress has been made in the suspicion, diagnosis and comprehensive care of children that suffered Ng, despite the fact that this form of CA could be very frequent and that its medium and long term consequences could be catastrophic.

We insist on the need to work in the development of a dynamic and effective intervention (geared towards the reduction and prevention of all CA forms) of all the professionals who attend and interact with children, adolescents, parents and teachers, as well as all the different government instances that develop actions to prevent or reduce the "social determinants" that affect the physical and intellectual health of children and adolescents, and that violet the rights of people in this age group.

REFERENCES

[1]   Gilbert, R., Kemp, A., Thoburn, J., Sidebotham, P., Radford, L., Glaser, D., McMillan, H. Recognising and responding to child maltreatment. *Lancet*, 2009; 373:167 - 80.

[2]   Dubowitz, H., Bennet, S. Physical abuse and neglect of children. *Lancet,* 2007; 369:1891 - 1899.

[3] Gilbert, R., Spatz, W. C., Browne, K., Fergusson, D., Webb, E., Janson, S. Burden and consequences of child maltreatment in high-income countries. *Lancet,* 2009; 373:68 - 80.

[4] American Academy of Pediatrics, Committee on child abuse and neglect. Distingishing sudden infant death syndrome from child abuse fatalities. *Pediatrics,* 2001; 107:437 - 41.

[5] Loredo Abdalá, A. *Maltrato en niños y adolescentes. [Abuse in children and adolescents]* Editores de Textos Mexicanos. Mexico. 2004.

[6] U.S. Department of health and human services administration for children and families administration on children, youth and families children's Bureau. *Child maltreatment.* Washington 2011: 22;24.

[7] U.S. Department of health and human services administration for children and families administration on children, youth and families children's Bureau. *Child Maltreatment 2014.* Washington 2016: 25.

[8] Loredo-Abdalá, A., Monroy-Llaguno, D. A., Casas-Muñoz, A. El maltrato infantil: Conceptos básicos de una patología médico social legal. [Child maltreatment: Basic concepts of a legal social medical pathology] *Rev. Fac. Med. UNAM,* 2013; 56:5 - 10.

[9] Loredo Abdalá, A. Maltrato al menor: Consideraciones clínicas sobre maltrato físico, agresión sexual y deprivación emocional. [Abuse of the minor: Clinical considerations about physical abuse, sexual aggression and emotional deprivation] *Gac. Med. Méx.,* 1999; 135: 611 - 620.

[10] Loredo-Abdalá, A., Casas-Muñoz, A., Monroy-Llaguno, D. A. Maltrato infantil: características clínicas usuales. [Child abuse: usual clinical characteristics] *Rev. Fac. Med. UNAM,* 2014; 57:15 - 23.

[11] Corchado, C. H. S., Loredo-Abdalá, A., Perea-Martínez, A., Villa, R. A. El niño maltratado: obstáculos médicos - legales en el diagnóstico y asistencia integral. [The abused child: medical - legal obstacles in the diagnosis and integral assistance] *Bol. Med. Hosp. Infant Mex.,* 2004; 61:412 - 422.

[12] Loredo-Abdalá, A., Trejo-Hernández, J., Castilla-Serna, L. Children injured: abuse or accident? Diagnosis through indicators. *Bol. Med. Hosp. Infant Mex.*, 2003; 60:368 - 379.

[13] Paul, A. R., Adams, M. A. Non-accidental trauma in pediatric patients: a review of epidemiology, pathophysiology, diagnosis and treatment. *Trans. Pediatr.*, 2014; 3:195-207.

[14] Loredo-Abdalá, A., Trejo-Hernández, J., Villa-Romero, A., López-Domínguez, J. M., Sánchez-Velázquez, A., Bobadilla-Mompala, M. E. Child abuse: risk factors associated with the macro and microenvironment in a suburban zone within Mexico City. *Bol. Med. Hosp. Infant Mex.*, 2003; 60:252 - 262.

[15] Clasificación *Internacional de Enfermedades 10 (CIE-10). Organización Panamericana de la Salud/Organización Mundial. [International Classification of Diseases 10 (ICD-10)].* Pan American Health Organization/World Organization.

[16] Allin, H., Wathen, C. N., Macmillan, H. Treatment of child neglect: a systematic review. *Canad. J. Psychiatr.*, 2005; 50:497 - 504.

[17] Sedlak, A. J., Mettenburg, J., Basena, M., Petta, I., MPherson, K., Greene, A., Li, S. *Fourth National Incidence Study of child abuse and neglect (NIS-4).* Washington, DC: US Department of Health and Human Services; 2010: 10 - 27.

[18] Loredo, A., Trejo, J., García, C., Portillo, A., López, A., Alcantar, M., Mendoza, O., Hernández, A., Sauceda, J., Capistrán, A., Carballo, R., Ramos, L., Llata, M., Sotelo, M., Guicho, E., Villanueva, H., Sotelo, T., Ortiz, S. Maltrato Infantil: una acción interdisciplinaria e interinstitucional en Mexico. Consenso de la Comisión para el Estudio y la Atención Integral al Niño Maltratado. Segunda parte. [Child Maltreatment: an interdisciplinary and inter-institutional action in Mexico. Consensus of the Commission for the Study and Integral Attention to Battered Children. Second part] *Salud Mental,* 2011; 34:67 - 73.

[19] Runyan, D. K., Hunter, W. M., Socolar, R. R. Children who prosper in unfavorable environments the relationship to social capital. *Pediatrics,* 1998; 101:12 - 18.

[20] Casas Muñoz, A. Negligencia: la forma más frecuente e inadvertida del maltrato infantil. En: Loredo Abdalá A. *Maltrato Infantil: Gravedad y Prevención.* [Negligence: the most frequent and unnoticed form of child abuse. In: Loredo Abdalá, *A. Child Abuse: Gravity and Prevention*] Editores de Textos Mexicanos. Mexico 2016.

[21] Child Welfare Information Gateway. *Definitions of child abuse and neglect.*

[22] U.S. Department of health and human services administration for children and families administration on children, youth and families children's Bureau. *Child Maltreatment 2014.* Washington 2016: 25.

[23] Polansky, N. A., Gaudin, J. M., Ammons, P. W., Davis, K. B. The psychological ecology of the neglectful mother. *Child Abuse Neglect,* 1985; 9:265 - 275.

[24] Gaudin, J. M., Polansky, N. A., Kilpatrick, A. C., Shilton, P. Family functioning in neglectful families. *Child Abuse Neglect,* 1996; 20: 363 - 377.

[25] Del Águila-Escobedo, A. Violencia y estrés infantil: ¿está en juego nuestro futuro? [Violence and child stress: is our future at stake?] *Acta Med. Peru,* 2015; 32:71 - 83.

[26] *Comisión Nacional de los Derechos Humanos.* Programa Nacional de Prevención y Protección de los Niños, Niñas y Adolescentes Víctimas de Maltrato y Conductas Sexuales. Mexico, 2005. [*National Commission for Human Rights.* National Program for the Prevention and Protection of Children and Adolescents Victims of Sexual Behavior and Behavior].

[27] Perea Martínez, A., Loredo Abdalá, A., Corchado, C. H. S. Situación actual de la atención a los menores víctimas de violencia. [Current situation of attention to minors victims of violence. In: *Faces of family violence* En: *Caras de la violencia familiar*] Universidad Autónoma de la Ciudad de México. Dirección General de Equidad y Desarrollo Social. Gobierno del Distrito Federal. México. 2005.

[28] *Código Penal Federal [Federal Penal Code of Mexico]* (2009) Artículos 335 y 339.

[29] *Ley General de Víctimas. Ley publicada en la Primera Sección del Diario Oficial de la Federación.* [General Law of Victims. Law published in the First Section of the Official Gazette of the Federation] Febrero, 2013.

[30] Modelo Integral de Atención a Víctimas. Diario *Oficial de la Federación.* Junio 2015. [Integral Model of Assistance to Victims. *Official Journal of the Federation*] June 2015.

[31] Olivien, G. Évaluation du rattrapage de la croissance chez les garçons d'âge préscolaire ayant souffert pendant une longue période de négligence et de maltraitance psychologique. *Child Abuse Neglect,* 2003; 103 - 108.

[32] INEGI. *Mujeres y hombres en Mexico 2014 – 2015.* [INEGI. *Women and men in Mexico 2014 - 2015*].

[33] Perea Martínez, A., Loredo Abdalá, A., López Negrete, G. E. y Jordán, G. N. ¿Negligencia o pobreza? El sobrediagnóstico de maltrato al menor. [Negligence or poverty? The over diagnosis of child abuse] *Acta Pediatr. Mex.,* 2007; 28:193 - 197.

[34] UNICEF - CONEVAL, *Pobreza y Derechos Sociales de Niños, Niñas y Adolescentes en Mexico.* [*Poverty and Social Rights of Children and Adolescents in Mexico*] UNICEF, 2010-2012.

[35] Gutiérrez, J. P., Rivera, D. J., Shamah, L. T., Villalpando, H. S., Franco, A., Cuevas, N. L., Romero, M. M., Hernández, A. M. *Encuesta Nacional de Salud y Nutrición 2012.* [*National Survey of Health and Nutrition 2012*] Cuernavaca, Mexico: Instituto Nacional de Salud Pública (MX), 2012.

[36] *X Consejo Nacional de Evaluación de la Política de Desarrollo Social. Informe de pobreza en Mexico, 2012.* [*X National Council for the Evaluation of Social Development Policy. Poverty report in Mexico, 2012*] Mexico DF, CONEVAL, 2013.

[37] Veilleux, L. N., Pouliot-Laforte, A., Lemay, M., Moira, S., Cheung, M. S., Glorieux, F. H., Rauch, R. The functional muscle–bone unit in patients with osteogenesis imperfecta type I. *Bone,* 2015; 79:52 - 57.

[38] Prentice, A. Nutritional rickets around the world. *J. Steroid Biochem.,* 2013; 136:201 - 206.

[39] Kolker, S., Christensen, E., Leonard, J. V., Greenberg, C. R., Boneh, A. Diagnosis and management of glutaricaciduria type I – revised recommendations. *J. Inherit. Metab. Dis.,* 2011; 34:677 - 694.

[40] Rodríguez-Merchan, E. C., Jimenez Yuste, G. The role of selective angiographic embolization of the musculo-skeletal system in haemophilia. *Haemophilia,* 2009; 15:864 - 8.

[41] Ethier, L. S., Milot, T. Effet de la durée, de l'âged'exposition à la négligence parentale et de la comorbidité sur le développement socioémotionnel à l'adolescence. *Neuropsychiat. Enfan.,* 2009; 57: 136 - 145.

[42] Dahlberg, L. L., Krug, E. G. *World report on violence and health.* Geneva, Switzerland: World Health Organization 2002:1 - 56.

[43] Instituto Nacional de las Mujeres. Embarazo adolescente y madres jóvenes en Mexico: *Una visión desde el Promajoven* [National Institute of Women. *Teen pregnancy and young mothers in Mexico*] 1a Ed. Secretaría de Educación Pública. Mexico 2012; 1 - 185.

[44] Belitzky, R., Cruz, C., Marinho, E., Tenzer, S. Resultados Perinatales en Madres Jóvenes: Estudio Comparativo en Maternidades Latinoamericanas. En: *La salud del Adolescente y el joven en las Américas* [Perinatal Results in Young Mothers: Comparative Study in Latin American Maternities. In: *Adolescent health and youth in the Americas*] Washington, DC: OPS/OMS. 1985; 221 - 72.

[45] Villalobos-Hernández, A., Campero, L. D., Suárez-López, L., Atienzo, E. E., Estrada, F. E., De La Vara-Salazar, E. Embarazo adolescente y rezago educativo: análisis de una encuesta nacional en Mexico [Adolescent pregnancy and educational backwardness: analysis of a national survey in Mexico] *Salud Pública de Méx.,* 2015; 57: 135 - 143.

[46] Trickett, P. K., McBride-Chang, C. The developmental impact of different forms of Child Abuse Neglect *Dev. Rev.,* 1995; 15:311 - 337.

[47] Chapple, C. L., Vaske, J. Child neglect, social context, and educational outcomes: examining the moderating effects of school and neighborhood context. *Violence Victims,* 2010; 25:470 - 485.

[48] Eckenrode, J., Laird, M., Doris, J. School performance and disciplinary problems among abused and neglected children. *Dev. Psychol.*, 1993; 29:53 - 62.

[49] Fantuzzo, J. W., Perlman, S. M., Dobbins, E. K. Types and timing of child maltreatment and early school success: A population-based investigation. *Child Youth Serv. Rev.*, 2011; 33:1404 - 1411.

[50] Messman-Morre, T., Walsh, K., DiLillo, D. Emotion dysregulation and risk sexual behavior in revictimization. *Child Abuse Neglect,* 2010; 34:967 - 976.

[51] Lansford, J. E., Dodge, K. A., Pettit, G. S., Bates, J. E., Crozier, J., Kaplow, J. A 12-year prospective study of the long-term effects of early child physical maltreatment on psychological, behavioral, and academic problems in adolescence. *Arch. Pediatr. Adolesc. Med.,* 2002; 156:824 - 830.

[52] Romano, E., Babchishin, L., Marquis, R., Fréchette, S. Childhood maltreatment and educational outcomes. *Trauma Violence Abuse,* 2015; 16:418 - 37.

[53] Wodarski, J. S., Kurtz, P. D., Gaudin, J. M. Jr., Howing, P. T. Maltreatment and the school-age child: major academic, socioemotional, and adaptive outcomes. *Soc. Work,* 1990; 35: 506 - 13.

[54] Dereck, S. Brown, X. F. Medical costs attributable to child maltreatment: a systematic review of short-and long-term effects. *Am. J. Prev. Med.,* 2011; 41:627 - 635.

[55] Irazusta, J. E., Mcjunkin, J. M., Danadian, K., Forest, A., Zhang, J. Outcome and cost of child abuse. *Child Abuse Neglect*, 1997; 21:751- 757.

[56] Brown, D. S., Fang, X., Florence, C. S. Medical costs attributable to child maltreatment, A systematic review of short- and long-term effects. *Am. J. Prev. Med.,* 2011; 41:627 - 635.

[57] United States Government Accountability Office. Child maltreatment: strengthening national data on child fatalities could aid in prevention. *GAO90.* 2011.

In: Child Abuse: Harm and Solutions   ISBN: 978-1-53614-271-6
Editors: Arturo Loredo Abdalá et al. © 2018 Nova Science Publishers, Inc.

Chapter 11

CHILD ABUSE: PREVENTIVE STRATEGIES IN ODONTOPEDIATRIC

Hilda Ceballos Hernández,*
Luis Fernando Rodríguez Campos
and Irene Martínez Soberanis
Servicio de Estomatología. Instituto Nacional de Pediatría.
Ciudad de Mexico, Mexico

ABSTRACT

Child abuse is a universal problem that affects children of all nationalities and social status. One of the indicators of abuse in children is the oral health which could affect the mouth head and/or the neck. In children, these areas are the most affected sites in child abuse, especially physical and sexual abuse. Usually, the pediatric victims are afraid to denounce the mistreatment and most often resort to introverted or violent behavior. Therefore, it is extremely important that a complete physical examination of the patient and a psychological assessment be carried out; bearing in mind that access to medical care in these cases is not

---

* Corresponding Author Email: hilda.ceballoshdz@gmail.com.

immediate. Assaults that affect oral health can occur in all forms such as physical abuse, sexual abuse and negligence.

It is essential to bear in mind that dental damage in childhood influences adult life. Therefore, it is very important to detect the warning signs, prevent continued abuse and treat the injuries. In this chapter, we will review how child abuse impact in oral health and pinpoint the etiological instruments in odontopediatric child abuse, its local and global incidence as well as the different forms of stomatognathic system lesions suggestive of CA and the preventive strategies to curb the phenomenon.

Keywords: dental damage, maxillofacial diseases, negligence, oral health, odontopediatric

INTRODUCTION

Child Abuse (CA) is a universal problem that affects children of all nationalities and social status. Its universality does not only refer to its global nature but also to its variable ways of presentation and to the different parts of the body which it affects. Within the body parts of its affectation are the oral cavity and the facial mass, areas that are the subject this chapter. Based on this, odontopediatricians should suspect child abuse whenever there is a traumatic lesion on the face and in the oral cavity of a child without convincing or consistent explanation by the relatives. With the establishment of such suspicion, a multidisciplinary team composed of a pediatrician, an odontologist, a traumatologist and a social worker must be constituted to evaluate the child and the relatives [1]. In the stomatological area, it has been observed that head, face and neck injuries occur in more than 50% of the cases of child abuse as demonstrated in Figure 1 depicting a facial injury as a result of physical abuse (PA). Therefore, in the light of head, facial and buccal trauma suspected to occur as a result of abuse and neglect, it is pertinent that a stomatologist be involved as part of the multidisciplinary team since such trauma demands professional, legal and ethical management. In this regard, the function of the stomatologistis to carry out the exploration of these areas in search of stomatognathic system lesions and provide timely treatment when they exist [2].

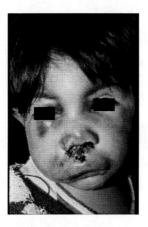

Figure 1. Photograph of patient with facial injuries.

In the evaluation, the stomatologist must make use of his knowledge in the diseases of these areas, comparing the subjective data with the objective data and then confirm the suspected abuse. It is extremely important that all victims of abuse, including child custody, be carefully examined for signs of oral trauma, caries, gingivitis and other oral problems of negligence character [3-6].It is crucial to bear in mind that doctors of other specialties have minimal training in oral health, oral and maxillofacial diseases and dentoalveolar trauma. Therefore, it is not advisable to put such evaluations in their hand as they may not easily detect the dental aspects of abuse or neglect as they do in abuse and child neglect that involve other areas of the body.

ETIOLOGY

Oral lesions may be inflicted with instruments such as kitchen utensils; feeding sets such as feeding bottles, cups, bottles, forks, knives and spoons; hands, fingers, spilled liquids or caustics [3-6]. Abuse may result in contusions; burns; lacerations of the tongue, lips, palate (soft and hard), oral mucosa and frenum; fractures or displacement; teeth avulsion and fractures of the face and jaw [3].

According to Naidoo [7], the most common site of oral injuries are lips (54%), oral mucosa (15%), teeth (12%), gum (12%) and tongue (7%). Moreover, in 25 cases of suspected CA reported by specialists of the American Commission of Pedodontics, it was found that the main oral lesions in cases of suspected CA was: tooth fracture (32%), bruising (24%), lacerations (14%), fractures of mandible or maxilla (11%) and burns (5%) [7-9]. As a result of previous trauma, teeth may exhibit color change (darker) indicating pulp necrosis [6-10].

Some serious lesions of the oral cavity, including posterior pharyngeal lesions and retropharyngeal abscesses, can be caused by parents or caregivers who suffer from factitious disorders such as Munchausen syndrome by proxy.

EPIDEMIOLOGY

A comprehensive data on CA is difficult to establish for its global nature and for the fact that it involves various parts of the body including the emotional part. Similarly, statistical data on child abuse with oral maxillofacial involvement specifically is difficult to obtain probably due to the inadequate way or reporting CA cases. In a study performed in a sample of 52 CA patients at the National Institute of Pediatrics (INP by its Spanish acronym), Mexico City, it was reported that 27 (54%) had head, face and mouth injuries [2].

In a retrospective observational study conducted by Dorfman et al. [11] in the United States which was published in 2017 and in which 2890 children were evaluated during 120 months for PA, it was found that 3.3% (n = 96) of them had oral lesions, 42% were between 0 and 12 months, 39% between 1 and 3 years and 18% were older than 3 years. The oral lesion was the principal reason for evaluation in 32 cases (33%). Of the 96 patients with oral lesions, 43% (42) had frenum lesions. Skeletal studies were done in 84% of the patients out of which 25% had hidden fractures. Neuroimaging was performed in 75% revealing a lesion in 38%. Retinal examination performed in 41% of children with oral lesions showed retinal hemorrhage in 24% of the tests. The study demonstrated that children with oral lesions are at high risk of having hidden injuries and that infants and preschoolers are the high risk population such injuries.

Cavalcanti reported in 2010 a study focusing on the prevalence and characteristics of head and orofacial region injuries in children and adolescents with PA [12]. The sample of the study consisted of 1070 reports of children and adolescents aged 0-17 years who were confirmed victims of this type of CA in northeastern Brazil. 52.8% settle the males and 47.2% were females. The author observed that the highest prevalence of victims of physical violence occurred in the age group 13 to 17 years (72.4%) followed by children aged 9-12 years (14.0%) in descending by those from 5-8 years (6.8%) and 0-4 years (6.7%).12.4% of the cases had intraoral injuries although, this was not statistically different between gender. Considering the oral regions affected, 55.6% of the lesions occurred in the superior maxilla, 35.5% were in the jaw and 9.0% in both regions. A total of 133 intraoral lesions were recorded. 94.8% of them were soft tissue lacerations, mainly in the upper lip (46.4%), the lower lip (34%) and oral mucosa (19.6%). In the victims with dental injuries (5.2%), coronal fracture was presented in all cases. Injuries to the upper incisors accounted for 84.6% of the cases of dental trauma. There was no record of injuries in the mandibular teeth.

A retrospective study of 66 pre-school children, aged 2 – 6 years, admitted between 1991 and 2004 in the Company Help the Children of Toronto (CHCT), Ontario, Canada, the prevalence of early childhood caries(ECC) and the oral health status were determined 37 (56%) of the children were boys and 29 (44%) girls. The average age of the patients was 4.1 years. The result of the study showed that none of the 66 infants had evidence of previous dental treatment except the untreated caries in the time of dental examination. Four (6%) of the children had evidence of dental trauma. ECC was observed in 58% of the children with CA (average decayed teeth was 5.63) compared to 30% in the school population of 5 years in the city of Toronto. This finding indicates that children with CA are more susceptible to higher levels of caries than those without CA [13].

Doria et al., published a transverse cut study of 104 children (52 children with a previous diagnosis of CA and 52 children without apparent CA) with an age range of 6-16 years. Clinical examinations consisting of muscle assessment, the presence of facets, temporomandibular joint, habits and Beck Anxiety Inventory (BAI) to determine the degree of anxiety were performed. The findings showed that abused children had 16 times greater chances of presenting a harmful habit of dental clenching and developing temporomandibular disorders in the future [14].

In the UK, Cairns et al., carried out a retrospective study of the medical records of children with suspected PA from 1998 to 2003 comprising of 390 records. They found that 59% (n = 230) of the children had signs of head, face or neck PA. About 23.4% (n = 54) had been punched or slapped on the head, neck or face, 17.4% (n = 40) had been hit with an object and 15.2% (n = 35) had multiple injuries of different types. Bruises were observed in the head, neck or face in 95.2% (n = 219) of the children and 32.6% (n=75) had abrasions. 65.2% (n= 150) of the bruises and 22.9% (n = 53) of the abrasions were on the face. The age range of the children with suspected PA was 23 days to 15 years. 45% of the examined children had less than 4 years and the median of age 2 years (12% of the total).There was significantly more boys than girls, 240 (61.5%) vs. 150 (38.5%).The only intraoral injury documented was frenum lip torn despite the fact that, in all cases, medical examiners verified intraoral injuries [15].

In Romania, a study with a sample of 299 abused subjects (218 boys and 81 girls) aged between 6 and 18 years was conducted. 62.11% of the population studied showed soft tissue injuries (contusions, bruises, bites) and 19.47% dentoperiodontal trauma (fractures, dislocations, concussions, avulsions, etc.); mandible injuries were found in 7.89%; facial bone fractures occurred in 7.89% while 2.63% suffered ATM injuries. It was found that, compared with other types of injuries, dental fractures had a higher rate (49%) and that the dentoperiodontal injury topographies were predominantly at the level of the central incisors 74% [16].

Kvist et al., in a study conducted in Sweden, reported dental care CA of 1.5 per 1000 children in a social service. 86% of the cases were in children who had had previous contact with social services [17].Sanger studied a group of 246 US odontopediatricians and found that only 9% had had reported cases of CA, although almost 90% knew about the problem [18].

CLASSIFICATION

CA maxillofacial injuries are classified into: accidents, physical abuse, sexual abuse, psychological abuse, bullying and neglect or omission [3, 6]

Accidents

Accidental injuries in the orofacial region may be caused primarily by falls, blows and car accidents. The latter are the most maxillofacial impact because children that are involved in car accidents at high speeds can suffer 39% skull fractures. This is a consequence of negligence in the care of a child hence, the importance of prevention by using safety belts and baby seat in the car. Small children should not be allowed to occupy the front seat and in no way should be permitted to ride on the rider's legs [19].

Physical Abuse

The oral cavity may be a central focus by PA. The following describes characteristic injuries of the anatomical parts of our interest:

Lips

They can be bruising, lacerations, scars from previous traumas, burns caused by hot food or cigarettes and in extreme cases caustics, bruises, abrasions and scabs. The clamp used in the mouth may result in bruises, lichenification or scarring in oral commissures [9, 20].

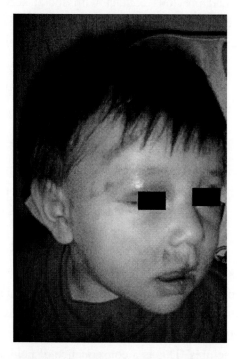

Figure 2. Patient with craniofacial injuries.

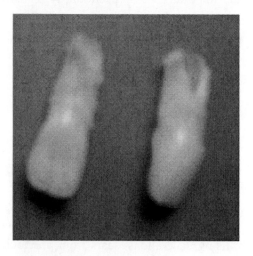

Figure 3. Dental avulsion secondary to trauma.

Oral Mucosa

The oral cavity can present clear lacerations of labial or lingual frenum caused by assault, gavage, covering the mouth of a child abruptly when the child is crying. Perioral hematoma is almost pathognomonic. Gums, tongue, palate, the floor of the mouth are not exempted from presenting lacerations and abrasions produced by the same mechanism as burns by caustic ingestion [5].

Teeth

Dental structure may have enamel and dentin fracture, complete fracture of the tooth avulsion, dislocation and discoloration. In Figure 2 and 3 show a CA victim patient with craniofacial injuries and dental avulsion secondary to trauma.

Maxillary and Jaw

Usually, early signs of fracture are observed during the diagnosis of the injury.

Sexual Abuse

Although the oral cavity is not a frequent site of SA in children, the presence of visible oral lesions or infections are not rare. When oral-genital contact is suspected, it is recommended that the child be referred to specialized clinical to perform additional tests (gonorrhea, human papillomavirus, chlamydia, syphilis and HIV +) [3,6,9,21].

Unexplained injury or petechiae palate, particularly at the junction of the hard palate and soft palate, and the presence of broken frenum may be evidence of forced oral sex. As in all presumptive cases of child abuse or neglect, when SA is suspected or diagnosed, the child should be reported to the child protection services and/or to the law enforcement agencies for the necessary research and action [3,5].

Other injuries that may occur include erythema, ulcers, vesicles with purulent drainage or pseudomembranous injury and condylomatous lips, tongue, palate and nasopharynx including symptoms such as sore throat and swallowing problem [3,6,21].

Within sexual abuse are also bite marks. These are suspected when elliptical or ovoid patterns of bruising, abrasion or laceration are presented. The inter canine distance less than 3 cm is also a sign of adult bite. Marks by bites appear with a central area of ecchymosis which can be caused by two phenomena: positive pressure by crushing teeth against the tissue causing disruption of small vessels, or by the negative pressure caused by sucking and the thrust of the tongue. Unlike dog and other animal bites, human bite does not usually tear tissues. It is characterized by tissue compression without avulsion [9, 21]. As a result, the bites can appear anywhere, but tend to focus on the cheek, arm, shoulder, buttocks or genitals [22].

Another aspect of SA is the behavior of the child during dental appointments. The range is from patients who behave quiet until the non-cooperative, as a result of oro-genital experiences. Itis important to note the patient's actions, behavior, movements and verbal and nonverbal communication when you ask them to open their mouth to perform treatments. SA antecedent is always a factor for the patient to develop fear and anxiety to dental consultation especially in cases of fellatio [21].The child may perform a visual impression since many abused children are fearful and constantly observes around for signs of danger. The face may be stationary, there is no spontaneous smiles, and usually no eye contact. It is possible to see if the child has difficulty getting on the dental unit or experiences pain when lifting [23].

It is essential to document injuries when sexual abuse is suspected. The injuries or marks and shooting must be completely described [22].

Psychological Abuse (PA)

PA can manifest when parents or caregivers express prejudicial comments to the child. Such comments can be on the poor state of the teeth or making fun of him if he cries during the medical practice or threatening him with punishments if he does not cooperate with the treatment. However, these types of isolated behaviors do not assume that the child suffered psychological abuse, but they will help the physician to reach a conclusion especially if there are also physical assaults or a suspicion of SA. CA victims are at increased risk of developing PTSD. According to Spatz, up to 37.5% of the victims of CA develop PTSD [24]. This can cause temporomandibular disorders such as bruxism, the rapid development of caries associated with depression that leads to disinterest to maintain oral health especially, in adulthood [25].The increase in the level of child anxiety can also be determined by continuous finger sucking and nail biting habit which the child uses to occlude the anxiety [23,26,27].

Within the PA, is bullying or peer abuse. According to American Academy of Odontopediatrics, 30% of the children in sixth to tenth grade reported having privacy/or harassing others. Children with abnormal orofacial or dental (including malocclusion) are often subject of bullying and as a result, they may suffer serious psychological consequences, including depression and suicidal ideation. It was found that children who reported PA, dating violence, forced sex and bullying also reported a bad oral health. Medical care providers (including odontopediatrics) may ask patients about bullying programs and advocate for anti-bullying in schools and other community settings.

Dental Neglect (DN)

The omission or DN affects the health of the child. The American Academy of Odontopediatrics defines dental neglect as "the voluntary fault of the parent or tutor to seek and to continue with the necessary treatment to assure a level of essential oral health for a suitable free function of pain and infection [3, 6]. If not treated; caries, periodontal diseases, mycosis, viral or bacterial diseases and other conditions can cause more serious conditions such as cellulitis or facial abscesses that can compromise the child's life. Figure 4 shows the presence of caries in several teeth, which suggests little care in oral health.

The dentist should be committed to ensure the preservation and integrity of the dental health of patients, especially children. The correct classification of lesions in the stomatognathic system, collaboration, exchange of information, knowledge, experience and good practice will contribute to improve the exercise of children's rights to health, welfare and life quality of a pediatric patient 5].

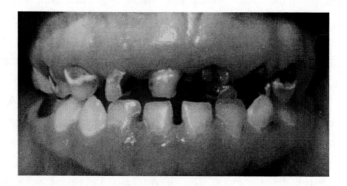

Figure 4. Presence of multiple caries. If not treated, they can cause cellulitis or facial abscesses.

DIAGNOSIS

All injuries should be reported in the medical record regardless the caregiver's reason. Unintentional or accidental injuries are common and should be distinguished from abuse. The history and mechanism of injury must be consistent with the characteristics of the lesion and the development capabilities of the child sometimes make the diagnosis difficult to establish.

Radiographic examination can also be very useful, because almost 50% of the patients are often repetitively abused. Therefore, in radiographic studies, previous injuries as root fractures poorly consolidated, obliteration pulp and alteration of tooth germs can be found.

Although dentists should be suspicious of all injuries, in children, they should be aware that the diagnosis of PA is never done on the basis of a sign as various diseases can be mistaken for abuse. Impetigo lesions may resemble cigarette burns, birthmarks can be mistaken for bruising and conjunctivitis can be confused with trauma. All children with a history of bruising should be attended by the pediatrician to rule out bleeding disorders. Unexplained, multiple or frequent fractures are rarely due to imperfect osteogenesis or family history, blue sclera and the presence of imperfect dentinogenesis and these can help to establish the diagnosis [3,5,28]. Parents who mistreat their children rarely take the child to the same doctor. However, they are not as cautious about dentists.

SIGNS OF SUSPICION

1. Physical appearance (outer clothing and hygiene) is usually misaligned, which could prove a lack of emotional care in their welfare.

2. Attendance to doctor's appointment or attention to treatment is generally delayed or spaced, sometimes after the date they were beaten.

3. The parents or guardians allege that injuries are accidental and there is a marked discrepancy between the data referred by parents and obtained by inspection and exploration.

4. The indifference is shown by the child. Often he is sad and makes fearful expression. During the examination, the child is found listless. Although he does not speak, tear escapes and sometimes, he can display an aggressive behave or tendency to develop violent behavior.

5. Itis common to find psychomotor limitations for his age, because of poor psychological and emotional stimulation by the mother [5,6].

LONG TERM PREVENTION

It is estimated that around 20% of patients seeking dental care may have experienced SA, so it is believed that dentists work, often unknowingly, with adult survivors of this modality of CA. This raises further interest in developing preventive strategies for CA prevention in any of its presentations [29].The purpose of prevention is to quickly identify cases of CA and embark on strategies of interventions to protect the children affected. This strategy is certainly a form of prevention and must be beneficial for the children and the families. However, it will not help to substantially reduce the CA incidence that could be achieved if strategies that address the root causes and contributing factors are implemented [30].

Moreover, not all countries have the same system of oral health and culture of oral care especially of deciduous teeth. So, many parents don't take their children to the dentist because of the belief that they are milk teeth and will fall at certain age. This added to the high cost of private dental services worsens the situation. It is a fact that if children under 6 years of age have caries-free primary teeth, they will have 83% chances of having caries-free adult teeth. Conversely, if the teeth present untreated cavities before 6 years, there is 94% probability of presenting caries in the teeth in adulthood. So, it is important to increase the issue of prevention tactics, promote affordable dental care costs and increase the number of dental health professionals [31].

Such strategies should include prevention campaigns and education in both social, community and individual levels. In addition, to reduce the incidence of child abuse, it is pertinent to launch global, national and local campaigns with stanzas on oral and school public health. Table 1 shows a list of suggestions for prevention strategies according to the level of care.

Table 1. Prevention Strategies

First Level	Second Level	Third Level	Fourth Level	Fifth Level
Health promotion and education	Specific protection	Diagnosis and early treatment	Limitation of damage	Rehabilitation
• Community campaigns. • Accessibility to oral health services. • Reduction of environmental risk factors. • Have qualified stomatologists to identify cases of abuse.	•Home visit programs for the population at risk. •Preparing children to avoid situations of abuse. • In order to reduce dental negligence: application of fluoride, placement of sealants, prophylaxis.	• Quick identification of cases of abuse. • Protection and treatment of the affected family. • Continue medical attention. •Stomatological treatment in cases of dental negligence: removal of caries, dentoalveolar trauma	• Prevent abuse from recurring. • Psychosocial and mental health support. • Stomatological treatment in cases of dental negligence: Pulpal treatments, extractions.	• Recovery and integration. • Protection and welfare of the child. •Stomatological treatment in cases of dental neglect: Placement of crowns, space maintainers, prosthesis
Primary prevention		Secondary prevention	Tertiary prevention	

CONCLUSION

In order to generate new knowledge about CA and provide the best dental care, dissemination of studies and/or research is necessary. It is extremely important to have available a statistical and descriptive information that will enrich the knowledge and awareness of the physicians and provide them with the required professional tools to detect and prevent not only odontopediatric-associated child abuse but also all kinds of abuse. The society must have the ethical and legal responsibility to report cases of CA in order to avoid their fatal outcomes. Likewise, it is important to sensitize the general population, especially parents, caregivers and teachers on the reality of CA and on the signs to suspect it so as to tackle the problem on time.

REFERENCES

[1]   Díaz, LM; Martínez, AA; Valdespino, CV; Leyva, YA. Oral injuries of child maltreatment in forensic dentistry. *Rev Elec Inv CICS-UST.*, 2014, 8(1),1-7.

[2]   Loredo-Abdalá, A; Monter-García, MA; Escudero-Castro, A; delaTeja-Ángeles, E. Orofacial indicators in the child abuse síndrome. *Acta Pediatr Mex*, 2003, 24, 240-4.

[3]   American Academy of Pediatrics Committee on Child Abuse, American Academy of Pediatric Dentistry. Guideline on oral and dental aspects of child abuse and neglect. *Reference Manual*, 1999, 37, 15-6.

[4]   Mouden, LD; Bross, DC. Legal issues affecting dentistry's role in preventing child abuse and neglect. *J Am Dent Assoc*, 1995,126, 1173-80.

[5]   Soria, EA; Perera, R. Forensic dentistry as an auxiliary science in child abuse in Mexico. *Rev Odontología Actual*, 2013,117, 26-32.

[6]   Fisher-Owens, SA; Lukefahr, JL; Tate, AR. American Academy of Pediatrics, Committee on Child Abuse and Neglect, & American Academy of Pediatric Dentistry. Oral and dental aspects of child abuse and neglect. *Pediatrics*, 2017,140, e20171487.

[7]   Naidoo S. A profile of the oro-facial injuries in child physical abuse at a children's hospital. *Child Abuse Neglect*, 2000, 24, 521-34.

[8]   John, V; Messer, LB; Arora, R; Fung, S; Hatzis, E; Nguyen, T. Child abuse and dentistry:a study of knowledge and attitudes among dentists in Victoria, Australia. *Aust Dent J*, 1999, 44, 259-267.

[9]   Costacurta, M; Benavoli, D; Arcudi, G; Docimo, R. Oral and dental signs of child abuse and neglect. *Oral Implantol*, 2015, 8, 68-73.

[10]   Tate, RJ. Facial injuries associated with the battered child syndrome. *Br J Oral Surg*, 1971, 9, 41-5.

[11]   Dorfman, MV; Metz, JB; Feldman, KW; Farris, R; Lindberg, DM. Oral injuries and occult harm in children evaluated for abuse. *Arch Dis Child*, 2017, 313400.

[12]   Cavalcanti AL. Prevalence and characteristics of injuries to the head and orofacial region in physically abused children and adolescents. A retrospective study in a city of the Northeast of Brazil. *Dent Traumatol*, 2010, 26, 149-53.

[13]   Valencia-Rojas, N; Lawrence, HP; Goodman, D. Prevalence of early childhood caries in a population of children with history of maltreatment. *J Public Health Dent*, 2008, 68, 94-101.

[14]   Doria, AM; Navarro, MI; Garzón, SL; Herrera, MC; Moreno, GC; Furman, E; Ayala, L. Dental tightening suggestive of child abuse in institutionalized children from 6 to 18 years. *Univ Odontol*, 2016, 35, 65-74.

[15]   Cairns, AM; Mok, JYQ; Welbury, RR. Injuries to the head, face, mouth and neck in physically abused children in a community setting. *Int J Paediat Dent*, 2005, 15, 310-318.

[16]   Savin, C; Petcu, A; Earar, K; Bălan, G; Maxim, A; Bălan, A. Child physical abuse from the perspective of pediatric dentistry. *Romanian J Oral Rehab*, 2010, 2, 17-20.

[17] Kvist, T; Cocozza, M; Annerbäck, EM; Dahllöf, G. Child maltreatment prevalence and characteristics of mandatory reports from dental professionals to the Social Services. *Int J Paediatr Dent*, 2016, 27, 3-10.

[18] Adair, SM; Yaresbi, S; Wray, IA; Hanes, CM; Sama, DR; Russell, CM. Demographic, educational, and experiential factors associated with dentist's decision to report hypothetical cases of child maltreatment. *Pediatr Dent*, 1997, 19, 466-9.

[19] Shah, M; Vavilala, MS; Feldman, KW; Hallam, DK. Motor vehicle crash brain injury in infants and toddlers: a suitable model for inflicted head injury. *Child Abuse Neglect*, 2005, 29, 953-967.

[20] Rupp, RP. The dentist's role in reporting suspected child abuse and neglect. *Gen Dent*, 2000, 48, 340-2.

[21] Stavrianos, C; Kokkas, A; Katsikogiani; H., Tretiakov; G. Dentist's action after identifying child sexual assault. *Res J Med Sci*, 2010, 4, 157-165.

[22] Wagner, GN. Bitemark identification in child abuse cases. *Pediatr Dent*, 1986,8, 96-100.

[23] Loredo-Abdalá, A; delaTeja-Ángeles, E; Escudero-Castro, A. The pediatric stomatologist in the comprehensive care of the abused child:a new intervention policy. *Abuse in children and adolescents*. Editores de Textos Mexicanos, Mexico 2004, 248-61.

[24] Spatz, C. Posttraumatic stress disorder in abused and neglected children grown up. *Am J Psychiatr*, 1999,156, 1223-1229.

[25] Friedlander, AH; Friedlander, IK; Marder, SR. Posttraumatic stress disorder:psychopathology, medical management, and dental implications. *Oral Surg Oral Med Oral Pathol Oral Radiol Endod*, 2004, 97, 5-11.

[26] Shetty, RM; Shetty, M; Shetty, NS; Deoghare, A. Three-alarm system:revisited to treat thumb-sucking habit. *Int J Clin Pediatr Dent*, 2015, 8, 82-86.

[27] Martagón, LR; Belmont, F; delaTeja, E; Téllez, J. Abused child syndrome with stomatological impact. A case report. *Rev Odont Mex*, 2016, 20, 98-106.

[28] Harris, J; Sidebotham, P; Welbury, R, Čuković-Bagić. *Child protection and the dental team: an introduction to safeguarding children in dental practice. 2010.* Available in: https: //bda.org/ childprotection/Resources/Documents/Childprotectionandthedentalte am_v1_4_Nov09.pdf.

[29] Dougall, A; Fiske, J. Surviving child sexual abuse:the relevance to dental practice. *Dent,* Update 2009, 36, 294-304.

[30] Butchart, A; Phinney, Harvey, A; Mian, M; Fürniss, T; Kahane, T. *Prevention of child abuse: what to do, and how to obtain evidence. World Health Organization. 2009.* Available in: http: //apps.who.int/ iris/bitstream/10665/44228/1/9789243594361_spa.pdf

[31] Li, Y; Wang, W. Predicting caries in permanent teeth from caries in primary teeth:an eight-year cohort study. *J Dent Res,* 2002, 81, 561-566.

ABOUT THE EDITORS

Arturo Loredo Abdalá
Director, Center for Advanced Studies on
Child Maltreatment-Prevention, National Institute of Pediatrics
(Centro de Estudios Avanzados sobre Maltrato Infantil-Prevención
del Instituto Nacional de Pediatría)
Mexico City, Mexico

Dr. Arturo Loredo Abdala is a pediatrician internist, and Founder and Director of the Abused Child Care and Prevention of the National Institute of Pediatrics since 1993. He is member of the National Academy of Medicine and National Academy of Pediatricians. He is Titular Researcher of the National Institute of Health, and Graduate Professor in Pediatrics at UNAM.

Hugo Juárez Olguín
Department of Pharmacology,
National Institute of Pediatrics and Faculty of Medicine
National Autonomous University of Mexico (UNAM)
(Laboratorio de Farmacología, Instituto Nacional de Pediatría,

Facultad de Medicina, Universidad Nacional Autónoma de Mexico)
Mexico City, Mexico

Dr. Hugo Juárez Olguín is a researcher in Medical Sciences, a position given by Health Ministry of Mexico, and Titular Professor of Pharmacology at Faculty of Medicine in National Autonomous University of Mexico (UNAM). He has twenty-eight years experience working as researcher in Clinical Pharmacology in the Hospital of Health Ministry and Teacher of Pharmacology/Faculty of Medicine, at the National Autonomous University of Mexico (UNAM). He belongs to the National System of Investigators.

Abigail Casas Muñoz
National Institute of Pediatrics
Coordinator, Center for Advanced Studies
on Child Maltreatment-Prevention
(Centro de Estudios Avanzados sobre Maltrato Infantil-Prevención
del Instituto Nacional de Pediatría)
Mexico City, Mexico

Abigail Casas Muñoz is a pediatrician, and has a Master in Medical Science by UNAM. She is a researcher at the Abused Child Care and Prevention of the National Institute of Pediatrics. Researcher by National Institutes of Health. Member of the National Academy of Pediatrician.

INDEX